First World War
and Army of Occupation
War Diary
France, Belgium and Germany

16 DIVISION
Headquarters, Branches and Services
Adjutant and Quarter-Master General
10 December 1915 - 30 November 1918

WO95/1957

The Naval & Military Press Ltd
www.nmarchive.com
Published in association with The National Archives

Published by

The Naval & Military Press Ltd

Unit 10 Ridgewood Industrial Park,
Uckfield, East Sussex,
TN22 5QE England
Tel: +44 (0) 1825 749494

www.naval-military-press.com
www.nmarchive.com

This diary has been reprinted in facsimile from the original. Any imperfections are inevitably reproduced and the quality may fall short of modern type and cartographic standards.

Contents

Document type	Place/Title	Date From	Date To
Heading	16th Division "A" & "Q" Branch Dec 1915-Nov 1918		
War Diary	Blackdown	10/12/1915	19/12/1915
War Diary	Chateau Drouvin	20/12/1915	31/12/1915
War Diary	Bomy	01/01/1916	07/01/1916
War Diary	Amettes	08/01/1916	26/02/1916
War Diary	Busnes	27/02/1916	08/03/1916
War Diary	Philomel	09/03/1916	27/03/1916
War Diary	Noeux Les Mines	27/03/1916	10/05/1916
War Diary	Noeux	11/05/1916	21/05/1916
War Diary	Noeux Les Mines	22/05/1916	30/06/1916
Heading	War Diary. "A" And "Q" Branch Headquarters, 16th (Irish) Division 1st July to 31st. July 1916 Volume.8		
War Diary	Noeux-Les Mines	01/07/1916	31/07/1916
Heading	War Diary. "A" & "Q" Branch 16th Div. Headquarters Month Of August, 1916 Volume, 9		
War Diary	Noeux-Les-Mines	01/08/1916	16/08/1916
War Diary	Corbie	12/08/1916	17/08/1916
War Diary	Hallen Court	18/08/1916	20/08/1916
War Diary	Westoutre	21/08/1916	24/08/1916
War Diary	Noeux-Les-Mines.	17/08/1916	27/08/1916
War Diary	Raimbert	28/08/1916	29/08/1916
War Diary	Corbie.	30/08/1916	30/08/1916
War Diary	Forked Tree Camp.	31/08/1916	31/08/1916
War Diary	Noeux-Les-Mines	01/08/1916	27/08/1916
War Diary	Raimbert	28/08/1916	29/08/1916
War Diary	Corbie.	30/08/1916	30/08/1916
War Diary	Forked Tree Camp.	31/08/1916	31/08/1916
Heading	War Diary. "A" and "Q" Branch 16th Division Month Of September 1916 Volume 10		
War Diary	Forked Tree Camp	01/09/1916	04/09/1916
War Diary	Citadel	05/09/1916	10/09/1916
War Diary	Corbie	11/09/1916	11/09/1916
War Diary	Westoutre.	25/09/1916	30/09/1916
Heading	War Diary Month Of October, 1916 Volume 11 "A" & "Q" Branch 16th Division		
War Diary	Westoutre (Belgium)	01/10/1916	12/10/1916
War Diary	Westoutre	13/10/1916	31/10/1916
Heading	War Diary For Month Of November, 1916. Volume 12 "A" & "Q" Branch 16th Division M.G. Vol 12		
War Diary	Westoutre	01/11/1916	30/11/1916
Heading	War Diary For Month Of December, 1916. Volume 13 "A" & "Q" Branch 16 Div H.Q. Vol 13		
War Diary	Westoutre.	01/12/1916	31/12/1916
Heading	War Diary for month of January, 1917 Volume 14. "A" & "Q" Branch 16th Division		
War Diary	Westoutre.	01/01/1917	31/01/1917
Heading	War Diary For Month Of February, 1917. Volume 15 Unit:- "A & Q" Branch 16th Division Original Vol 15		
War Diary	Westoutre	01/02/1917	28/02/1917

Heading	War Diary For Month Of March, 1917 Volume 16 Unit:- "A & Q" Branch 16th (Irish) Division		
War Diary	Westoutre	01/03/1917	31/03/1917
Operation(al) Order(s)	16th. Division Administrative Order No. 4. Reference. 16th Division Operation Order No. 89	26/03/1917	26/03/1917
Miscellaneous	Table To Accompany 16th. Division Administrative Order No. 4		
Heading	War Diary For Month Of April, 1917. Volume. 17 Unit:- "A & Q" Branch 16th D.H.Q		
War Diary	Locre	01/04/1917	30/04/1917
Operation(al) Order(s)	16th. Division Administrative Order No. 6. Reference 16th. Division Operation Order No. 96 d/-11/4/17	11/04/1917	11/04/1917
Miscellaneous	A Area. RECQUES. Brigade Group.		
Operation(al) Order(s)	16th. Division Administrative Order No. 7	15/04/1917	15/04/1917
Operation(al) Order(s)	Distribution of 16th. Division Administrative Order No. 7		
Operation(al) Order(s)	16th. Division Administrative Order No. 8 Reference 16th. Division Operation Order No. 100 D/-23-4-17	23/04/1917	23/04/1917
Operation(al) Order(s)	16th. Division Administrative Order No. 10 Reference 16th Divl. Artillery Operation Order No. 66 D/-22/4/17	26/04/1917	26/04/1917
Miscellaneous	16th. Division Administrative Order No. 10 Reference 16th Divl. Artillery Operation Order No. 66 d/-22/4/17	26/04/1917	26/04/1917
Operation(al) Order(s)	16th. Division Administrative Order No. 11 Reference 16th Divl. Artillery Operation Order No. 103 Dated 29-4-17	29/04/1917	29/04/1917
Operation(al) Order(s)	Distribution of 16th Div. Administration Order No. 11		
Heading	War Diary For Month Of May, 1917. Volume:- 18 Unit:- A & Q. Branch 16th Div H.Q. (Original)		
War Diary	Locre	01/05/1917	31/05/1917
Heading	War Diary For Month Of June, 1917 Volume:- 19 Unit:- "A & Q" Branch 16th Division		
War Diary	Locre.	01/06/1917	06/06/1917
War Diary	Mont Rouge	07/06/1917	11/06/1917
War Diary	Locre.	12/06/1917	12/06/1917
War Diary	Merris	13/06/1917	16/06/1917
War Diary	Locre	17/06/1917	17/06/1917
War Diary	Merris	18/06/1917	19/06/1917
War Diary	Godewaers Velde	20/06/1917	21/06/1917
War Diary	Zeggers Cappel.	22/06/1917	30/06/1917
Heading	War Diary For Month Of July, 1917 Volume:- 20 Unit "A & Q" Branch 16th D.H.Q. Original		
War Diary	Zeggers Cappel.	01/07/1917	23/07/1917
War Diary	Poperinghe	24/07/1917	31/07/1917
Heading	War Diary For Month Of August, 1917. Volume 21 Unit "A & Q" 16 Div Headqrs. Duplicate.		
War Diary	Poperinghe	01/08/1917	04/08/1917
War Diary	Brandhoek.	05/08/1917	17/08/1917
War Diary	Watou	18/08/1917	21/08/1917
War Diary	Achiet-Le-Petit	22/08/1917	31/08/1917
Miscellaneous	The following is the statement of casualties to all units in the Division, from 1st to 31st August 1917, (both dates inclusive).		
Heading	War Diary For Month Of 1917 Volume 22 Unit "A & Q" Branch 16 Div H.Q. Original		
War Diary	Moyenneville	01/09/1917	18/09/1917
War Diary	Behagnies	19/09/1917	30/09/1917

Heading	War Diary For Month Of October, 1917 Unit "A & Q" Branch 16 Division Volume Number 23 Original		
War Diary	Behagnies	01/10/1917	31/10/1917
Heading	War Diary For Month Of December, 1917 Volume:- 25 Unit:- "Q" Branch 16th Division		
Heading	War Diary For Month Of November, 1917 Volume:- 24 Unit:- "A & Q" Branch 16th D.H.Q		
War Diary	Behagnies	01/11/1917	30/11/1917
Heading	16th Division Q. Administrative Instructions.		
Miscellaneous	16th Division No. Q/307/8/5 O.C., VI Corps Ammunition Park	05/11/1917	05/11/1917
Miscellaneous	47th Infantry Bde. 48th Infantry Bde. 16th Division No. A.M. 1009-6-11-1917	06/11/1917	06/11/1917
Miscellaneous	Amendment To 16th Divisional Administrative Instruction No. 7	07/11/1917	07/11/1917
Heading	Q302/13/3 7/11/17 Ref. Ref. Wire Cutters		
Miscellaneous	47th Infantry Brigade. 48th Infantry. Brigade. 16th Division No. Q 302/13/3	07/11/1917	07/11/1917
Miscellaneous	16th. Division VI. Corps No. SQ/381	17/11/1917	17/11/1917
War Diary	Behagnies	01/12/1917	02/12/1917
War Diary	Little Wood near Ytres	03/12/1917	04/12/1917
War Diary	Flamicourt	05/12/1917	06/12/1917
War Diary	Villers Faucon	07/12/1917	31/12/1917
Heading	War Diary For Month Of January, 1918 Volume:- 26 Unit:- "A & Q" Brch, 16th D.H.Q.		
War Diary	Villers Faucon.	01/01/1918	21/01/1918
War Diary	J.17.b.8.8. (Sheet 62c.) near Tincourt.	22/01/1918	31/01/1918
Heading	War Diary for Month of February, 1918. Volume:- 27 Unit:- "A & Q" Branch 16th D.H.Q.		
War Diary	Terrace Camp, Near Tincourt J.17.b.8.8	01/02/1918	28/02/1918
Heading	16th Division Administrative. A. & Q. 16th Division March 1918 Appendices Attached:- Administrative Notes On Operations.		
War Diary	Tincourt	01/03/1918	22/03/1918
War Diary	T 17. Central	22/03/1918	22/03/1918
War Diary	Doingt	23/03/1918	23/03/1918
War Diary	Cappy	24/03/1918	24/03/1918
War Diary	Morlancourt	25/03/1918	25/03/1918
War Diary	Lamotte-En-Santerre	25/03/1918	26/03/1918
War Diary	Hamel	26/03/1918	27/03/1918
War Diary	Fuilloy	27/03/1918	31/03/1918
Miscellaneous	Administrative Notes On Recent Operations East Of Amiens.	13/05/1918	13/05/1918
War Diary	Fuilloy	01/04/1918	03/04/1918
War Diary	Saleux	04/04/1918	04/04/1918
War Diary	Cerisy	05/04/1918	09/04/1918
War Diary	Gamaches	09/04/1918	10/04/1918
War Diary	Fauquem-Bergues	10/04/1918	15/04/1918
War Diary	Aire.	16/04/1918	15/05/1918
Diagram etc	Aire Samer	16/05/1918	16/05/1918
War Diary	Samer	19/05/1918	18/06/1918
War Diary	Boulogne	18/06/1918	30/06/1918
War Diary	Samer	01/08/1918	19/08/1918
War Diary	Monchy Cayeux	20/08/1918	22/08/1918
War Diary	Ruitz	23/08/1918	28/08/1918
War Diary	K25c. 4.2	29/08/1918	31/08/1918

Miscellaneous	Table of Moves and Entrainment of 16th Division Appendix I		
Miscellaneous	Appendix II 16th Div. No. A.409. Supply Arrangements For Move Of 47th Infantry Brigade Group, Consisting Of:-	17/08/1918	17/08/1918
Miscellaneous	Administrative Instructions To Accompany 16th Division Order No. 239. Appendix III	17/08/1918	17/08/1918
Operation(al) Order(s)	Reference Administrative Instructions To Accompany 16th. Divisional Order No. 239	17/08/1918	17/08/1918
Miscellaneous	Administrative Instruction No. 2 Appendix IV	17/08/1918	17/08/1918
Operation(al) Order(s)	Amendment To Location List Issued On 17-8-18, To Accompany 16th Divisional Order No. 239	19/08/1918	19/08/1918
Miscellaneous	16th. Division Administrative Instruction. No. 3 Supply Arrangements To Move Of 49th. Brigade Group. Appendix V	17/08/1918	17/08/1918
Miscellaneous	16th Division Administrative Instructions No. 4 Appendix VI	17/08/1918	17/08/1918
Miscellaneous	16th Division Administrative Instructions. Appendix VII	18/08/1918	18/08/1918
Miscellaneous	Details of Officers "Taken on" or "Struck off" Strength		
Miscellaneous	Division. A. 22/1. Appendix VIII	31/08/1918	31/08/1918
War Diary	Ruitz K 25 C.4.2	01/09/1918	22/09/1918
War Diary	Drouvin	23/09/1918	30/09/1918
Miscellaneous	Notes On Administration In The Event Of An Advance Appx. I	01/09/1918	01/09/1918
Miscellaneous	16th Division Administrative Instructions, No. 7. Appendix II	05/09/1918	05/09/1918
Miscellaneous	16th Division Appendix III	07/09/1918	07/09/1918
Miscellaneous	Details of Officers "Taken on" or "Struck off" Strength.		
Operation(al) Order(s)	13th Division. Weekly Disposition Report No. 2. Appx IV	09/09/1918	09/09/1918
Miscellaneous	Appendix V		
Miscellaneous	Administrative Instruction No. 8 Appendix VI	17/08/1918	17/08/1918
Miscellaneous	16th Division Appx VII	28/09/1918	28/09/1918
Miscellaneous	Changes In Nominal Rolls Of Officers.		
Miscellaneous	Salvage Organisation In 16th Divisional Area. Appx VIII	28/09/1918	28/09/1918
Miscellaneous	Divisional Salvage Company Administration. 16th. Div. No. Q.61/3	28/09/1918	28/09/1918
Map	Sketch Map Illustrating Salvages Organisation In 16th Divl. Area.		
War Diary	Drouvin	01/10/1918	06/10/1918
War Diary	Chateau Des Pres	07/10/1918	16/10/1918
War Diary	Billy	17/10/1918	18/10/1918
War Diary	Phalempin	19/10/1918	21/10/1918
War Diary	Templeuve	22/10/1918	31/10/1918
Miscellaneous	16th Division. Arrangements For The Collection Of Stores In Event Of All Advance Appendix I	02/10/1918	02/10/1918
Miscellaneous	Distribution		
Miscellaneous	16th Division. Strength Return Made Up To 12 Noon Saturday 12th October 1918 Appx II	12/10/1918	12/10/1918
Miscellaneous	16th Division. Strength Return Made Up To 12 Noon Saturday 26th October 1918 Appx III	26/10/1918	26/10/1918
War Diary	Templeuve	01/11/1918	09/11/1918
War Diary	Taintignies	10/11/1918	15/11/1918
War Diary	Attiches	16/11/1918	27/11/1918
War Diary	Avelin.	28/11/1918	30/11/1918

16TH DIVISION

'A' & 'Q' BRANCH

DEC 1915-NOV 1918

Confidential

A & Q.

16th Div.

Instructions regarding War Diaries and Intelligence Summaries are contained in F. S. Regs., Part II. and the Staff Manual respectively. Title pages will be prepared in manuscript.

WAR DIARY
or
~~INTELLIGENCE SUMMARY.~~
(Erase heading not required.)

Army Form C. 2118.

Place	Date	Hour	Summary of Events and Information	Remarks and references to Appendices
BLACKDOWN.	10/12/15.	P.M. 9.40	Signed copy of W.O. telegram recd from A.T.C. stating that embarkation commences about 17th ordering Ad. Parties to be warned. Southampton party Dec. 12th. Folkestone party Dec. 14th.	
"	11/12/15	12 noon	Forwarding letter from H.Q., A.T.C., containing W.O. letter withdrawing 1st S. African Inf. Bgde, 49th Inf. & Artillery not to proceed with Divn.	
"	12/12/15	12 noon	Adv. Party left for Southampton.	
"	13/12/15	12 noon	Divnl Route March. Orders recd. for units to start moving Friday 17/12/15. Detail of how units move given (no ~~train~~tables).	
"	14/12/15	12 noon	Divnl Motors & Adv Party left for Boulogne. ~~Time~~ Train tables arrvd.	
"	15/12/15	12 noon	- - - - - - - - - - -	
"	17/12/15	12 noon	47th Inf. Bgde. moved out 1st Train load 7 A.M.	
"	18/12/15	12 noon	Moved from Blackdown with Div. H.Q. to SOUTHAMPTON for HAVRE.	
"	19/12/15	12 noon	Arrd. HAVRE 8 A.M. Left 11.50 P.M. Destination unknown.	
CHATEAU DROUVIN	20/12/15		Arrd. CHATEAU DROUVIN 9.30 P.M.	

2353 Wt. W2514/1454 700,000 5/15 D. D. & L. A.D.S.S./Forms/C. 2118.

Instructions regarding War Diaries and Intelligence Summaries are contained in F. S. Regs., Part II. and the Staff Manual respectively. Title pages will be prepared in manuscript.

WAR DIARY
or
INTELLIGENCE SUMMARY.
(Erase heading not required.)

Army Form C. 2118.

Place	Date	Hour	Summary of Events and Information	Remarks and references to Appendices
CHATEAU DROUVIN	21/12/15.	5.P.M	Division billeted as follows :-	

Hd.Qrs. CHATEAU DROUVIN.

Formation	Unit	Billet	Strength	Total
47th Inf.Bgde	6th Rl.Irish Regt.	DROUVIN	34 Offrs. 996 O.R.	TOTAL 132 offrs. 3833 O.R.
	6th Conn.Rangers	HESDIGNEUL	35 " 941 "	
	7th Leinster Regt	GOSNAY	31 " 948 "	
	8th R. Muns. Fus.	VERQUIN	32 " 948 "	
48th Inf.Bgde	7th R.Ir.Rifles	NOEUX-LES-MINES / HOUSHIN	Not yet arrd.	
	9th R.Muns.Fus.	NOEUX-LES-MINES		
	8th R.Dub.Fus.	HOUSHIN		
	9th R.Dub.Fus.			

Unit	Billet
16TH DIV TRAIN	HESDIGNEUL (Tents)
155 Coy R.E.	PHILOSOPHE
156 Coy R.E.	NOEUX-LES-MINES
157 Coy R.E.	MAZINGARBE
11th Hants. (Pioneers)	NOEUX-LES-MINES
S.I.HORSE	LABUISSIERE
16th Div Cyclists	HOUSHIN
111th Fd. Amb.	LABUISSIERE
112th Fd. Amb.	HOUSHIN.

2353 Wt. W2544/1454 700,000 5/15 D. D. & L. A.D.S.S./Forms/C. 2118.

Army Form C. 2118.

WAR DIARY
or
INTELLIGENCE SUMMARY.
(Erase heading not required.)

Instructions regarding War Diaries and Intelligence Summaries are contained in F. S. Regs., Part II. and the Staff Manual respectively. Title pages will be prepared in manuscript.

Place	Date	Hour	Summary of Events and Information	Offrs.	O. R.	Remarks and references to Appendices
CHATEAU DROUVIN	25/12/15	5 PM	H.Q. Div. Engineers	2	10	
			155 Coy. R.E.	6	220	
			156 " "	6	221	
			157 " "	6	218	
			16th Div. Signal Co.	5	172	
			16th " Cyclists Co.	8	192	
			16th " Train	20	450	
			111th Field Ambulance	10	178	
			112th " "	10	180	
			Santy. Sectn.	1	27	
			Mob. Vet. Sectn.	1	23	
			First casualty reported 2/Lt. P.S. McMAHON 8th Rl. MUNS FUSrs.			
"	26/12/15	"	No change.			
"	27/12/15	"	No change.			
"	28/12/15	"	Units under instruction in trenches.			
"	29/12/15	"	New area decided upon. Following units moved neighbourhood of NEDONCHELLE. S.I.Horse, 8th R. Dublins and 9th Rl. Muns. Fusrs.			

2353 Wt. W2544/1454 700,000 5/15 D. D. & L. A.D.S.S./Forms/C. 2118.

Army Form C. 2118.

Instructions regarding War Diaries and Intelligence Summaries are contained in F. S. Regs., Part II. and the Staff Manual respectively. Title pages will be prepared in manuscript.

WAR DIARY
or
INTELLIGENCE SUMMARY.
(Erase heading not required.)

Place	Date	Hour	Summary of Events and Information	Remarks and references to Appendices
CHATEAU DROUVIN	29/12/15	6 PM	Move of Divn. proceeding. BOMY fixed as Hd.Qrs. of Divn. Following moved today:- 7th Bn. Leinster Regt. 6th Rl. IRISH Rifles 8th Rl. MUNS. FUSrs.	
"	30/12/15	"	No change.	
"	31/12/15	"	No change.	
~~B O M Y~~	~~1/1/16~~		~~Hd. Qrs. of Divn. moved from CHATEAU DROUVIN to BOMY.~~	

[illegible] Lt Col
for Maj Gen
Cdg 16th Divn

Confidential

A + Q.

Instructions regarding War Diaries and Intelligence Summaries are contained in F. S. Regs., Part II. and the Staff Manual respectively. Title Pages will be prepared in manuscript.

WAR DIARY
or
~~INTELLIGENCE SUMMARY~~

(Erase heading not required.)

16th Divn
Jan 1916

Army Form C. 2118

Place	Date	Hour	Summary of Events and Information	Remarks and references to Appendices
BOMY	1/1/16	5.PM	Hd Qrs 16th Divn moved to BOMY.	
"	~~1/1/16~~ 2/1	"	Casualties. 7th R.I. Rifles 1.O.R. slightly wounded. 9th R Dub Fus 1.O.R. killed. Joined HQ. 1st London Arty. 1/1 1/2 & 1/3 Bgdes + 10th D.A.C. HQ at ECQUEDECQUES.	
BOMY	2.1/16			
"	3/1/16	"	Major ~~G.R.~~ Sa G.P.B ROBINSON posted to 6th Bn Con. Rangers. Casualties 7th R.I. Rifles 2.O.R wounded.	
"	4/1/16	"	Casualties 8th R Dub Fus 1.O.R. killed 1.O.R. wounded 7th R.I.R. 2 O.R. wounded. 1st Army ask if we can exchange Div HQ to HONENGHEN CHATEAU at FEBVIN PALFART.	
"	5/1/16	"	No changes.	
"	6/1/16	"	Orders received for shift of Hd Qrs of Divn. BOMY struck out of Divnl area.	

1875 Wt. W593/826 1,000,000 4/15 J.B.C. & A. A.D.S.S./Forms/C. 2118.

Instructions regarding War Diaries and Intelligence Summaries are contained in F. S. Regs., Part II. and the Staff Manual respectively. Title Pages will be prepared in manuscript.

WAR DIARY
or
~~INTELLIGENCE~~ SUMMARY
(Erase heading not required.)

Army Form C. 2118

Place	Date	Hour	Summary of Events and Information	Remarks and references to Appendices
BOMY	7/1/16	6PM	No Change.	
AMETTES	8/1/16	"	Arrival of HdQrs of Divn at this station	
"	9/1/16	"	Distribution in Billets of units 16th Divn as follows.	
			Dw HQ AMETTES	
			C. Sqd S.I. Horse — WESTREHEM	
			HQ Dw Arty. — EGQUEDECQUES	
			1/3 London Bgde RFA. — LIERE	
			16th D.A.C (less 3 sections) — LES PESSES	
			155 Fd Coy RE — PHILOSOPHE	
			156 " " " — NOEUX LES MINES	
			157 " " HQ & 2 secs — MAZINGARBE	
			2 secns of 157 CoRE — AMETTES.	
			47th Inf Bgde HQ — HONENGHEM CHATEAU	
			6th R Irish Regt — FEBVIN PALFART & MONT CORNET.	
			6th Con. Rangers — HESDIGNEUL	
			7th Leinster Regt — LAIRES	
			8th R. Muns. FUS. — BEAUMETZ LES AIRES	

1875 Wt. W593/826 1,000,000 4/15 J.B.C. & A. A.D.S.S./Forms/C. 2118.

Instructions regarding War Diaries and Intelligence Summaries are contained in F. S. Regs., Part II. and the Staff Manual respectively. Title Pages will be prepared in manuscript.

Army Form C. 2118

WAR DIARY
or
~~INTELLIGENCE SUMMARY~~
(Erase heading not required.)

Place	Date	Hour	Summary of Events and Information	Remarks and references to Appendices
"	"	"	48th Inf Bgde HQ. — FONTAINE LES HERMANS.	
			7th R. Irish Rifles — AMES	
			9th Rl Muns Fusn — NOEUX LES MINES	
			8th Rl Dub Fusn — " " "	
			9th Rl Dub. Fusn. — BELLERY.	
			11th Hants (Pioneers) — LES BREBIS	
			16th Cyclist Coy — MINX.	
			16th Div Train (less 145 Coy) — AUCHY AU BOIS	
			16th Div Train ([illegible] 5th 145 Coy) — HESDIGNEUL	
			47th Mob Vet Sectn. — 36A. T 13d. 3, 5.	
			81st San Sectn. — AUCHY-AU-BOIS	
			111 FD Ambulance — ECQUEDECQUES.	
			112 " " — AUCHY-AU-BOIS	
			16th Div MOTOR AMBce Workshop. — AUCHY-AU-BOIS	

1875 Wt. W593/826 1,000,000 4/15 J.B.C. & A. A.D.S.S./Forms/C. 2118.

Instructions regarding War Diaries and Intelligence Summaries are contained in F. S. Regs., Part II. and the Staff Manual respectively. Title Pages will be prepared in manuscript.

WAR DIARY
or
~~INTELLIGENCE SUMMARY~~
(Erase heading not required.)

Army Form C. 2118

Place	Date	Hour	Summary of Events and Information	Remarks and references to Appendices
			Started Batt at AMETTES for HdQrs 2 Sec[ns] 157 Fd Coy R.E + Signals. No Rain.	
"	11/1/16	"	No change	
"	12/1/16	"	H.Q. 47th Inf Bgde + 6th Bn Royal Irish Regt left FEBVIN PALFART to march up for attachment to 15th Division for the trenches.	
"	13/1/16	"	Med Officer reports 4 cases of measles in 6th RI Irish Regt since 12/1/16. Sent at once to ADMS 16th Divn for opinion + requesting ADMS 15th Div to be informed.	
"	14/1/16	"	No Change.	

1875 Wt. W593/826 1,000,000 4/15 J.B.C. & A. A.D.S.S./Forms/C. 2118.

Instructions regarding War Diaries and Intelligence Summaries are contained in F. S. Regs., Part II. and the Staff Manual respectively. Title Pages will be prepared in manuscript.

WAR DIARY
or
~~INTELLIGENCE SUMMARY~~
(Erase heading not required.)

Army Form C. 2118

Place	Date	Hour	Summary of Events and Information	Remarks and references to Appendices
AMETTES	15/1/16	6PM	No Change.	
"	16/1/16	"	~~No change~~ Sw.	
"	~~[illegible]~~	"	Total evacuation: sick + wounded for the Division to this date 201. Two hundred and one.	
"	17/1/16	"	Orders recd for the following officers to join. They have been appointed as below.	
			Lt-Col T.S. ~~LAMBERT~~ (Sw) LAMBART 2nd Bn E. Lancs. Regt to command 47th Inf Bgde.	
			Temp Lt-Col F.W. RAMSAY MIDDLESEX Regt to command 48th Inf Bgde.	
"	18/1/16	"	~~No Change~~ Sw. Lt-Col T.S. LAMBART reported sick. The name of Lt-Col G.E. PEREIRA CMG. DSO substituted.	
"	19/1/16	"	No Change.	

1875 Wt. W593/826 1,000,000 4/15 J.B.C. & A. A.D.S.S./Forms/C. 2118.

Instructions regarding War Diaries and Intelligence Summaries are contained in F. S. Regs., Part II. and the Staff Manual respectively. Title Pages will be prepared in manuscript.

WAR DIARY
or
~~INTELLIGENCE~~ SUMMARY
(Erase heading not required.)

Army Form C. 2118

Place	Date	Hour	Summary of Events and Information	Remarks and references to Appendices
AMETTES	20/1/16	6 PM	No change.	
"	21/1/16	"		
"	22/1/16	"		
"	23/1/16	"	Br Gen F W RAMSAY DSO. assumed Comd 48th Inf Bgde.	
"	24/1/16	"	Orders received for 48th Inf Bgde to proceed to front lines for trenches. The first Bn (9th Rl Muns Fus) moves on 26th. 16th Divnal Signal Coy inspected by GOC at 10.30AM Turn out v. good. horses in good condition. Shoeing good.	
"	25/1/16	"	No change.	
"	26/1/16	"	16th Div Train inspected by GOC 11AM Turn out v good horses in excellent condition. Major G.W. LE PAGE 6th Rl Irish Regt reported killed 9 30 am this day.	

1875 Wt. W593/826 1,000,000 4/15 J.B.C. & A. A.D.S.S./Forms/C. 2118.

Instructions regarding War Diaries and Intelligence Summaries are contained in F. S. Regs., Part II. and the Staff Manual respectively. Title Pages will be prepared in manuscript.

WAR DIARY
or
~~INTELLIGENCE~~ SUMMARY
(Erase heading not required.)

Army Form C. 2118

Place	Date	Hour	Summary of Events and Information	Remarks and references to Appendices
AMETTES	27/1/16	6 PM	Total Casualties for 16th Divn from wounds including accidental and self inflicted to this date are as follows:	

Unit	Officers Kd	Officers Wd	Officers Md	Other ranks Kd	Other ranks Wd	Other ranks Md
6th Bn Rl Irish Regt	1	-	-	2	13	-
6th Bn Con. Rangers	-	-	-	-	2	-
7th Bn LEINSTER REGT	-	-	-	-	15	-
8th Bn Rl Muns. Fusrs	2	1	-	1	5	-
7th Bn RL IRISH RIFLES	-	1	-	-	7	-
9th Bn RL MUNS FUSrs	-	1	-	2	10	-
8th Bn RL DUB. FUSrs	-	-	-	5	19	-
9th Bn RL DUB. FUSrs	-	4	-	5	13	-
11th HANTS (PIONEERS)	-	1	-	1	24	-
16th Div Cyclists Coy	-	-	-	-	2	-
155 Fd COY R.E	-	-	-	1	6	-
157 Fd COY R.E	-	2	-	-	4	-
1/1 LONDON Bde RFA	-	-	-	1	5	-
1/2nd LONDON Bde R.FA	-	-	-	-	1	-
1/3rd LONDON BDE RFA	-	-	-	-	2	-
Total	3	10	-	18	128	-

1875 Wt. W593/826 1,000,000 4/15 J.B.C. & A. A.D.S.S./Forms/C. 2118.

Instructions regarding War Diaries and Intelligence Summaries are contained in F. S. Regs., Part II. and the Staff Manual respectively. Title Pages will be prepared in manuscript.

WAR DIARY
or
~~INTELLIGENCE SUMMARY~~
(Erase heading not required.)

Army Form C. 2118

Place	Date	Hour	Summary of Events and Information	Remarks and references to Appendices
AMETTES	28/1/16	6PM	NO CHANGE.	
"	29/1/16	"	" "	
"	30/1/16	"	Visited LES BREBIS. and 2 Coys 11th Hants (Pioneers). The Country has now dried up considerably owing to spell of fine weather. Roads have improved a lot in this area. Capt G.E. BOSTOCK (Temp) - 8th Bn R. Innis Fus killed	
"	31/1/16	"	Proceeded to HESDIGNEUL the H.Q. of 7th Bn Rl Irish Rifles to pick up The Lord Primate of IRELAND who is visiting Irish troops at the front. Saw working party on flying ground afterwards went to IV Corps H.Q. where his lordship paid visit to Corps Commander. Returned with him to Divnl HdQrs 1.30 P.M.	

[signature]
for Major Gen
Cdg 16th Divn

1875 Wt. W593/826 1,000,000 4/15 J.B.C. & A. A.D.S.S./Forms/C. 2118.

Confidential

A & Q.

16th Divn

Army Form C. 2118

Instructions regarding War Diaries and Intelligence Summaries are contained in F. S. Regs., Part II. and the Staff Manual respectively. Title Pages will be prepared in manuscript.

WAR DIARY
or
~~INTELLIGENCE SUMMARY~~

(Erase heading not required.)

Place	Date	Hour	Summary of Events and Information	Remarks and references to Appendices
AMETTES	1/2/16	6 PM	Lt Col H. WILLIAMS Cdg 9th Bn Rl MUNSTER Fus. reported as wounded (at duty) on this date. Visited No 8 Ordonance repair workshop LABEUVRIERE, Found it very full with repairs 1st Divn. many 18 PR guns in for repairs.	
"	2/2/16	"	Hard frost. Visited 16th Dn Bomb school at LAIRES. Saw two parties (under instruction) throwing. Up to 40 yds frequently thrown in this school.	
"	3/2/16	"	No change.	
"	4/2/16	"	" "	
"	5/2/16	"	News received of transference of this Division from 4th to 1st Corps.	
	6/2/16	"	No change	
	7/2/16	"	" "	

1875 Wt. W593/826 1,000,000 4/15 J.B.C. & A. A.D.S.S./Forms/C. 2118.

Instructions regarding War Diaries and Intelligence Summaries are contained in F. S. Regs., Part II. and the Staff Manual respectively. Title Pages will be prepared in manuscript.

WAR DIARY
or
INTELLIGENCE SUMMARY
(Erase heading not required.)

Army Form C. 2118

Place	Date	Hour	Summary of Events and Information	Remarks and references to Appendices
AMETTES	8/2/16	6PM	Notification received that 49th Infantry Bgde is to come from ENGLAND on 16/2/16. ditto 16th Divnl Artillery	
AMETTES	9/2/16	"	Weather bad, ~~more~~ rain than usual, wind high & West. most of the Regiments undergoing instruction in Trench warfare with 4th Corps.	
AMETTES	10/2/16	"	Weather clearer, Definite orders received that we come under the orders of 1st Corps on 15th/2/16 at 12 Noon, visited the baths at BELLERY, found them clean and in good working order, the men seemed to be thoroughly enjoying their bath.	
AMETTES	11/2/16		Weather dark & heavy rain at various intervals. Advanced parties of the 49th Inf Bde and 16th Divisional Artillery expected to arrive on the 14th/2/16. General inspected two Companies of the Divisional train & was very pleased with the turn out, especially the horses.	
AMETTES	12/2/16	"	Weather bad heavy rain practically all day, out door work impossible. Connaught Rangers passed through on their way	

1875 Wt. W593/826 1,000,000 4/15 J.B.C. & A. A.D.S.S./Forms/C. 2118.

Instructions regarding War Diaries and Intelligence Summaries are contained in F. S. Regs., Part II. and the Staff Manual respectively. Title Pages will be prepared in manuscript.

WAR DIARY
or
INTELLIGENCE SUMMARY
(Erase heading not required.)

Army Form C. 2118

Place	Date	Hour	Summary of Events and Information	Remarks and references to Appendices
			from the front line, all looked fit & well & certainly very clean, after their good work, the whole Regt had a bath at BELLERY.	
[?]METTES	13/2/16		Weather clears no change	
"	14/2/16		Strong wind but no rain. Staff Captain 49th Inf Bde and Staff Captain 16th Div Arty arrived at AIRE and reported in the afternoon to Div. H. Q, they both went out to their areas, after reporting. G. OC inspected 155 Field Coy after their two months in the front line the men were clean & smart and very bright after their trying time. Col Brown took over command of the 9th Royal Munster Fusiliers.	
"	15/2/16		Wind high, but weather clear & bright, 9th Royal Munsters and H Q 48 Inf Bde moved to FLECHIN, to make room for the 49th Inf Bde due to arrive on the 19th 20th & 21st/2/16.	
"	16/2/16		A very high wind 50 m.P.H, with occasional bursts of 60 m.P.H. a few wagons were turned over at the dumps. Went with the G OC to inspect the 9th Munsters, they turned out very well indeed the men were all clean & bright, and showed no signs of their spell of the front line trenches.	

Army Form C. 2118

Instructions regarding War Diaries and Intelligence Summaries are contained in F. S. Regs., Part II. and the Staff Manual respectively. Title Pages will be prepared in manuscript.

WAR DIARY
or
INTELLIGENCE SUMMARY
(Erase heading not required.)

Place	Date	Hour	Summary of Events and Information	Remarks and references to Appendices
AMETTES	17/2/16		Still a high wind but not so strong as yesterday. Went with the G.O.C. to inspect the 16th Div Cavalry & Cyclists, both turned out well, and the Cavalry horses looked very fit. On our way back we went to the Ambulance work shop, the arrangements were excellent, and everything clean and tidy.	
AMETTES	18/2/16		Weather clear, 16th Div ARTY HQ arrived at 8 30 PM.	
"	19/2/16		No Change.	
"	20/2/16		" "	
"	21/2/16		" "	
"	22/2/16		Heavy fall of snow followed by severe frost. Notification received that 16th Divn is to be transferred to 3rd Corps.	
"	23/2/16		Another fall of snow on frozen roads. All traffic very difficult. Snow to a depth of 3 to 4 inches in most places. Transfer of 16th Divn to 3rd Corps Cancelled.	

1875 Wt. W593/826 1,000,000 4/15 J.B.C. & A. A.D.S.S./Forms/C. 2118.

Army Form C. 2118

WAR DIARY
or
INTELLIGENCE SUMMARY
(Erase heading not required.)

Instructions regarding War Diaries and Intelligence Summaries are contained in F. S. Regs., Part II. and the Staff Manual respectively. Title Pages will be prepared in manuscript.

Place	Date	Hour	Summary of Events and Information	Remarks and references to Appendices
AMETTES	24/2/16	-	Very heavy frost. Traffic very difficult. Move of 1st London Divnal Artillery to 56th Divn 3rd Army Commenced today to be completed tomorrow.	
"	25/2/16	-	Much snow, roads almost blocked.	
"	26/2/16	6PM	Forty ninth Infantry Bgde moved today to new area Heavy thaw set in.	
BUSNES	27/2/16	-	Head Qrs. of Divn moved to CHATEAU BUSNES. At 12 noon thaw order brought into force making all moves very difficult. Thaw order affects nearly all roads in our late area.	
BUSNES	28/2/16	"	Snow clearing off country very water logged.	
"	29/2/16	-	Fine day warmer snow almost completely gone. Last units of the Divn. moved into new Reserve area today. Thaw orders ceased at 6 AM today	

G. Webb Lt Col for Lt Col
Cdg 16th Divn.

1875 Wt. W593/826 1,000,000 4/15 J.B.C. & A. A.D.S.S./Forms/C. 2118.

Cont.

Instructions regarding War Diaries and Intelligence Summaries are contained in F. S. Regs., Part II. and the Staff Manual respectively. Title Pages will be prepared in manuscript.

A+Q.

WAR DIARY
or
~~INTELLIGENCE~~ SUMMARY

(Erase heading not required.)

~~16th Divn~~ A+Q 16th Divn Vol 4

Army Form C. 2118

Place	Date	Hour	Summary of Events and Information	Remarks and references to Appendices
BUSNES	1/3/16	6PM.	Orders rcd for move at an early date into another reserve area. Weather improving steadily. Fine spring day and much sunshine. Country drying up.	
BUSNES	2/3/16		8TH MUNSTERS moved into St HILAIRE. 7th and 8th INNIS. FUS. moved forward and were attached to 15th DIVN for trench instruction.	
BUSNES.	3/3/16		156 Coy. R.E. attached to 1st Division.	
BUSNES	4/3/16		8th/IRISH FUS. moved from GONNEHEM and are attached to 1ST DIVN. for trench instruction. Instruction to be given first by Platoons, then by Companies, and then by battalions, the battalion taking over and holding a portion of the line for three days. Training to be complete on 23rd.	
BUSNES	5/3/16		157 Coy. R.E. to forward area for attachment to 12th DIVN. 11th HANTS moved from BOURECQ to forward area for attachment to 15th DIVN.	

1875 Wt. W593/826 1,000,000 4/15 J.B.C. & A. A.D.S.S./Forms/C. 2118.

Instructions regarding War Diaries and Intelligence Summaries are contained in F. S. Regs., Part II. and the Staff Manual respectively. Title Pages will be prepared in manuscript.

WAR DIARY
or
~~INTELLIGENCE~~ SUMMARY

(Erase heading not required.)

Army Form C. 2118

Place	Date	Hour	Summary of Events and Information	Remarks and references to Appendices
BUSNES	6/3/16		No change.	
BUSNES	7/3/16		No change.	
BUSNES	8/3/16		H.D.Qrs. R.A. to ECQUECDEQUES. 77th R.F.A. to LIERES. 177th R.F.A. to ECQUECDEQUES. 180th R.F.A. to AMES. 182nd R.F.A to BELLERY, 16th D.A.C. to LESPESSES, 155 Coy. R.E. to LE REVEILLON. 47th INF. BDE. HD. QRS. to ALLOUAGNE. 6th R. IRISH to ALLOUAGNE. 7th LEINSTERS to ALLOUAGNE 8th MUNSTERS to HAUT RIEUX and BAS RIEUX, HD. QRS. 49th INF. BDE. to MAZINGARBE (forward area) 111TH F. AMB. to ALLOUAGNE. 16th D.S.C LILLERS 16TH A.S.P. AUCHEL.	
PHILOMEL	9/3/16		DIVL. HD.QRS. to PHILOMEL. DIVL. CAV. to HURIONVILLE. 16th CYCLIST Coy. to HURIONVILLE. HD. QRS. 48th INF. BDE. to MARLES LES MINES, 7th IRISH RIFLES and 9th DUBLINS to LAPUGNOY, 8th DUBLINS and 9th MUNSTERS to MARLES LES MINES. 145 Coy. A.S.C to LILLERS. 112th F.A. to LILLERS	

1875 Wt. W593/826 1,000,000 4/15 J.B.C. & A. A.D.S.S./Forms/C. 2118.

Army Form C. 2118

Instructions regarding War Diaries and Intelligence Summaries are contained in F. S. Regs., Part II. and the Staff Manual respectively. Title Pages will be prepared in manuscript.

WAR DIARY
or
~~INTELLIGENCE SUMMARY~~
(Erase heading not required.)

Place	Date	Hour	Summary of Events and Information	Remarks and references to Appendices
PHILOMEL	9/3/16		113TH F. AMB. to RAIMBERT, 81st SANITARY SECTION to LILLERS, 47th M.V.S. to Sheet 36 A. U.16d. 16th F.A.W.U. to LILLERS.	
PHILOMEL	10/3/16		9th DUBLINS to forward area for attachment to 12th DIVN. 16th DIVL. TRAIN. (less one Coy.) to RAIMBERT. EVACUATION of 1st CORPS reserve area complete.	
PHILOMEL	11/3/16		Attachment of 6th CONN. RANGERS to 12th DIVN. complete. they return to ALLOUAGNE. 6th R. IRISH move forward for attachment to 12th DIVN.	
PHILOMEL	12/13/3/16		No change.	
PHILOMEL	14/3/16		6th R. IRISH recalled from 12th DIVN and return to BURBURE. Ditto. 9th DUBLINS who returned to LAPUGNOY.	

1875 Wt. W593/826 1,000,000 4/15 J.B.C. & A. A.D.S.S./Forms/C. 2118.

Instructions regarding War Diaries and Intelligence Summaries are contained in F. S. Regs., Part II. and the Staff Manual respectively. Title Pages will be prepared in manuscript.

WAR DIARY
or
~~INTELLIGENCE SUMMARY~~
(Erase heading not required.)

Army Form C. 2118

Place	Date	Hour	Summary of Events and Information	Remarks and references to Appendices
PHILOMEL	15.3.16		156 Coy R.E complete attachment to 12th DIVN and return to LAPUGNOY.	
			157 Coy R.E attachment to 12th DIV completed they return to CAUCHY A LA TOUR.	
PHILOMEL	17.3.16		No change	
PHILOMEL	18.3.16		No change	
PHILOMEL	19.3.16		No change.	
PHILOMEL	20.3.16		Hd Qrs 49th BRIGADE to DIV. AREA from attachment to 15th DIV.	
PHILOMEL	21.3.16		7th INNIS. FUSILIERS return to DIV. area from attachment 15th DIVISION.	
			7th IRISH FUSILIERS -"- -"- 12th DIVISION.	
PHILOMEL	22.3.16		8th INNIS FUSILIERS -"- -"- 15th DIVISION.	
PHILOMEL	23.3.16		8th IRISH FUSILIERS finish attachment to 1st DIVISION & proceed to billets at NOEUX les MINES.	

1875 Wt. W593/826 1,000,000 4/15 J.B.C. & A. A.D.S.S./Forms/C. 2118.

Instructions regarding War Diaries and Intelligence Summaries are contained in F. S. Regs., Part II. and the Staff Manual respectively. Title Pages will be prepared in manuscript.

WAR DIARY
or
~~INTELLIGENCE SUMMARY~~
(Erase heading not required.)

Army Form C. 2118

Place	Date	Hour	Summary of Events and Information	Remarks and references to Appendices
PHILOMEL	24.3.16		Advanced parties of 47th Infantry Brigade, 155 Coy R.E. and 111th Field Ambulance moved from ALLOUGANE to NOEUX les MINES. — dismounted portion by bus remainder by road.	
	25.3.16		47th Infantry Brigade, 155 Coy R.E., 111th Field Ambulance, advanced parties of 48th Inf. Bde 156 Coy R.E., 113 Field Ambulance ~~143 Coy ASC~~ moved to NOEUX les MINES, dismounted portion by rail from LILLER, remainder by road. 143 Coy ASC to VAUDRICOURT	
	25/26.3.16	night.	47th Infantry Brigade & 155 Coy R.E. moved forward & relieved 45 Infantry Bde & 91st Field Coy R.E. in 14 Bis Sector.	
	26.3.16		48th Infantry Brigade, 156 Coy R.E. 113 Field Ambulance, billeting parties of 49th Inf Bde 157 Coy R.E. & 112 Field Ambulance moved to NOEUX les MINES Hd Qrs 16th Div Train & 145 Coy A.S.C. to VAUDRICOURT — dismounted portion by rail from LAPUGNOY, remainder by road	
	26/27.3.16	night.	48th Infantry Brigade & 156 Coy R.E. forward in relief of 46th Infantry Bde & 74 Coy R.E. in HULLUCH Sector.	
NOEUX les MINES	27.3.16		Hd Qrs Division moved to NOEUX les MINES. 49th Infantry Brigade 157 Coy R.E. & 112th Field Ambulance moved to NOEUX les MINES dismounted party by rail from LAPUGNOY remainder by road. 142 & 144 Coys ASC from RAIMBERT to VAUDRICOURT less supply wagons of 16th Div Artillery 11th Hants Pioneers relieved the 9th Gordon Highlanders at MAZINGARBE 1 Section Reserve Park from BAS RIEUX to VAUDRICOURT & 16th D.S.C. from LILLERS to MINX	

1875 Wt. W593/826 1,000,000 4/15 J.B.C. & A. A.D.S.S./Forms/C. 2118.

Instructions regarding War Diaries and Intelligence Summaries are contained in F. S. Regs., Part II. and the Staff Manual respectively. Title Pages will be prepared in manuscript.

WAR DIARY
or
~~INTELLIGENCE~~ SUMMARY
(Erase heading not required.)

Army Form C. 2118

Place	Date	Hour	Summary of Events and Information	Remarks and references to Appendices
26 NOEUX les MINES	28·3·16			
NOEUX les MINES	29·3·16			
NOEUX les MINES	30/31·3·16	night	Advanced parties, Lewis Gun detachments, all available trained personnel of Light Trench Mortars of 49th Infantry Brigade relieved similar personnel of 47th INF BRIGADE	
	31·3·16 / 1·4·16	night	49th INF BRIGADE relieved 47th INF BRIGADE in the 14th BIS SECTION	
	~~1·4·16~~		~~47th B INF. BRIGADE arrived into billets in MAZINGARBE + NOEUX les MINES 31st 35 in NOEUX les MINES~~	

G. W. Abbott Col for Major Gen
Comdg 16th Divn

1875 Wt. W593/826 1,000,000 4/15 J.B.C. & A. A.D.S.S./Forms/C. 2118.

Instructions regarding War Diaries and Intelligence Summaries are contained in F. S. Regs., Part II. and the Staff Manual respectively. Title Pages will be prepared in manuscript.

A & Q

WAR DIARY
or
~~INTELLIGENCE~~ SUMMARY
(Erase heading not required.)

16th Div

Army Form C. 2118

A & Q
Vol 5

Place	Date	Hour	Summary of Events and Information	Remarks and references to Appendices
NOEUX-LES-MINES	1/4/16	6 P.M.	47th Inf Bgde moved into billets in MAZINGARBE + NOEUX-LES-MINES. H.Q in NOEUX-LES-MINES.	
"	2/4/16	"	No Change.	
"	3/4/16	"	Capt. G.M. Jackson 9th R. Ir. Rifles killed in trenches today. Weather very fine + warm. Country quite dried up.	
"	4/4/16	"	The 9th Rl Muns Fus down to a strength of 33 offrs + 691 O.R. Wired base asking when reinforcements this unit may be expected. This has been quietest day for many weeks in so far as gun fire was concerned.	
"	5/4/16	"	No Change.	
"	6/4/16	"	48th Inf Bgde relieved tonight by 47th Inf Bgde. Visited trenches with Div Comdr. Heavy strafe on 49th Inf Bgde section. Some damage done. Weather cold + fine.	
"	7/4/16	"	No Change	
"	8/4/16	"	NOEUX-LES-MINES heavily shelled all day with various, some 8" armour piercing. Weather cold + very fine. Small draft 62 received during week for 9th Rl Muns Fus	

1875 Wt. W593/826 1,000,000 4/15 J.B.C. & A. A.D.S.S./Forms/C. 2118.

Instructions regarding War Diaries and Intelligence Summaries are contained in F. S. Regs., Part II. and the Staff Manual respectively. Title Pages will be prepared in manuscript.

WAR DIARY
or
~~INTELLIGENCE SUMMARY~~
(Erase heading not required.)

Army Form C. 2118

Place	Date	Hour	Summary of Events and Information	Remarks and references to Appendices
NOEUX LES MINES	9/4/16	6 PM	Weather fine + cold. Visited MAZINGARBE + canteen there, also DUMP. Some few shells again fell in NOEUX. Applied to 1st Corps for reinforcements for 9th R. Mune Flsrs	
"	10/4/16	"	Very cold but fine. Visited Div Laundry BETHUNE. New washing machine provided by 16th Divn working satisfactorily. Wringer not success. NOEUX-LES-MINES station shelled today after all supply waggons had left yard. 3 Aeroplane bombs dropped no damage.	
"	11/4/16	"	Cold + wet. Supply train late owing to accident. Issued 47 Inf Bgde with preserved ration. Two other Brigades as usual.	
"	12/4/16	"	Cold, wet + stormy. 48th Inf Bgde relieve 49th Inf Bgde front trenches tonight.	
"	13/4/16	"	Cold, wet + stormy. PHILOSOPHE heavily shelled, some billets destroyed. Ascertained to be 8" howitzer, nose cap armour piercing shell produced by advanced station 113 Fd Amb ce.	
"	14/4/16	"	Very stormy. Cold + wet.	
"	15/4/16		No change	
"	16/4/16		" "	

1875 Wt. W593/826 1,000,000 4/15 J.B.C. & A. A.D.S.S./Forms/C. 2118.

Instructions regarding War Diaries and Intelligence Summaries are contained in F. S. Regs., Part II. and the Staff Manual respectively. Title Pages will be prepared in manuscript.

A & Q

WAR DIARY
or
~~INTELLIGENCE SUMMARY~~
(Erase heading not required.)

16th Divn

Army Form C. 2118

Place	Date	Hour	Summary of Events and Information	Remarks and references to Appendices
NOEUX-LES-MINES	17/4/16	6PM	Visited 16th Inf Base Depot ETAPLES by order of Div Comdr. Condition of Depot appeared very good & training well carried out as far as can be done in the time. Asked for more arm drill and instruction in saluting.	
"	18/4/16	"	About 260 men inspected by 1st Army Comdr and Cast. as unfitted for service at the front.	
"	19/4/16	"	Very wet cold & stormy. Enemy blew camouflet at about 10.30 AM. Casualties four sappers.	
"	20/4/16	"	Weather variable cold & showery. Enemy shelled NOEUX-LES MINES today with smaller stuff than usual. Damage slight. MAZINGARBE shelled, some damage.	
	21/4/16	"	Deluge of rain, very cold.	
	22/4/16	"	More rain & trenches flooded again. Issued 900 boots to 49th Inf Bde.	
	23/4/16	"	Weather fine and ground drying up. NOEUX-LES-MINES & MAZINGARBE ROAD now shelled daily. Ration traffic stopped until after 6.30 PM.	

1875 Wt. W593/826 1,000,000 4/15 J.B.C. & A. A.D.S.S./Forms/C. 2118.

Instructions regarding War Diaries and Intelligence Summaries are contained in F. S. Regs., Part II. and the Staff Manual respectively. Title Pages will be prepared in manuscript.

Army Form C. 2118

WAR DIARY
or
~~INTELLIGENCE SUMMARY~~ A & Q 16th Division.
(Erase heading not required.)

Place	Date	Hour	Summary of Events and Information	Remarks and references to Appendices
NOEUX LES MINES	24/4/16	6 p.m.	Fine bright day BRAQUEMONT and station shelled for a little in the morning.	
"	25/4/16	"	Fine + warm, 45th M.G. company arrived. Visited MAZINGARBE and Divisional Laundry.	
"	26/4/16	"	Visited trenches 14 BIS sector 48th Infantry Bde	
"	27/4/16	"	Fine + warm with N.E. breeze. Germans attacked along 16th Division front	
"	~~28/4/16~~	"	at about 5.15 a.m having bombarded trenches especially support for over an hour previously also MAZINGARBE and PHILOSOPHE they penetrated our trenches in the vicinity of CHALK PIT WOOD and ESSEX LANE but were driven out again in about ½ hour. The attack was made under cover of smoke balls and gas also lachrymatory shells. Many dead Germans were left on our parapet. Our casualties were about 440 officers + men. Situation became normal about 11.30 a.m.	
	28/4/16	"	47th and 48th M.G. Companies arrived, 48th billeted at HOUCHAIN, 47th at NOEUX LES MINES. (Huts).	
	29/4/16	"	Fine + warm with fairly strong breezes from N.W. to N.E. Germans made a gas attack, gas reached our trenches, remained stationary and finally was blown back by change of wind, causing Germans to retire from the craters	

1875 Wt. W593/826 1,000,000 4/15 J.B.C. & A. A.D.S.S./Forms/C. 2118.

Instructions regarding War Diaries and Intelligence Summaries are contained in F. S. Regs., Part II. and the Staff Manual respectively. Title Pages will be prepared in manuscript.

Army Form C. 2118

WAR DIARY
or
~~INTELLIGENCE SUMMARY~~

A + Q 16th Division

(Erase heading not required.)

Place	Date	Hour	Summary of Events and Information	Remarks and references to Appendices
NOEUX LES MINES	29/4/16	6p.m	behind which they were massing, in doing so they appeared to suffer very heavy casualties from our artillery. Our casualties about 800 killed wounded and gassed. 49th Machine Gun Coy arrived and was billeted at NOEUX LES MINES. 6th (S) Bn Cameron Highlanders (15th Division) attached to Division in support of 7/Leinsters also on account of heavy AB: Casualties ~~approximately 800 killed~~ took place of 8/Inniskilling Fus as a temporary measure. 47th Bde relieved 48th Inf Bde in 14 Bis Section. 47th + 48th M.G. Cos went up into the line.	
	30/4/16	"	Fine + warm, Situation normal.	

G A Cobb Lieut Colonel
A.A + Q.M.G. for G.O.C.

30.4.16

1875 Wt. W593/826 1,000,000 4/15 J.B.C. & A. A.D.S.S./Forms/C. 2118.

Instructions regarding War Diaries and Intelligence Summaries are contained in F. S. Regs., Part II. and the Staff Manual respectively. Title Pages will be prepared in manuscript.

WAR DIARY
or
INTELLIGENCE SUMMARY
(Erase heading not required.)

Army Form C. 2118

16 DW A&Q
VOL 6

Place	Date	Hour	Summary of Events and Information	Remarks and references to Appendices
NOEUX-LES-MINES	1/5/16	6PM.	Wind in E. Gas Alert in force. Quiet day some shells fell here. Gas Expert from 1st Army took away 12 P.H. helmets for examination. These were helmets men were gassed in.	
"	2/5/16	"	Wind in E. gas alert in force. Total Casualties Officers & OR in bulk for actions of 27/4/16 & 29/4/16 are as below. Officers killed 11 wounded 46 missing 1 Other ranks killed ~~384~~ 392 wounded 1028 missing 43 Grand Total 1521. situation normal	
"	3/5/16	"	Fine light breezes from S.W. Situation normal Army commander attended lecture on "Gas" at the Cinema NOEUX LES MINES.	
"	4/5/16		Fine & warm - situation normal. 49th I.Bde relieved 6/Camerons in HULLUCH section and 6/Camerons rejoined 15th Div.	

Army Form C. 2118

Instructions regarding War Diaries and Intelligence Summaries are contained in F. S. Regs., Part II. and the Staff Manual respectively. Title Pages will be prepared in manuscript.

WAR DIARY
or
~~INTELLIGENCE SUMMARY~~
(Erase heading not required.)

Place	Date	Hour	Summary of Events and Information	Remarks and references to Appendices
Noeux les Mines	5/5/16	6 p.m.	Fine & very warm. The C in C accompanied by G.O.C. 1st Corps inspected 1 company of 8/R. Dublin Fusiliers and 1 Coy. 9th R. Dublin Fus and 1 Coy. 9th R. Munster Fus. 48th Bde held a horse and transport show which was also visited.	
	6/5/16	"	Fine, cooler with more wind from the south. The C of G.S visited 16th Div. Hd Qrs from England. 48th I. Bde relieved 49th I. Bde in HULLUCH section of 16th Div. Cyclists returned to NOEUX LES MINES. Situation normal.	
	7/5/16	"	Dull with drizzling rain. attended conference at I Corps Head Quarters. Situation normal.	
	8/5/16	"	Cloudy with moderate wind. 1 Coy R.E + 1 Tunnelling Coy arrived from 12th Division to be attached for work on lines & billeted in MAZINGARBE.	
	9.5.16	"	Rained nearly all day. nothing to report except a small German raid on 47th Bde taking 2 prisoners.	
	10.5.16	"	Wind + rain – attended 1st Corps conference subject "collection of supplies on a forward move" appointment of "area" officers etc.	

Instructions regarding War Diaries and Intelligence Summaries are contained in F. S. Regs., Part II. and the Staff Manual respectively. Title Pages will be prepared in manuscript.

WAR DIARY
or
~~INTELLIGENCE SUMMARY~~

(Erase heading not required.)

Army Form C. 2118

Place	Date	Hour	Summary of Events and Information	Remarks and references to Appendices
NOEUX	11/5/16	6 p.m.	Fine & cool day. Conference at 1st Corps Hdqrs on the subject of collecting stores etc in case of a forward advance	
	12/5/16	"	Execution carried out at Mazingarbe this morning. Weather cloudy & cool	
	13.5.16	"	Wet day. Notified G.O.C 1st Army will present medals on 18th inst.	
	14.5.16	"	Cold & dull. Proceeded to WERMHOULT on business with regard to economy of petrol.	
	15.5.16	"	Situation normal. D.C. Entrenching Battn, a new Battn formed out of amalgamation of 9th and 15th Divns, reported. At present billetted at VERQUIN. Expects to move Hdqrs and 2 Companies up to MAZINGARBE soon.	
	16.5.16	"	Presentation of medal ribbons postponed until 17th. Fine & hot. Wind S.W. Situation normal	
	17.5.16	"	Fine & warm. Presentation of medals on Church Square, NOEUX-LES-MINES at 4 p.m by G.O.C. 1st Corps. 49th Brigade relieved 47th & 2nd Brigades in the Loos Sector.	
	18.5.16	"	Went round with C.R.E to all wagon lines to arrange for water supply. Engaged on 1st Corps scheme for re-organization of artillery. Situation normal. Warm & sunny.	
	19.5.16	"	Visited local cultivators to ascertain possibility procuring green forage which is difficult to obtain. A hot day. Wind Easterly.	
	20.5.16	"	Situation normal. A hot & sunny day. Wind S.E. Visited 8th Siege Batty re movements of Kite Balloon section re farms at grass damaging their drainage operations.	
	21.5.16	"	Proceeded to Wormhoult on duty. In evening at 6.15 p.m enemy dropped shells of heavy calibre into NOEUX LES MINES. Considerable damage done to buildings near Monument. Casualties reported 6 or 18 killed & wounded.	

1875 Wt. W593/826 1,000,000 4/15 J.B.C. & A. A.D.S.S./Forms/C. 2118.

Instructions regarding War Diaries and Intelligence Summaries are contained in F. S. Regs., Part II. and the Staff Manual respectively. Title Pages will be prepared in manuscript.

WAR DIARY
or
~~INTELLIGENCE SUMMARY~~
(Erase heading not required.)

Army Form C. 2118

Place	Date	Hour	Summary of Events and Information	Remarks and references to Appendices
NOEUX LES MINES	22.5.16	6 p.m	Weather fine & hot. Wind S.W. Sergt Major Pantol of 10th Cw. Bdgr died of wounds received on 21st. Our Artillery active at Mazingarbe. Went to Mazingarbe on Board to enquire into condition of 68 tins of biscuits. All tins condemned as unfit for food.	
"	23.5.16	[illegible]	Funeral of Sergt Major Pantol at 2.30 p.m. Our artillery active from Mazingarbe to Philosophe & Vermelles in the evening between 9.30 & 10.30 p.m. Heavy bombardment heard during the night from direction of Vimy. Weather fine in morning, rain in afternoon. Wind S.S.E.	
"	24.5.16	6 pm	Fine in morning. Rain in afternoon & evening. Intermittent bombardment heard north & south of NOEUX. Wind S.S.E. veering to E.	
"	25.5.16	6 pm	Enemy again shelled NOEUX-LES-MINES in the afternoon at 4.30 p.m for about 20 minutes. One house in Rue National destroyed. Otherwise situation normal. Wind S.W.	
"	26.5.16	"	8th Royal [illegible] Fusiliers moved back from line into DROUVIN. This Battalion was relieved by the 5th Royal Berkshire. Lecture on Traffic Control at 2.30 p.m. Enemy again shelled NOEUX-LES-MINES at 4 p.m. Horses of 190 Bde. R.F.A. were stampeded down Rue d'Arras. Weather fine & cool. Wind S.W.	
"	27.5.16	"	Hot & fine. Wind N.E. to E. In accordance with scheme for re-organization of artillery wagons left for Palais. Situation normal.	

1875 Wt. W593/826 1,000,000 4/15 J.B.C. & A. A.D.S.S./Forms/C. 2118.

Instructions regarding War Diaries and Intelligence Summaries are contained in F. S. Regs., Part II. and the Staff Manual respectively. Title Pages will be prepared in manuscript.

WAR DIARY
or
INTELLIGENCE SUMMARY
(Erase heading not required.)

Army Form C. 2118

Place	Date	Hour	Summary of Events and Information	Remarks and references to Appendices
NOEUX LES MINES	28.5.16	9 p.m.	Fine & cool. Wind N.E. veering to N.W. Went to WORMHOUDT on business in connection with Divl Cinema. 9th Royal Inniskilling Fusiliers entrained at BETHUNE at 4.30 p.m. for CONDETTE. 9th Munsters went into billets at DROUVIN. [illegible] Batteries(?) R.F.A. arrived in divisional area. A quiet day.	
"	29.5.16	"	Intermittent artillery fire both by enemy & ourselves all day. The road between ~~[struck out]~~ BRACQUEMONT and PETIT SAINS was heavily shelled by enemy about 2.45 p.m. otherwise enemy's fire did not seem to be directed at any particular target. Company of 11th Hants still billetted at MAZINGARBE under orders to move to LOOS. Weather fine in morning, cloudy in afternoon. Wind N.N.W.	
"	30.5.16		A quiet day. Weather fine & cool. Wind N.W. to W. Orders received for 11th Hants to move from MAZINGARBE to LOOS and for Headquarters of 16th Div. Artillery to move back from MAZINGARBE to NOEUX-LES-MINES.	
	31.5.16	"	Weather fine & cool. 33rd Division asked for 4000 Mills grenades to be sent up to MAZINGARBE KEEP. Situation quiet. Wind N.W.	

Instructions regarding War Diaries and Intelligence Summaries are contained in F. S. Regs., Part II. and the Staff Manual respectively. Title pages will be prepared in manuscript.

WAR DIARY
or
~~INTELLIGENCE SUMMARY~~.
(Erase heading not required.)

"A" and "Q" Branch, 16th Division.

Army Form C. 2118.

Vol 7

Place	Date	Hour	Summary of Events and Information	Remarks and references to Appendices
NOEUX LES MINES	1.6.16	9.p.m	A fine, clear day. Steady breeze from W. MAZINGARBE ROAD heavily shelled at 11.a.m	
	2.6.16	"	2 Companies 7th Suffolk arrived in MAZINGARBE, and are billeted there. 49th Brigade moved back into Divisional Reserve. 47th Bde in 14 Bis Section, 48th Bde in LOOS Section. Wind steady from W and N.W. Bright sunshine all day.	
"	3.6.16	"	Wind steady from N.W. Situation normal. News received by wireless about naval engagement between German & British fleets. Heavy British losses reported.	
"	4.6.16	"	Steady westerly breeze. Presentation of medals on SHOW GROUND at 3 p.m by Corps Commander. Situation very quiet.	
"	5.6.16	"	Wind strong from W. 16th Divisional Coy moved out of their quarters in Rue National, NOEUX-LES-MINES, into other quarters in Rue d'Lessin [illegible] 15th Divisional [illegible] Staff occupied quarters in Rue d'Lessin previously allotted to 15 Div Coy. 2 new 3" Stokes guns were received. Arrangements made for inspection of 49th Brigade by Corps Commander. 7th Suffolks relieved 6th Royal Berkshire Regiment. Situation normal.	
"	6.6.6	"	Strong wind from W. Went to 16th Div Bomb Store to inspect 2" Trench Mortar Bombs, and to arrange as far as possible that trench explodes are fitted to trench mortar bombs & R.L. explodes to R.L. bombs. Arranged that Transport of 5 R. Berks to be moved from Show Ground, NOEUX-LES-MINES to HOUCHIN and Transport of 7th Suffolks from HOUCHIN to Show Ground NOEUX-LES-MINES [illegible] latter coming under 49. Bde. 2 guns of C/177th Bde R.A. condemned by [illegible] sent to [illegible]	

2353 Wt. W2544/1454 700,000 5/15 D. D. & L. A.D.S.S./Forms/C. 2118.

Instructions regarding War Diaries and Intelligence Summaries are contained in F. S. Regs., Part II. and the Staff Manual respectively. Title pages will be prepared in manuscript.

WAR DIARY
or
~~INTELLIGENCE SUMMARY~~.
(Erase heading not required.)

"A" and "Q" Branch, 16th Division.

Army Form C. 2118.

Place	Date	Hour	Summary of Events and Information	Remarks and references to Appendices
NOEUX LES MINES	6.6.16	9 pm	Instructions received that the 181st Brigade R.F.A. of 40th Divisional Artillery will commence to train with 16th Divisional Artillery on June 7th. G.O.C. 1st Army visited NOEUX, but did not inspect troops owing to wet weather. Strong westerly wind. Situation normal. Nothing to report.	
"	7.6.16	"	Strong wind from N.W. 4 sections 181st Brigade R.F.A., less guns, moved in from 40th Divn for instruction with 16th Div Artillery.	
"	8.6.16	"	9th R. Fusiliers relieved 7th Suffolks and were attached to the 49th Infantry Brigade. The 11th Middlesex Regiment relieved the 5th Royal Berkshire Regiment and are attached for work on defences to C.R.E. 16th Division. The 9th R. Fusiliers & 11th Middlesex are billeted in MAZINGARBE. The 7th Suffolks & 5th Royal Berkshires rejoined their own Brigades in area of Reserve ~~Div~~ Division. One section of B/63, one section C/63 & one section of B/62 of 12 Division R.F.A. moved out of 16th Divisional area.	
"	9.6.16		Strong wind from N.W. Situation very quiet. 229 Coy R.E. moved into Divisional area.	
	10.6.16	"	Wind N.W. Rain and thunder. 1 Sec A Echelon 40 D.A.C arrived at 16th Divisional area. 1 Coy West Yorks also came into 16th Divisional area. 1 Sec D63 and 2 Secs D.A.C 12th Division left Divisional area. Situation normal.	
"	11.6.16	"	Wind N.W. Heavy rain at intervals. Went to WORMHOULT on duty. 1 Section B Echelon, 40th D.A.C arrived in 16th Divisional area today. Situation normal.	
	12.6.16	"	Very quiet day. Much rain. Wind N.W. Nothing to report.	
	13.6.16	"	Cold with heavy rain. Wind strong from N.E. The 5th Northants Pioneer Regt, 11th Middlesex Regt & 8th Royal Fusiliers rejoined the 12th Divn. 6th Connaught Rangers temporarily placed at disposal of 47th Brigade. Situation normal.	

Instructions regarding War Diaries and Intelligence Summaries are contained in F. S. Regs., Part II. and the Staff Manual respectively. Title pages will be prepared in manuscript.

WAR DIARY
or
~~INTELLIGENCE SUMMARY.~~

(Erase heading not required.)

"A" and "Q" Branch, 16th Division.

Army Form C. 2118.

Place	Date	Hour	Summary of Events and Information	Remarks and references to Appendices
NOEUX-LES-MINES	14.6.16	9 p.m	Cold & heavy rain. Wind NNE. 8th Royal Inniskilling Fusiliers returned from CAMBETTE to PHILOSOPHE. 61 men of Cyclist Coy of 12th Division went up to LOOS. Situation normal.	
	15.6.16	9 p.m	Abnormally cold. Wind N.E. 5th Northants left Divisional area. 3 Companies 12th Yorks came in and are billeted at MAZINGARBE. Situation normal.	
	16.6.16	9 p.m	8th Royal Inniskilling Fusiliers relieved the 9th Royal [illegible] Fusiliers in left sub-section of 14 Bis section. Abnormally cold with wind from NE veering to E. Situation normal.	
	17.6.16	"	Cold wind from NE. 3 sections of A Echelon 49th D.A.C. came into Divisional area. Enemy shelled BRACQUEMONT with heavy shells between 4.30 p.m and 5.30 p.m.	
	18.6.16	"	Cold wind from NE. Proceeded to WORMHOUDT on duty. Enemy aeroplane appeared over SAILLY-LA-BOURSE at 6 p.m and was driven back by our anti-aircraft guns. Situation normal. No 1 Section 4th Reserve Park moved from GOSNAY to HESDIGNEUL. 47th Bde relieved the 48th Bde in LOOS Section.	
	19.6.16	"	Wind N.W. 9th [illegible] Motor Machine Gun Battery, 12th Division moved from MAZINGARBE to VERDUN. G.O.C. 1st Army inspected 1st Munsters & 9th Dub Fusiliers at NOEUX. Situation normal.	
	20.6.16	"	Wind NW. Situation normal. Nothing to report.	
	21.6.16	"	Wind NW. G.O.C. 1st Corps inspected horse & wagon lines in NOEUX. Situation normal.	
	22.6.16	"	Wind S.E. 48th Bde held a demonstration of the effects of Smoke Candles & P. Smoke grenades on the Bombing ground in NOEUX. Enemy shelled the MAZINGARBE-NOEUX road during the forenoon. Situation normal elsewhere.	

2353 Wt. W2544/1454 700,000 5/15 D. D. & L. A.D.S.S./Forms/C. 2118.

WAR DIARY
or
~~INTELLIGENCE~~ SUMMARY.
(Erase heading not required.)

Army Form C. 2118.

"A" and "Q" Branch, 16th Division.

Instructions regarding War Diaries and Intelligence Summaries are contained in F. S. Regs., Part II. and the Staff Manual respectively. Title pages will be prepared in manuscript.

Place	Date	Hour	Summary of Events and Information	Remarks and references to Appendices
NOEUX-LES-MINES	23.6.16	9 p.m	Sultry with thunder. Enemy shelled MAZINGARBE in vicinity of abattoir. Demonstration of effect of [illegible] & [illegible] Grenades by 48 & 49th Brigades. Enemy aeroplanes active after 10 p.m & from 4.30 a.m to 7.30 a.m. Situation otherwise quiet.	
"	24.6.16	"	Wind W.S.W. Proceeded to BETHUNE to make arrangements for accommodation at BETHUNE of men proceeding on leave. Proceeded at 6 p.m to 47th & 49th Bdes in connection with supply of grenades & smoke candles. Our aeroplanes active in evening over enemy lines E of MAZINGARBE. Situation quiet.	
"	25.6.16	"	Wind S.W. Proceeded to MERVILLE, [illegible], LILLERS and BETHUNE on duty. Situation quiet. Nothing to report. Wind dropped to calm in evening.	
"	26.6.16	"	Wind S.W. by W up to 3 p.m then dropped to calm with rain. Situation calm. Nothing to report.	
"	27.6.16	"	49th Bde came back into Reserve on night of 26th/27th and were relieved by the 48th Bde. Wind W.N.W. veering to N. Steady breeze up to 6 p.m then falling at night time to slight current of air. Our artillery active along the whole of Divl front.	
	28.6.16	"	Wind W.N.W. Nothing to report.	
	29.6.16	"	Wind SSW. Our artillery active along whole of our front. Nothing further to report.	
	30.6.16	"	Wind S.W. Our artillery still active along whole of our front. 229 Coy R.E. left the Division area also 3 Coys of 12th Yorks.	

G. A. [illegible] Lt Col
AA & QMG 16th Div
for G.O.C.

July

16/

AQ 16 Dn
Vol 8

— Original —

W A R   D I A R Y.

"A" AND "Q" BRANCH
H E A D Q U A R T E R S,
16TH. (IRISH) DIVISION

1st. July to 31st. July 1916.

VOLUME 8.

Instructions regarding War Diaries and Intelligence Summaries are contained in F. S. Regs., Part II. and the Staff Manual respectively. Title pages will be prepared in manuscript.

WAR DIARY
or
~~INTELLIGENCE SUMMARY.~~

(Erase heading not required.)

Army Form C. 2118.

Place	Date	Hour	Summary of Events and Information	Remarks and references to Appendices
NOEUX-LES-MINES	1.7.16	[illegible]	Wind S.W. [illegible] enemy aeroplanes over [illegible] at 6 p.m. [illegible] torpedoes from 1st Army [illegible] workshop. [illegible] Our artillery very active along the whole of our front.	
	2.7.16	"	Proceeded to WORMHOUDT on duty. Steady wind from WSW to 7.30 p.m. then dropped [illegible]. Our artillery active along whole of our front. At 6.30 p.m. enemy dropped a few shells near [illegible] CHURCH and the station at [illegible]. Feeding strength of division 29725 men, 707 H.D. horses and 6106 L.D. horses.	
	3.7.16	"	The 47th Inf. Bde. relieved the 49th Inf. Bde. in the [illegible] SECTION [illegible]. Wind moderate varying from S.E. to W.S.W. [illegible] Feeding strength men 20716 Horses H.D. 697 L.D. 6105.	
	4.7.16	"	[illegible] S.E. to S.S.W. [illegible] Battalion [illegible] Relieved by [illegible] Div. Men in trenches 8788. [illegible] shelled by enemy at 10.20 a.m.	
	5.7.16	"	Wind N.W. Feeding strength 20582 men, 697 H.D. horses, 6091 L.D. horses. No new units were rationed to-day, but all A.T.A. units belonging to 16th Div with the exception of 7/181 loaded [illegible] for the last time. Order of groups at refilling point, 48th Bde, 49th Bde, Div. Troops, 47th Bde. Men in trenches 8895.	
	6.7.16	"	Wind WSW. Enemy shelled MAZINGARBE. Some shells fell very near 16th Div Bomb Store. Feeding strength of division 19290 men. 698 H.D. horses. 6734 L.D. horses. Men in trenches 7812.	
	7.7.16	"	Wind S.E. 255 [illegible] by R.E. increased by 200 men. Feeding strength 19439 men. H.D. horses 693. L.D. 6717. Men in trenches 8309.	

Instructions regarding War Diaries and Intelligence Summaries are contained in F. S. Regs., Part II. and the Staff Manual respectively. Title pages will be prepared in manuscript.

WAR DIARY
or
~~INTELLIGENCE SUMMARY.~~

(Erase heading not required.)

Army Form C. 2118.

Place	Date	Hour	Summary of Events and Information	Remarks and references to Appendices
NOEUX-LES-MINES	8.7.16	9.p.m	Wind S.W. MAZINGARBE heavily shelled last night but not near 1st Div. Bomb Store. Bomb Store has been depleted of most heavy explosives, i.e. 3" Stokes, 2" T.M., MILLS grenades & rifle grenades on account of proximity of Filling Holes. Feeding strength 19147 Horses H.D. 848. L.D. 4618 Men in trenches 8219	
"	9.7.16	9.p.m	Wind S.W. Enemy shelled MASINGARBE at 6.10 p.m. Feeding strength of Division 19069 men. H.D. horses 840. L.D. horses 4650. Nothing further to report.	
"	10.7.16	"	Wind S.W. Feeding strength 19087. H.D. Horses 841. L.D. 4627. No new units were attached or left Division. Situation quiet on our front.	
	11.7.16	"	48th Bde relieved to night by 47th. Feeding strength 18963 men. H.D. Horses 842. L.D. 4626. Men in trenches 7532.	
	12.7.16	"	Wind W.S.W. 4" Stokes guns ordered to be withdrawn by Corps in order to make alteration in mountings. Feeding strength 19053 men. H.D. horses 845 L.D. horses 4642. Men in trenches 7873	
	13.7.16	"	Strong wind W.S.W. 22nd H.L.I. & 1st Home Counties Field Coy R.E. attached this day to the Division & drew rations for 1st time. 255 Coy R.E. drew rations from this Division for the last time on transfer to 40th Div. Feeding strength of Div. 19555 men. H.D. horses 701. L.D. horses 4686. Men in trenches 7180.	
	14.7.16	"	Wind W.N.W. 173 Coy R.E. joined to-day from 40th Division in place of 255 Coy R.E. and are attached to Divnl Troops for supply purposes. Parade on square & march past before Divisional Commander. Feeding strength 19411 men. [illegible] H.D. horses 4658 L.D. horses. Men in trenches 7028.	
	15.7.16	"	Wind N.W. 1 section B/77 & 1 section D/77 left but are still attached to us for supplies. 22nd H.L.I. moved out last evening, but for convenience of the Division they drew rations from us this morning. X16 Trench Mortar Battery also [illegible] for the [illegible] Relief. Enemy shelled Railway station at 4 p.m. & 7.30 p.m.	

Instructions regarding War Diaries and Intelligence Summaries are contained in F. S. Regs., Part II. and the Staff Manual respectively. Title pages will be prepared in manuscript.

WAR DIARY
or
~~INTELLIGENCE SUMMARY.~~
(Erase heading not required.)

Army Form C. 2118.

Place	Date	Hour	Summary of Events and Information	Remarks and references to Appendices
NOEUX LES MINES	16.7.16	9 a.m.	Wind WNW. Feeding strength 19624 men, 675 Heavy Draft horses. 4546 L.D. horses. Following reinforcements are received. 7th Leinsters 48 men. 6th Connaught Rs 6 men. 1st R. Munsters 10 men. 7th R. Inniskilling Fusiliers 26 men. 6th R. Irish Regt 84 men. 8th R. Munster Fus 16 men. 8th R. Dublin Fus 6 men. 7 R. Irish Fus 11 men. Total 253 men. These men are transferred from the 7th Brigade.	
"	17.7.16	"	Wind WNW. Feeding strength 19230 men. H.D. horses 667. L.D. horses 4681. Men in trenches 7529. Following units became Corps Troops for Rations from tomorrow 170th & 173rd Coys (Tunnelling) R.E. Following units attached to us for rations from tomorrow:- 1st Corps Cavalry. 1st Corps Cyclist Battn. 2nd T. M. G. Battery. 48th Brigade held jumping competition and other military sports on show ground	
"	18.7.16	"	Wind NNE. 16th Ammn. Sub Park, 170 Coy R.E. and 173 Coy R.E. left and joined 1st Corps for ration rationing purposes. Enemy shelled MAZINGARBE heavily in afternoon. Feeding strength of Division 18611 men. H.D. horses 675. L.D. horses 5126. Men in trenches 7323.	
"	19.7.16	"	Wind WNW. Feeding strength 19650 men. HD Horses 661. LD horses 5087. Men in trenches 7399. Tunnelling Coys 170. 173 rejoined this Division for supply purposes. 48th Bde relieved the 49th Brigade in the LOOS SECTION. 49th Billetted in MAZINGARBE & NOEUX. HdQrs in NOEUX	
"	20.7.16	"	Wind NW. Feeding strength 19457 men. H.D. horses 662. L.D. horses 5096. Men in trenches 7614. Enemy dropped a few shells in neighbourhood of Station about 6 p.m.	
"	21.7.16	"	16th Division moved one section up north, taking over HULLUCH SECTION and moving out of LOOS SECTION. Feeding strength 19376 men. HD horses 660. LD horses 5063. Men in trenches 7775. 49th Bde moved out of Reserve into HULLUCH SECTION, so that all Brigades are in line.	

2353 Wt. W2544/1454 700,000 5/15 D. D. & L. A.D.S.S./Forms/C. 2118.

Instructions regarding War Diaries and Intelligence Summaries are contained in F. S. Regs., Part II. and the Staff Manual respectively. Title pages will be prepared in manuscript.

WAR DIARY
or
~~INTELLIGENCE SUMMARY.~~
(Erase heading not required.)

Army Form C. 2118.

Place	Date	Hour	Summary of Events and Information	Remarks and references to Appendices
NOEUX LES MINES	22.7.16	9 p.m.	Wind N.W. Men in trenches 19406. H.D. horses 665. L.D. horses 5085. Men in trenches 8732. Two units left or joined the Division to-day. Lt. Commander 32nd Div. visited Village Line to-day	
	23.7.16	"	Wind W.N.W. Feeding strength of Div. 18965 men. H.D. horses 667. L.D. horses 5110. Men in trenches 8725. The 49th Bde T.M. Battery & 49th Bde M.G. ~~Batty~~ Coy were relieved by the 48th T.M. Batty & 48th M.G. Coy.	
"	24.7.16	"	The 48th Inf. Bde relieved the 49th Inf. Bde on night of 23rd/24th. 182nd Bde R.A. moved out to Sailly La BOURSE & VERQUINEUL to-day. Feeding strength 19176. H.D. horses 669. L.D. horses 5103 men in trenches 8437.	
	25.7.16	"	6th Connaughts relieved the 6th Royal Irish Regt in the right subsection of 14 Bis section. Feeding strength of Division 18987. H.D. horses 663 L.D. horses 5101. Men in trenches 7393.	
	26.7.16	"	The 8th Munsters relieved the 7th Leinsters in the left subsection of 14 Bis section. Feeding strength of Division 19009. H.D. horses 626. L.D. horses 5152. Men in trenches 7281. Corps Ordnance dump & 16th Div. Salvage store were destroyed by fire this evening.	
	27.7.16	"	11th Hants were relieved last night from LOOS by the Pioneer Battalion of the 32nd Div. 3 Companies of the 11th Hants are billeted in PHILOSOPHE E. Headquarters & 1 Coy in NOEUX-LES-MINES. Feeding strength of 16 Div 18805 men. H.D. horses 625. L.D. horses 5137. Men in trenches 7281	
	28.7.16	"	Feeding strength of Division 18775 men. H.D. horses 620. L.D. horses 5108. Men in trenches 7313. Enemy dropped 5 shells in NOEUX, 4 of which were "blinds", about 7.15 p.m.	
	29.7.16	"	Feeding strength of Division 18734 men H.D. horses 616. Men in trenches 7312. 15th H.L.I. 2 sections 214 Coy R.E and C/155 R.F.A joined this Division to-day. H.L.I billeted at MAZINGARBE. 2 sections R.E at PHILOSOPHE.	

2353 Wt. W2544/1454 700,000 5/15 D. D. & L. A.D.S.S./Forms/C. 2118.

Instructions regarding War Diaries and Intelligence Summaries are contained in F. S. Regs., Part II. and the Staff Manual respectively. Title pages will be prepared in manuscript.

WAR DIARY
or
~~INTELLIGENCE SUMMARY.~~
(Erase heading not required.)

Army Form C. 2118.

Place	Date	Hour	Summary of Events and Information	Remarks and references to Appendices
NOEUX LES MINES	30.7.16	9.pm	Men in trenches 7179. Feeding strength 19549. H.D. horses 684. L.D. horses 5297. A quiet day. Nothing of importance to report.	
"	31.7.16	"	49th Inf. Bde relieved the 47th Inf. Bde. in the 14 BIS SECTION. 2 Battns 47th Inf Bde in MAZINGARBE and 2 in NOEUX LES MINES. Feeding strength of Divn 19651 men. H.D. horses 625. L.D. horses 5288. Men in trenches 6678.	

C Knipe Capt
for A. A. & Q. M. G.
16th Division

2353 Wt. W2544/1454 700,000 5/15 D. D. & L. A.D.S.S./Forms/C. 2118.

Vol 9

W A R D I A R Y.

"A" & "Q" Branch 16th Div Headquarters

MONTH OF AUGUST, 1916.

VOLUME:- 9.

Instructions regarding War Diaries and Intelligence Summaries are contained in F. S. Regs., Part II. and the Staff Manual respectively. Title pages will be prepared in manuscript.

WAR DIARY
or
~~INTELLIGENCE SUMMARY.~~
(Erase heading not required.)

Army Form C. 2118.

Place	Date	Hour	Summary of Events and Information	Remarks and references to Appendices
	August			
NOEUX -les-MINES	1st.	9.pm.	Colonel BUCKLEY, 7th Leinster Regiment, proceeded to England on leave. Feeding strength of Division: men 19620: H.D.Horses 641: L.D.Horses 5291: men in trenches 6627. Oats changed on lorries of Supply Column.	
-do-	2nd.	-do-	Feeding strength of Division; men 19613: H.D.Horses 634: L.D.Horses 5280: men in trenches 5280: enemy aeroplane dropped a bomb in NOeux last night.	
-do-	3rd.	-do-	A.A.& Q.M.G., visited Divisional Bomb Store to inspect precautions taken against spontaneous combustion of incendiary and smoke bombs. A large ~~number~~ quantity of salved grenades and bombs were handed into bomb store some of which was buried. Feeding strength of Division : men 19564: H.D.Horses 651: L.D.Horses 5286: men in trenches 6716.	
-do-	4th.	-do-	Brig-General READY, D.A.& Q.M.G., I Corps, visited this office with Brigadier-General ANDERSON, who relieves him. 118 Bangalore Torpedoes supplied to 48th Brigade by First Army R.E.Workshop. Feeding strength of Division: men 19344: H.D.Horses 645: L.D.Horses 5277: men in trenches 7209:	
-do-	5th.	-do-	Lieut-Colonel CROCKETT proceeded to England on leave. Situation normal: nothing of importance to report.	
-do-	6th.	-do-	Special Parade, Divine Service, held in GRAND PLACE, BETHUNE, this morning at 10.45.a.m. First Army Commander attended. German aeroplane flew over NOEUX at 8.a.m., but was driven off by our aeroplanes and anti-aircraft guns.	
-do-	7th.	-do-	Enemy shelled the railway station at NOEUX at 9.30.a.m., and again at 4.30.p.m. Some shells of large calibre were fired into BETHUNE doing heavy damage in the GRAND PLACE and No. 33 Casualty Clearing Station. There were numerous casualties among the civilian and military inhabitants. Feeding strength of Division; men 18680: H.D.Horses 617: L.D.Horses 5265: men in trenches 7076. Wood could not be cleared this morning from railway station owing to hostile shell fire. Presentation of medal ribbons by Corps Commander on Show Ground at NOEUX.	

8th:-

2353 Wt. W2544/1454 700,000 5/15 D. D. & L. A.D.S.S./Forms/C. 2118.

Instructions regarding War Diaries and Intelligence Summaries are contained in F. S. Regs., Part II. and the Staff Manual respectively. Title pages will be prepared in manuscript.

WAR DIARY
or
~~INTELLIGENCE SUMMARY~~.
(Erase heading not required.)

Army Form C. 2118.

Place	Date	Hour	Summary of Events and Information	Remarks and references to Appendices
NOEUX -les- MINES	8th.	9.pm.	Heavy retaliation on enemy for damage done to BETHUNE. D.A.Q.M.G., went to VERMELLES in connection with the handing over 16th Div. T.M.Bomb Store to 8th Division. Also visited 16th Div Bomb Store at MAZINGARBE. 30 boxes for salved Newton rifle grenades asked for from First Army R.E.Workshop. Refilling point changed from railway station to point on NOEUX-BETHUNE road	
-do-	9th.	-do-	Situation normal: feeding strength of Division; men 19045: H.D.Horses 627: L.D.Horses 5281.	
-do-	10th.	-do-	A quiet day. Feeding strength of Division; men, 19737: H.D.Horses 632: L.D.Horses 5380. Following units loaded with us for last time today:- Corps Cavalry, Cyclists, 2 M.M.G.Batteries, and reverted to Corps Troops. 17th Northumberland Fusiliers, and half of 96th M.M.G.Battery drew for first time; these came from 40th Division.	
-do-	11th.	-do-	Divisional Commander proceeded to LOOS to inspect defences. A quiet day. Situation normal.	
-do-	12th.	-do-	D.A.A.& Q.M.G., proceeded to 14 BIS section on tour of inspection: 100 cyclists attached for duty to Commandant, LOOS. Feeding strength of Division; men 18938.	
-do-	13th.	-do-	No change.	
-do-	14th.	-do-	Feeding strength of Bivision; men 18989: H.D.Horses 617: L.D.Horses 4871: men in trenches 10428. Two 3.7" T.M.left in LOOS bomb store by 40th Division have to be collected and sent back to D.A.D.O.S. Situation normal.	
-do-	15th.	-do-	Enemy shelled MAZINGARBE. Feeding strength of Division; men 18945: H.D.Horses 612: L.D.Horses 4876: men in trenches 9618. Situation normal.	
-do-	16th.	-do-	Feeding strength of Division; men 18911: H.D.Horses 610: L.D.Horses 4880; men in trenches 9035. Situation normal. Nothing to record.	

17th:-

2353 Wt. W2544/1454 700,000 5/15 D. D. & L. A.D.S.S./Forms/C. 2118.

Instructions regarding War Diaries and Intelligence Summaries are contained in F. S. Regs., Part II. and the Staff Manual respectively. Title pages will be prepared in manuscript.

WAR DIARY
or
INTELLIGENCE SUMMARY.
(Erase heading not required.)

Army Form C. 2118.

Place	Date	Hour	Summary of Events and Information	Remarks and references to Appendices
CORBIE	12th	9pm	Weather fine: a quiet day: nothing to report. Feeding strength 12,218 including 34th Div.D.S.C.	
do.	13th	9pm	Weather fine: a quiet day: reinforcements received from 11th September to 13th inclusive, 7 officers and 268 Other Ranks.	
do.	14th	9pm	A quiet day: weather fine and dry: nothing to report.	
do.	15th	9pm	A fine day: Division still resting in CORBIE area: nothing to report.	
do.	16th	9pm	Weather still fine and cold. Total reinforcements to date for Division 12 officers and 621 men.	
do.	17th	9pm	16th Division Transport and Mounted personnel moved out of CORBIE area between 1.p.m. and 3.p.m. proceeding to LA CHAUSSEE and PICQUINY, where they billeted for the night. Destinations were reached by 12 midnight.	
~~HALLENCOURT 18th 9pm~~ HALLEN COURT	18th	9pm	Divisional Headquarters and the Infantry of the Division moved by bus out of the CORBIE area into back area. Divisional Headquarters at HALLENCOURT. Casualties of the Division during tour in SOMME AREA: Officers:- killed,67: wounded 160: missing 14. Other Ranks:- killed, 581: wounded 2673: missing 845: TOTAL:- Officers 241: Other Ranks 4,099:	
do.	19th	9pm	Division resting in back area. Nothing to report.	
do.	20th	9pm	Nothing to report.	
WESTOUTRE	(21st (22nd	9pm	Division started entraining for IX Corps area at 0.45.a.m. on 21st. Divisional Headquarters at WESTOUTRE. The whole of the Division were settled into new area by evening of 22nd. Total reinforcements of Division to date: 25 Officers, 954 Other Ranks.	
do.	23rd	9pm	48th and 49th Brigades took over portion of line from 4th Canadian Division. 47th Brigade in Reserve; weather fine.	
do.	24th	9pm	Weather fine. D.A.Q.M.G. visited horse lines. Second Army Commander inspected various units of the Division.	

2353 Wt. W2514/1454 700,000 5/15 D. D. & L. A.D.S.S./Forms/C. 2118.

25th:-

Army Form C. 2118.

Instructions regarding War Diaries and Intelligence Summaries are contained in F. S. Regs., Part II. and the Staff Manual respectively. Title pages will be prepared in manuscript.

WAR DIARY
or
INTELLIGENCE SUMMARY.
(Erase heading not required.)

Place	Date	Hour	Summary of Events and Information	Remarks and references to Appendices
NOEUX -les- MINES.	17th	9.pm	Feeding strength of Division: men 18,787: H.D.Horses 610: L.D.Horses 4,883: men in trenches 10,215: Situation normal. No change.	
	18th	9.pm.	Situation normal. No change: feeding strength; men, 18,643: H.D.Horses 609: L.D.Horses 4,912: men in trenches 10,116.	
	19th	9.pm.	Supply of 2" T.M.Ammunition now ample, after slight shortage. Consumption of Very Lights above normal: feeding strength of Division; men, 18,638: H.D.Horses 609: L.D.Horses 4,902: men in trenches 10,599. A quiet day. Board of Survey condemned 800 lbs of Potatoes.	
	20th	9.pm.	Feeding strength of Division: men 18,602: men in trenches 10,082: Lecture of Courts Martial procedure at PHILOSOPHE CHATEAU. Quiet day: no change.	
	21st	9.pm	Enemy shelled BETHUNE RAILWAY STATION with 5.9 shells about 6.30.p.m. Feeding strength of Division 18,536 men: H.D.Horses 612: L.D.Horses 4,881: men in trenches 10,071.	
	22nd	9.pm.	No change in situation. Nothing to record.	
	23rd	9.pm.	8th Royal Inniskilling Fusiliers moved today from MAZINGARBE to HOUCHIN. 7th Leinster Regiment moved from MAZINGARBE to HAILLICOURT. Men in trenches 10,071. Feeding strength of Division; men 18,433.	
	24th	9.pm.	A quiet day: nothing to report.	
	25th	9.pm.	Preparations being made to move to new area: otherwise no change.	
	~~26th~~	~~9.pm.~~	~~D.A.A.& Q.M.G., proceeded to RAIMBERT to arrange billets: D.A.Q.M.G. also went.~~	
	26th	9.pm.	A quiet day: nothing to report. Handed over Bomb Store to 112th Brigade.	
	27th	9.pm.	D.A.A.& Q.M.G., proceeded to RAIMBERT to arrange billets: D.A.Q.M.G. also went.	

28th:-

Instructions regarding War Diaries and Intelligence Summaries are contained in F. S. Regs., Part II. and the Staff Manual respectively. Title pages will be prepared in manuscript.

WAR DIARY
or
INTELLIGENCE SUMMARY.
(Erase heading not required.)

Army Form C. 2118.

Place	Date	Hour	Summary of Events and Information	Remarks and references to Appendices
RAIMBERT	28th	9.pm.	16th Division commenced to move out of area into back billets. All staff left except Captain KNIPE and Lieutenant COLTHURST. Representative of 3rd Division arrived to take over offices etc. Captain KNIPE and Lieutenant COLTHURST proceeded to RAIMBERT.	
	29th	9.pm.	Divisional Headquarters less Captain KNIPE and Major CLEMENTI left RAIMBERT for CORBIE. Division commenced entraining.	
CORBIE.	30th	9.pm.	Major CLEMENTI and Captain KNIPE proceeded from RAINBERT to CORBIE. A very wet day.	
FORKED TREE CAMP.	31st	9.pm.	Divisional Staff left CORBIE in forenoon. Arrived FORKED TREE CAMP at 12.noon. Weather clear and fine. Roads very cut up in places. Flies very troublesome and numerous. Water supply bad: has to be fetched by hand from 1½ miles distant.	

C. Knipe Capt
for D.A.Q.M.G.
16th Divn

Duplicate

Instructions regarding War Diaries and Intelligence Summaries are contained in F. S. Regs., Part II. and the Staff Manual respectively. Title pages will be prepared in manuscript.

WAR DIARY

or

~~INTELLIGENCE SUMMARY~~.

(Erase heading not required.)

Army Form C. 2118.

Place	Date	Hour	Summary of Events and Information	Remarks and references to Appendices
	August			
NOEUX -les-MINES	1st.	9.pm.	Colonel BUCKLEY, 7th Leinster Regiment, proceeded to England on leave. Feeding strength of Division: men 19620: H.D.Horses 641: L.D.Horses 5291: men in trenches 6627. Oats changed on lorries of Supply Column.	
-do-	2nd.	-do-	Feeding strength of Division; men 19613: H.D.Horses 634: L.D.Horses 5280: men in trenches 5280: enemy aeroplane dropped a bomb in NOeux last night.	
-do-	3rd.	-do-	A.A.& Q.M.G., visited Divisional Bomb Store to inspect precautions taken against spontaneous combustion of incendiary and smoke bombs. A large ~~number~~ quantity of salved grenades and bombs were handed into bomb store some of which was buried. Feeding strength of Division : men 19564: H.D.Horses 651: L.D.Horses 5286: men in trenches 6716.	
-do-	4th.	-do-	Brig-General READY, D.A.& Q.M.G., I Corps, visited this office with Brigadier-General ANDERSON, who relieves him. 118 Bangalore Torpedoes supplied to 48th Brigade by First Army R.E.Workshop. Feeding strength of Division: men 19344: H.D.Horses 645: L.D.Horses 5277: men in trenches 7209:	
-do-	5th.	-do-	Lieut-Colonel CROCKETT proceeded to England on leave. Situation normal: nothing of importance to report.	
-do-	6th.	-do-	Special Parade, Divine Service, held in GRAND PLACE, BETHUNE, this morning at 10.45.a.m. First Army Commander attended. German aeroplane flew over NOEUX at 8.a.m., but was driven off by our aeroplanes and anti-aircraft guns.	
-do-	7th.	-do-	Enemy shelled the railway station at NOEUX at 9.30.a.m., and again at 4.30.p.m. Some shells of large calibre were fired into BETHUNE doing heavy damage in the GRAND PLACE and No. 33 Casualty Clearing Station. There were numerous casualties among the civilian and military inhabitants. Feeding strength of Division; men 18680: H.D.Horses 617: L.D.Horses 5265: men in trenches 7076. Wood could not be cleared this morning from railway station owing to hostile shell fire. Presentation of medal ribbons by Corps Commander on Show Ground at NOEUX.	

8th:-

Instructions regarding War Diaries and Intelligence Summaries are contained in F. S. Regs., Part II. and the Staff Manual respectively. Title pages will be prepared in manuscript.

WAR DIARY

or

~~INTELLIGENCE SUMMARY~~.

(*Erase heading not required.*)

Army Form C. 2118.

Place	Date	Hour	Summary of Events and Information	Remarks and references to Appendices
NOEUX -les- MINES	8th.	9.pm.	Heavy retaliation on enemy for damage done to BETHUNE. D.A.Q.M.G., went to VERMELLES in connection with the handing over 16th Div. T.M.Bomb Store to 8th Division. Also visited 16th Div Bomb Store at MAZINGARBE. 30 boxes for salved Newton rifle grenades asked for from First Army R.E.Workshop. Refilling point changed from railway station to point on NOEUX-BETHUNE road	
-do-	9th.	-do-	Situation normal: feeding strength of Division; men 19045: H.D.Horses 627: L.D.Horses 5281.	
-do-	10th.	-do-	A quiet day. Feeding strength of Division; men, 19737: H.D.Horses 632: L.D.Horses 5380. Following units loaded with us for last time today:- Corps Cavalry, Cyclists, 2 M.M.G.Batteries, and reverted to Corps Troops. 17th Northumberland Fusiliers, and half of 96th M.M.G.Battery drew for first time: these came from 40th Division.	
-do-	11th.	-do-	Divisional Commander proceeded to LOOS to inspect defences. A quiet day. Situation normal.	
-do-	12th.	-do-	D.A.A.& Q.M.G., proceeded to 14 BIS section on tour of inspection: 100 cyclists attached for duty to Commandant, LOOS. Feeding strength of Division; men 18938.	
-do-	13th.	-do-	No change.	
-do-	14th.	-do-	Feeding strength of Division; men 18989: H.D.Horses 617: L.D.Horses 4871: men in trenches 10428. Two 3.7" T.M.left in LOOS bomb store by 40th Division have to be collected and sent back to D.A.D.O.S. Situation normal.	
-do-	15th.	-do-	Enemy shelled MAZINGARBE. Feeding strength of Division; men 18945: H.D.Horses 612: L.D.Horses 4876: men in trenches 9618. Situation normal.	
-do-	16th.	-do-	Feeding strength of Division; men 18911: H.D.Horses 610: L.D.Horses 4880; men in trenches 9035. Situation normal. Nothing to record.	

17th:-

2353 Wt. W2544/1454 700,000 5/15 D. D. & L. A.D.S.S./Forms/C. 2118.

Instructions regarding War Diaries and Intelligence Summaries are contained in F. S. Regs., Part II. and the Staff Manual respectively. Title pages will be prepared in manuscript.

WAR DIARY
or
INTELLIGENCE SUMMARY.
(Erase heading not required.)

Army Form C. 2118.

Place	Date	Hour	Summary of Events and Information	Remarks and references to Appendices
NOEUX -les- MINES.	17th	9.pm	Feeding strength of Division: men 18,787: H.D.Horses 610: L.D.Horses 4,883: men in trenches 10,215: Situation normal. No change.	
	18th	9.pm.	Situation normal. No change: feeding strength; men, 18,643: H.D.Horses 609: L.D.Horses 4,912: men in trenches 10,116.	
	19th	9.pm.	Supply of 2" T.M.Ammunition now ample, after slight shortage. Consumption of Very Lights above normal: feeding strength of Division; men, 18,638: H.D.Horses 609: L.D.Horses 4,902: men in trenches 10,599. A quiet day. Board of Survey condemned 800 lbs of Potatoes.	
	20th	9.pm.	Feeding strength of Division: men 18,602: men in trenches 10,082: Lecture of Courts Martial procedure at PHILOSOPHE CHATEAU. Quiet day: no change.	
	21st	9.pm	Enemy shelled BETHUNE RAILWAY STATION with 5.9 shells about 6.30.p.m. Feeding strength of Division 18,536 men: H.D.Horses 612: L.D.Horses 4,881: men in trenches 10,071.	
	22nd	9.pm.	No change in situation. Nothing to record.	
	23rd	9.pm.	8th Royal Inniskilling Fusiliers moved today from MAZINGARBE to HOUCHIN. 7th Leinster Regiment moved from MAZINGARBE to HAILLICOURT. Men in trenches 10,071. Feeding strength of Division; men 18,433.	
	24th	9.pm.	A quiet day: nothing to report.	
	25th	9.pm.	Preparations being made to move to new area: otherwise no change.	
	~~26th~~	~~9.pm.~~	~~D.A.A.& Q.M.G., proceeded to RAIMBERT to arrange billets: D.A.Q.M.G. also went.~~	
	26th	9.pm.	A quiet day: nothing to report. Handed over Bomb Store to 112th Brigade.	
	27th	9.pm.	D.A.A.& Q.M.G., proceeded to RAIMBERT to arrange billets: D.A.Q.M.G. also went.	

28th:-

Instructions regarding War Diaries and Intelligence Summaries are contained in F. S. Regs., Part II. and the Staff Manual respectively. Title pages will be prepared in manuscript.

WAR DIARY
or
INTELLIGENCE SUMMARY.
(Erase heading not required.)

Army Form C. 2118.

Place	Date	Hour	Summary of Events and Information	Remarks and references to Appendices
RAIMBERT	28th	9.pm.	16th Division commenced to move out of area into back billets. All staff left except Captain KNIPE and Lieutenant COLTHURST. Representative of 3rd Division arrived to take over offices etc. Captain KNIPE and Lieutenant COLTHURST proceeded to RAIMBERT.	
	29th	9.pm.	Divisional Headquarters less Captain KNIPE and Major CLEMENTI left RAIMBERT for CORBIE. Division commenced entraining.	
CORBIE.	30th	9.pm.	Major CLEMENTI and Captain KNIPE proceeded from RAINBERT to CORBIE. A very wet day.	
FORKED TREE CAMP.	31st	9.pm.	Divisional Staff left CORBIE in forenoon. Arrived FORKED TREE CAMP at 12.noon. Weather clear and fine. Roads very cut up in places. Flies very troublesome and numerous. Water supply bad: has to be fetched by hand from 1½ miles distant.	

C Knipe Capt
for D.A.D.M.S.
16th Divn

W A R   D I A R Y .

"A" and "Q" Branch / 16th Division

MONTH   OF SEPTEMBER. [redacted],   1916.

VOLUME:- 10

VOL 10

Army Form C. 2118.

Instructions regarding War Diaries and Intelligence Summaries are contained in F. S. Regs., Part II. and the Staff Manual respectively. Title pages will be prepared in manuscript.

WAR DIARY
or
INTELLIGENCE SUMMARY.

(Erase heading not required.)

Place	Date	Hour	Summary of Events and Information	Remarks and references to Appendices
	Septbr.			
Forked Tree Camp.	1st	9.pmm	Day spent in cleaning Camp. Canteen opened at Divisional Headquarters. Weather dry, and fine.	
do.	2nd	9pm	Weather fine and dry. 47th Brigade attached to 20th Division. Improvement in Camp continued. Trench Boards laid down. D.A.C. moved up to HAPPY VALLEY.	
do.	3rd	9pm	Heavy fighting in progress: reports shew satisfactory progress by us. Weather cloudy and cool.	
do.	4th	9pm	D.A.A.& Q.M.G. went to CITADEL to inspect camp into which Divisional Headquarters are moving to-morrow. Weather cloudy and cool.	
CITADEL	5th	9pm	16th Divisional Headquarters moved out of FORKED TREE CAMP at 8.a.m. Advanced Headquarters proceeded to MINDEN POST. Remainder of Headquarters in CITADEL. D.A.D.O.S. remained behind at FORKED TREE CAMP. Fine in morning, wet in afternoon. Heavy fighting all along our front. French on our right reported to be meeting with great success.	
do.	6th	9pm	Heavy fighting still proceeding on whole if Divisional front. A fine day. Feeding strength of Division 14,896 men.	
do.	7th	9pm	Rear portion of 16th Divisional Headquarters moved to another area in CITADEL. Feeding strength of Division 15,000	
do.	8th	9pm	Strength 15,000 men. A fine day. Heavy fighting on the Divisional front. A fine day. Heavy Artillery fire on the whole Divisional front.	
do.	9th	9pm	16th Division attacked and took GINCHY. Division was then relieved in the line by GUARDS DIVISION. Weather fine after foggy morning.	
do.	10th	9pm	Division commenced to move back to CORBIE area, to rest and refit. Weather fine.	
CORBIE	11th	9pm	16th Divisional Headquarters moved to CORBIE. 47th Brigade Headquarters at VAUX. 48th Brigade Headquarters at CORBIE. 49th Brigade Headquarters at SAILLY-le-SEC. Feeding strength 10,129 men. Weather fine.	

12th :-

2353 Wt. W2544/1454 700,000 5/15 D. D. & L. A.D.S.S./Forms/C. 2118.

Instructions regarding War Diaries and Intelligence Summaries are contained in F. S. Regs., Part II. and the Staff Manual respectively. Title pages will be prepared in manuscript.

WAR DIARY
or
INTELLIGENCE SUMMARY.
(Erase heading not required.)

Army Form C. 2118.

Place	Date Sept.	Hour	Summary of Events and Information	Remarks and references to Appendices
WEST OUTRE.	25th	9pm	Second Army Commander visited WESTOUTRE in forenoon. Reinforcements received on 23rd.,24th., and 25th., 32 Officers, 179 Other Ranks: weather fine.	
do.	26th	9pm	Weather fine and bright: orders out that 16th Division front will be held by the three Brigades in line. 47th Brigade on left: 48th Brigade in centre: 49th Brigade on right. All moves to be completed by noon on 28th instant. Reinforcements: 1 officer and 24 O.R. 60.O.R. sent to 16th Divisional Artillery who are still with XIV CORPS.	
do.	27th	9pm	D.A.Q.M.G. inspected horse lines: D.A.A.& Q.M.G. to DUNKIRK with Lieut.WILLIAMS to look for machinery for Divisional Laundry. German observation baloon broke adrift and was shot down in flames in our lines east of KEMMEL at 5.30.p.m. Reinforcements 15 officers and 11.O.R. 1 Officer and 9.O.R. diverted to Divisional Artillery.	
do.	28th	9pm	Weather fine: 2 officers and 285 O.R. received as reinforcements for the Division. A.Q.M.G. IX Corps visited "Q" Branch, 16th Division.	
do.	29th	9pm	Weather cloudy and hazy: D.A.A.& Q.M.G. visited Observation post on KEMMEL HILL: nothing to report.	
do.	30th	9pm	Court of Inquiry held at Headquarters, 1st Canadian Tunnelling Company on loss of Motor Cycle spare parts: weather fine.	

C. Knipe
Captain,
for D.A.A.& Q.M.G., 16th (Irish) Division.

5552
SB

W A R D I A R Y

MONTH OF OCTOBER, 1916.

VOLUME 11

"A & Q" Branch 16th Division

Vol 11

Army Form C. 2118

Instructions regarding War Diaries and Intelligence Summaries are contained in F. S. Regs., Part II. and the Staff Manual respectively. Title Pages will be prepared in manuscript.

WAR DIARY
or
~~INTELLIGENCE~~/~~SUMMARY~~
(Erase heading not required.)

Administrative Branch,
16th.Division Headquarters.

Place	Date	Hour	Summary of Events and Information	Remarks and references to Appendices
WESTOUTRE (BELGUIM)	1-10-16		A fine day. Reinforcements received - 2 Officers, 42 'O.R.' ANZACS raided German trenches last night. A quiet day. Nothing to report.	
"	2-10-16		No change - nothing to report.	
"	3-10-16		D.A.Q.M.G. visited all Brigade Bomb Stores in the morning. Total reinforcements for 2nd. and 3rd. 8 Officers - 108 'O.R.' - Weather - wet.	
"	4-10-16		A wet day. A.A. & Q.M.G. proceeded to G.H.Q. on duty. D.A.A. & Q.M.G. went to I.Corps today on duty. A quiet day on Divisional front.	
"	5-10-16		A quiet day - nothing to report.	
"	6-10-16		A fine day. Captain H.A.B. QUARE, 1st.Munsters appointed G.S.O. III., 41st. Division.	
"	7-10-16		Court of Enquiry on loss of vouchers and documents of 16th.Div. Laundry. Divisional Commander proceeded to LA TOUQUET on one day's leave. D.A.Q.M.G. proceeded to STEENVORDE with A.D.V.S. to draw 35 remounts. Stormy day.	
"	8-10-16		Court of Enquiry mentioned above re-assembled and concluded. A.A. & Q.M.G. proceeded on leave to England with Lt-Col. Crockett, O.C.,11th. Hants. Reinforcements received today - 3 Officers and 29 men.	
"	9-10-16		a fine day - nothing to report.	
"	10-10-16		Weather fine. Inspector of Catering paid a visit to "Q" Office to arrange for inspection tomorrow. D.A.Q.M.G. inspected Laundry at HOSPICE, LOCRE. Difficulty with engine. Will probably soon be overcome. MMMMMMMMMMMMMM D.A.D.M.S. returned from leave.	
"	11-10-16		Inspector of Catering visited 47th., 48th. and 49th. Brigade Transport Lines and was satisfied with the working arrangements seen. Weather fine. Reinforcements - 4 Officers, 145 'O.R.'	
"	12-10-16		Weather fine and windy. All medium T.M's left behind by 16th.Division by order of I. Corps at NOEUX-les-MINES were this day restored to the Division.	

1875 Wt. W593/826 1,000,000 4/15 J.B.C. & A. A.D.S.S./Forms/C. 2118.

WAR DIARY or ~~INTELLIGENCE/SUMMARY~~ Sheet 2. Army Form C. 2118

(Erase heading not required.)

Instructions regarding War Diaries and Intelligence Summaries are contained in F. S. Regs., Part II. and the Staff Manual respectively. Title Pages will be prepared in manuscript.

Administrative Branch,
16th. Divisional Headquarters.

Place	Date	Hour	Summary of Events and Information	Remarks and references to Appendices
WESTOUTRE	13-10-16		9th. R.Dublin Fusiliers relieved 8th.R.Dublin Fusiliers. 1st.R.Munster Fusiliers relieved 7th. Royal Irish Rifles. 8th.R.Dublin Fusiliers on relief to KLONDYKE FARM and ROSSIGNOL WOOD. 7th. Royal Irish Rifles to LOCRE. Weather fine.	
"	14-10-16		No change in situation. 2nd. Royal Irish Regiment joined 49th.Inf.Bde. 7th. and 8th.Bns. Royal Irish Fusiliers amalgamated and called 7th/8th. Royal Irish Fusiliers. O.C. Lt-Col. GREGORIE.	
"	15-10-16		Reinforcements today - 84 'O.R.' IX. Corps Commander visited Divisional Commander. Court of Enquiry held as to circumstances connected with wounding of 2 Belgian boys by a grenade. Weather fine	
"	16-10-16		A fine and coldday. Feeding strength of Division 17,307 men. Horses 566 H.D. 4396 L.D.	
"	17-10-16		Rain most of the day. 2nd. R.Irish Regt.relieved 8th.R.Inniskilling Fusiliers who moved into Divisional Reserve at LOCRE. Feeding strength of Division 17320 men. Horses 558 H.D. 4614 L.D. 8th. R.Munster Fusilier relieved a portion of the 6th. Connaught Rangers, whose Headquarters are at SIEGE FARM.	
"	18-10-16		A damp day with rain at intervals. D.A.Q.M.G. to BETHUNE on duty connected with Laundry. Allotment of 6 tons of anthracate coal for LOCRE Laundry. 180th. Brigade and No.3. Section, 16th.D.A.C. was withdrawn from the 16th. Division and transferred to 1st. A.N.Z.A.Corps . C/77 relieved D/180. 2 Section B/177 relieved 2 Sections B/180. 1 Section B/177 relieved 1 Section A/180.	
"	19-10-16		A wet day. D.A.A. & Q.M.G. and A.P.M. proceeded on leave. No change in situation. Feedings strength of Division 15726 men. 526 H.D. horses and 3478 L.D. Horses.	
"	20-10-16		Weather bright and cold. 59th. Siege Battery rationed by first time by 16th.Division. Feeding strength of Division 15779 men. 7th/8th.R.Irish Fusiliers relieved 2nd.R.Irish Regt. in Left Sub-Sector. 8th.R.Inniskilling Fusiliers relieved 7th.R.Inniskilling Fusiliers in Right Sub-Sector.	
"	21-10-16		Weather clear - frost at night - Reinforcements from 16th. to 21st. inclusive - 6 Officers, 213 'O.R.' Feeding Strength of Division 16263 men - 730 H.D. Horses, 3444 L.D. Horses. Enemy aeroplanes active. Total reinforcements for 16th.Division from Sept.11th. to date inclusive Officers 143, O.R. 2457.	

1875 Wt. W593/826 1,000,000 4/15 J.B.C. & A. A.D.S.S./Forms/C. 2118.

557a

Army Form C. 2118

WAR DIARY
or
INTELLIGENCE/SUMMARY
(Erase heading not required.)

Instructions regarding War Diaries and Intelligence Summaries are contained in F. S. Regs., Part II. and the Staff Manual respectively. Title Pages will be prepared in manuscript.

Administrative Branch,
16th.Divisional Headquarters.

Place	Date	Hour	Summary of Events and Information	Remarks and references to Appendices
WESTOUTRE	22-10-16		A bright day - cold and frosty. Nothing to report re situation. Test alarm at 2a.m.	
"	23-10-16		Weather fine. Wind S.E. Gas alert on. Feeding strength 16080 men .	
"	24-10-16		A wet day. No change in situation. 373 horses arrived for Division.	
"	25-10-16		A wet day. Fedding strength of Division 16406 men. H.D. horses 605, L.D. 3406. Gas alert on.	
"	26-10-16		Wind S.E. in morning, change in the afternoon to N.W. Wet in morning, fine in afternoon. Feeding Strength 16531 men, H.D. horses 613, L.D. horses 3749.	
"	27-10-16		Wind S.E. blowing a gale. Nothing to report.	
"	28-10-16		Wind S.E. Port of Boulogne closed until further notice. Feeding strength of Division 16594 men, H.D. horses 602. L.D. horses 3748. Reinforcements from 22nd. to 28th. inclusice, 39 Officers, 361 men.	
"	29-10-16		Raid on enemy's trenches carried out successfully at 5-45p.m. 4 Prisoners captured. Visited No. 4 D.S.C. with D.A.Q.M.G. 3 "Q" cars in dock. High wind from S.E.	
"	30-10-16.		D.A.Q.M.G. and D.A.D.O.S. proceeded on leave. Wind S.W. Gas alert off. No change in situation.	
"	31-10-16		Strong wind from S.W. Lecture on Horse-mastership by O.C. 47th.Mobile Vet. Section at LOCRE. No change in situation. Reinforcements from 29th. to 31st. inclusive. 9Officer, 86 'O.R.' Feedings strngth of the Division 16196 men, H.D. horses 602, L.D. horses 3732.	

C. Knipe Capt
for Major-General,

October 31st. 1916.

Commanding 16th. (Irish) Division.

558a

W A R D I A R Y .

F O R

MONTH OF NOVEMBER, 1916.

VOLUME 12

"A & Q." Branch 16th Div H.Q.

Vol 12

Army Form C. 2118.

WAR DIARY
or
INTELLIGENCE SUMMARY.
(Erase heading not required.)

"A" & "Q" BRANCH, 16th Division.

Instructions regarding War Diaries and Intelligence Summaries are contained in F. S. Regs., Part II. and the Staff Manual respectively. Title pages will be prepared in manuscript.

Place	Date	Hour	Summary of Events and Information	Remarks and references to Appendices
WESTOUTRE	Novr. 1st	9.pm.	Wind S: last of series of lectures on Horsemastership by O.C., 47th Mob.Vety.Section,at LOCRE. 176th Siege Battery joined 16th Division today.	
do.	2nd	do.	Wind S.W.: lecture on adjustment of Gas masks at 2.30.p.m. at WESTOUTRE; feeding strength of Division, 16762 men: H.D.Horses 603: L.D.Horses 3732.	
do.	3rd	do.	Wind S.E.: gas alert on : Observation balloon seen drifting from South to North: feeding strength 16558 men: no change in situation.	
do.	4th	do.	Wind strong from S.E.: H.R.H.The Duke of Connaught inspected 8th Dublin Fusiliers in afternoon: feeding strength of Division 16637 men: no change in situation.	
do.	5th	do.	Gale from S.E.: conference at "Q" Office attended by all Staff Captains, subject:- IX Corps Circulars. British aeroplane which descended last evening in field near Divisional Laundry, WESTOUTRE was repaired and proceeded; feeding strength of Division 16445 men: H.D.Horses 602: L.D.Horses 3701.	
do.	6th	do.	Strong wind from S.E. with some rain: A.A.& Q.M.G., attended IX Corps "Q" Conference: no change in situation.	
do.	7th	do.	A very strong gale from S.W. with heavy rain all day: feeding strength of Division 16451 men: H.D.Horses 601: L.D.Horses 3697: Reinforcements for Division from Nov.1st to Nov. 7th inclusive 4 officers and 53 men.	
do.	8th	do.	Wet and stormy: wind S.by W: nothing to report: Feeding strength of Division 16385 men: H.D.Horses 601: L.D.Horses 3691:	
do.	9th	do.	Fine day: nothing to report: feeding strength of Division 16378 men: H.D.Horses 605: L.D. horses 3705.	
do.	10th	do.	A very fine, bright day: conference of O's C. Divisional Trains was held at IX Corps H.Q., on question of Local purchase of straw: the Corps Reserve Area was divided up amongst 16th, 25th, and 36th Divisions for purposes of purchases.	

Instructions regarding War Diaries and Intelligence Summaries are contained in F. S. Regs., Part II. and the Staff Manual respectively. Title pages will be prepared in manuscript.

WAR DIARY
or
INTELLIGENCE SUMMARY.
(Erase heading not required.)

Army Form C. 2118.

Sheet 2.

Place	Date	Hour	Summary of Events and Information	Remarks and references to Appendices
WESTOUTRE	Novr. 11th	9.pm.	A fine, dull day: slight westerly breeze: feeding strength of Division 16443 men: H.D.Horses 604: L.D.Horses 3703:	
do.	12th	9.pm.	Dull day, no rain: conference at IX Corps on Road maintenance and repairs attended by D.A.Q.M.G: feeding strength of Division 15834 men: H.D.Horses 606: L.D.Horses 3708:	
do.	13th	do.	Dull day, slight westerly breeze: feeding strength of Division 16172 men: H.D.Horses 606: L.D.Horses 3690:	
do.	14th	do.	Wind S.E.: gas alert on: Captain C.A.M.Alexander, Bde.Major 48th Infantry Brigade, left on transfer: feeding strength of Division 16280 men: H.D.Horses 605: L.D.Horses 3673: intimation received that the 2nd Royal Dublin Fusiliers are to entrain tomorrow to join 16th Division on transfer from 4th Division, FOURTH ARMY: reinforcements for Division from 8th to 14th Novr inclusive, 6 officers, and 243 O.R.	
do.	15th	do.	Wind N.E.: very cold: slight frost during the night: Major C.T.BRADSHAW, A.P.M., left on transfer to 2nd Reserve Cavalry Regiment: Captain G.M.STEVENSON-REECE assumed his duties as A.P.M.: feeding strength of Division 15991 men: H.D.Horses 607: L.D.Horses 3660:	
do.	16th	do.	WindE: very cold: Major W.S.TRAILL, G.S.O.2, left the 16th Division on appointment as G.S.O.1 3rd Division: 2nd Royal Dublin Fusiliers arrived from 10th Brigade 4th Division on transfer to the 16th Division: feeding strength of Division 16195 men: H.D.Horses 607: L.D.Horses 3645:	
do.	17th	do.	Wind E: very cold: frost all day: feeding strength of the Division 17007 men: H.D.Horses 620: L.D.Horses 3679: nothing to report:	
do.	18th	do.	Slight fall of snow during the night: turned into rain and continued all day: Wind E: feeding strength of Division 16949 men: H.D.Horses 628: L.D.Horses 3679: nothing to report.	
do.	19th	do.	Wind S.E.: showery: noth ng to report: feeding strength of Division 17249 men: H.D.Horses 622: L.D.Horses 3674:	

Army Form C. 2118.

Instructions regarding War Diaries and Intelligence Summaries are contained in F. S. Regs., Part II. and the Staff Manual respectively. Title pages will be prepared in manuscript.

WAR DIARY
or
INTELLIGENCE SUMMARY.
(Erase heading not required.)

Sheet 3.

Place	Date	Hour	Summary of Events and Information	Remarks and references to Appendices
WESTOUTRE	Novr. 20th	9.pm.	Wind S.E: dull with a little rain: nothing to report: feeding strength of Division 17190 men: H.D.Horses 628: L.D.Horses 3674:	
do.	21st	do.	Light Wind E.: fine day: reinforcements for Division from 15th to 21st inclusive, 4 officers, and 689 O.R. feeding strength of Division 17388 men: H.D.Horses 612: L.D.Horses 3666: orders received that no more straw was to be purchased in Belgium, and amounts already purchased but not carried away to be handed back: 173rd Siege Battery drew rations for last time:	
do.	22nd	do.	Wind W: absorption of 8th R.Munster Fusiliers into the 1st R.Munster Fusiliers completed today: feeding strength of Division 17423 men: H.D.Horses 612: L.D.Horses 3668: part of 185th Battery left Divisional area.	
do.	23rd	do.	Wind S.W.: gas alert off: A.A.& Q.M.G. attended conference in morning on Trench Tramways: leave allotment increased to 39 places: feeding strength of Division 17254: H.D.Horses 602: L.D.Horses 3671.	
do.	24th	do.	Dull day: Wind S.E.: gas alert on: Reinforcements from 22nd to 24th inclusive 4 officers and 156 O.R.: Divisional School drew rations for first time: no change in situation:	
do.	25th	do.	A wet day: Court of Enquiry at WIPPENHOEK on certain rations which had been withdrawn from KEMMEL DEFENCES. Feeding strength of Division 17,800 men: H.D.Horses 608: L.D.Horses 3721:	
do.	26th	do.	No change: nothing to report:	
do.	27th	do.	D.A.Q.M.G. to BAILLEUL to attend conference on roads: Brig-Gen LEVESON GOWER proceeded to PARIS on leave: aeroplanes, both British and enemy, active over Divisional Headquarters.	
do.	28th	do.	Wind S.E.: gas alert on: feeding strength of Division 17834 men: H.D.Horses 591: L.D.Horses 3620: A.A.& Q.M.G., attended IX Corps Conference at BAILLEUL.	
do.	29th	do.	Wind S.E.: and dangerous: No.19 Motor Machine Gun Battery drew rations for first time today: no change in situation.	
do.	30th	do.	Wind S.E., and dangerous: A.A.& Q.M.G. proceeded to England on special leave: reinforcements from 25th to 30th inclusive officers 4, O.R. 76: No change in situation.	

1/12/16.

C. Hicke Captain
for A.A. & Q.M.G. 16 Div.

2353 Wt. W2544/1454 700,000 5/15 D. D. & L. A.D.S.S./Forms/C. 2118.

WAR DIARY FOR MONTH OF DECEMBER, 1916.

VOLUME 13

"A & Q" Branch 16 Div H.Q.

Vol 13

Army Form C. 2118

Instructions regarding War Diaries and Intelligence Summaries are contained in F. S. Regs., Part II. and the Staff Manual respectively. Title Pages will be prepared in manuscript.

WAR DIARY
or
INTELLIGENCE SUMMARY
(Erase heading not required.)

"A" & "Q" BRANCH, 16th Division.

Place	Date	Hour	Summary of Events and Information	Remarks and references to Appendices
	Decr.16.			
WESTOUTRE.	1st	9.pm.	General Protard of the French Army visited 16th Division this afternoon: Wind S.E. & dangerous.	
do.	2nd	9.pm.	Wind S.E. & dangerous: feeding strength of Division 17633 men: H.D. horses 599: L.D.Horses 3626: No. 25 Kite Balloon Section drew for first time today.	
do.	3rd	9.pm.	Owing to train failing to arrive at Railhead before noon, supplies were drawn from reserve Refilling took place at MONT NOIR: A.A.& Q.M.G. returned from special leave today. Wind S.E., dangerous.	
do.	4th	9.pm.	Wind S.W., safe: nothing to report.	
do.	5th	9.pm.	Wind N.E., dangerous: 16th Division took over the SPANBROEK Section of the 36th Division tonight: feeding strength of Division 17,841 men: H.D.Horses 585: L.D.Horses 3711: enemy aeroplane dropped bombs to north of WESTOUTRE in evening.	
do.	6th	9.pm.	Wind N.E., dangerous: lecture on Aerial photography at 16th Divisional School: no change in situation.	
do.	7th	9.pm.	Wind N.E., dangerous: No.19 Motor Machine Gun Battery drew for last time today: reinforcements from Dec 1st to Dec.7th inclusive: 12 officers, 118, O.R.: Officers' Club opened by Army Commander in BAILLEUL today: no change in situation.	
do.	8th	9.pm.	Wind S.W., safe: 176 Siege Battery drew for 1st time today: feeding strength of Division 17,466 men: H.D.Horses, 582: L.D.Horses 3,689.	
do.	9th	9.pm.	Wind S.W., safe: Nothing to report.	
do.	10th	9.pm.	Wind S.E., dangerous: conference of Brigadiers at Divisional Headquarters: reinforcements from 8th to 10th inclusive, 11 officer, 482 O.Ranks.	
do.	11th	9.pm.	No change.	
do.	12th	9.pm.	Heavy fall of snow: semi-finals of Divisional Boxing Competition: Court of Enquiry on shortage of Coal at CANADA CORNER: feeding strength of Division 18,110 men: 591 H.D.Horses: 3717,L.D.Horses.	

1875 Wt. W593/826 1,000,000 4/15 J.B.C. & A. A.D.S.S./Forms/C. 2118.

Instructions regarding War Diaries and Intelligence Summaries are contained in F. S. Regs., Part II. and the Staff Manual respectively. Title Pages will be prepared in manuscript.

WAR DIARY
or
INTELLIGENCE SUMMARY
(Erase heading not required.)

Army Form C. 2118

Place	Date	Hour	Summary of Events and Information	Remarks and references to Appendices
	Dec.16.			
WESTOUTRE.	13th	9.pm.	Wind S.E., dangerous: no change in situation.	
do.	14th	9.pm.	Wind S.E., dangerous: Divisional Boxing Competition commenced at BAILLEUL.	
do.	15th	9.pm.	Wind S.E., dangerous: feeding strength of Division 17,867 men: final of Divisional Boxing Competition at BAILLEUL: reinforcements from 11th to 16th inclusive, 7 Officer, 213, O.Ranks.	
do.	16th	9.pm.	Wind S.W., safe: no change.	
do.	17th	9.pm.	Wind S.W.: feeding strength of Division 18,245 men: H.D.Horses 591: L.D.Horses 3,720: Divisional Claims Officer proceeded to GODEWAERSVELDE and MONT NOIR on duty.	
do.	18th	9.pm.	Wind S.W.: billets being arranged for 2 ~~battalions~~ batteries 6" Howitzers and 2 Batteries 60 pounders, which are being placed in Divisional Area: 176 Battery R.G.A., left Division today.	
do.	19th	9.pm.	Wind S.W.: fall of snow in afternoon: feeding strength of Division, 18,0004 men: H.D.Horses 590: L.D.Horses 3,720:	
do.	20th	9.pm.	Wind S.E., dangerous: Commander-in-Chief visited Divisional front in the afternoon; feeding strength of Division 18,736 men.	
do.	21st	9.pm.	Wind, S.W.: safe: reinforcements from 16th to 21st inclusive: 1 officer: 922 O.Ranks.	
do.	22nd	9.pm.	Wind S.W., safe: feeding strength of Division 18,625 men: H.D.Horses 589: L.D.Horses 3692: no change.	
do.	23rd	9.pm.	Nothing to report.	
do.	24th	9.pm.	Wind, S.E.: safe : feeding strength of Division 18,610 men: H.D.Horses 588: L.D.Horses 3791:	
do.	25th	9.pm.	Wind, S.E., safe: Special Xmas dinner for Staff Clerks and others: reinforcements from 22nd to 25th inclusive 2 Officer, 207 Other Ranks:	

1875 Wt. W593/826 1,000,000 4/15 J.B.C. & A. A.D.S.S./Forms/C. 2118.

Instructions regarding War Diaries and Intelligence Summaries are contained in F. S. Regs., Part II. and the Staff Manual respectively. Title Pages will be prepared in manuscript.

WAR DIARY
or
INTELLIGENCE SUMMARY
(Erase heading not required.)

Army Form C. 2118

Place	Date	Hour	Summary of Events and Information	Remarks and references to Appendices
	Dec.16.			
WESTOUTRE.	26th	9.pm.	Wind S.E., safe: No change.	
	27th	9.pm.	Wind, S.W., dangerous: feeding strength of Division 19528 men: Final of Corps Boxing Competition Trench Mortar Bombardment by Division in afternoon: Kemmel shelled by enemy. 180th Brigade and 4th Section D.A.C., rejoined Division today.	
	28th	9.pm.	Wind W.S.W., safe: No change in situation.	
	29th	9.pm.	Captains HART and ROSWELL arrived for attachment to Division: wind blowing a gale from W.S.W., feeding strength of Divsion 19,714 men:	
	30th	9.pm.	Nothing to report.	
	31st	9.pm.	Wind S.W., safe: reinforcements from 26th to 31st inclusive, 38 Officers and 360 Other Ranks: feeding strength of Division 19, 387 men: H.D.Horses 602: L.D.Horses 3702.	

C. Knipe Capt
for Lieut Colonel
~~Major-General~~,
~~Commanding 16th (Irish)~~ Division.
AA & QMG 16th Division

1875 Wt. W593/826 1,000,000 4/15 J.B.C. & A. A.D.S.S./Forms/C. 2118.

W A R   D I A R Y   for month of JANUARY, 1917.

VOLUME 14

A & Q Branch 16th Division

Vol 14

[illegible] War Diaries and Intelligence [illegible] contained in F. S. Regs., Part II. [illegible] the Staff Manual respectively. Title Pages will be prepared in manuscript.

WAR DIARY
or
INTELLIGENCE SUMMARY
(Erase heading not required.)

Army Form C. 2118

"A" & "Q" BRANCH, 16th Div.Headquarters.

Place	Date	Hour	Summary of Events and Information	Remarks and references to Appendices
WESTOUTRE.	Jany. 1917.			
	1st	9.pm.	Wind S.E. and safe. Court of Enquiry held on fire at KEMMEL SHELTERS by which 3 huts and Company store were destroyed: first list of New Year's Honours published: Lieut-Colonel G.A.C.WEBB, A.A.& Q.M.G., 16th Division, awarded D.S.O.	
	2nd	9.pm.	Wind S.W. and safe: feeding strength of Division 19801 men: H.D.Horses 594: L.D.Horses 3455:	
	3rd	9.pm.	Wind S.W. and safe: nothing to report.	
	4th	9.pm.	Wind S.W. and safe: no change in situation.	
	5th	9.pm.	Wind S.W. and safe: a fine day and much aerial activity: Divisional Band instruments arrived, and unpacked: reinforcements from 1st to 5th inclusive, 8 Officers 255.O.R: feeding strength of Division 20051 men: H.D.Horses 596: L.D.Horses 3453:	
	6th	9.pm.	Wind S.E. and dangerous: no change in situation: Claims Officer proceeded to KEMMEL to investigate damage done to houses in village.	
	7th	9.pm.	Wind S.W., safe: aeroplane fight in view of Divisional Headquarters: British plane forced down in flames.	
	8th	9.pm	Wind S.E.,dangerous: percentage of frozen meat now very small: feeding strength of Division 20407 men.	
	9th	9.pm.	Wind S.E., dangerous: no change.	
	10th	9.pm.	Wind S.E., dangerous: Kite Balloon on MONT ROUGE brought down in flames by enemy aeroplane, in afternoon: reinforcements from 6th to 10th inclusive, 10 Officers, 121 O.R.	
	12th	9.pm.	Wind S.W. morning, changing to N.W., evening: Court of Enquiry held at LA CLYTTE on fire which occurred at 250th Tunnelling Coy. H.Q., on 29.11.16; Colonel ANDERSON, Inspector of Fires, President	

1875 Wt. W593/826 1,000,000 4/15 J.B.C. & A. A.D.S.S./Forms/C. 2118.

War Diaries and Intelligence ... contained in F. S. Regs., Part II. ... the Staff Manual respectively. Title Pages will be prepared in manuscript.

WAR DIARY
or
INTELLIGENCE SUMMARY

(Erase heading not required.)

Army Form C. 2118

Sheet 2.

Place	Date	Hour	Summary of Events and Information	Remarks and references to Appendices
WESTOUTRE	Jan. '17.		President: Raid by 49th Brigade in evening: 79 men of 176 Siege Battery joined today: feeding strength of Division 19764 men: H.D.Horses 613: L.D.Horses 4448:	
	13th	9.pm.	Wind N.E., snow, sleet and gale: nothing to report.	
	14th	9.pm.	Wind S., safe: reinforcements from 10th to 14th inclusive, 12 officers, 103,O.R.	
	15th	9.pm.	Second Army Commander inspected camps, horse lines, etc: fall of snow in evening: wind S.E., dangerous.	
	16th	9.pm.	Wind E., by S.E.: Commandant, Divisional School proceeded on leace: Old Marlburian dinner at BAILLEUL in evening: Colonel MONCK-MASON, 1st.R.Muns.Fus., returned from leave.	
	17th	9.pm.	Wind N.E., dangerous: heavy fall of snow: A.A.& Q.M.G., and O.C., 11th Hants, proceeded on leave: feeding strength of Division 20100 men: H.D.Horses 620: L.D.Horses 4573:	
	18th	9.pm.	Wind N.E., dangerous: Brig-General PERREIRA, 47th Infantry Brigade, proceeded on leave: reinforcements from 15th to 18th inclusive: 10 Officers, 283 O.R. H.Qrs., 77th., B/77th, C/77th and C/180 Batteries R.F.A., left Division today.	
	19th	9.pm.	Wind N.E., dangerous: no change in situation: nothing to report:	
	20th	9.pm.	Wind N.E., dangerous: very cold: no change in situation.	
	21st	9.pm.	Wind N.E., dangerous: severe frost: D.A.A.& Q.M.G., proceeded to Divisional School and LOCRE to inspect canteens.	
	22nd	9.pm.	Wind N.N.E., dangerous: frost still severe: Claims Officer proceeded to LOCRE to investigate claims of Farmer THIBAUT DECOOKEK: advance guard of 256th Siege Battery joined Division today.	
	23rd	9.pm.	Wind N.E., dangerous: continued frost: reinforcements from 19th to 23rd inclusive: 30 Officers and 71.O.R: feeding strength of Division 19,836 men: 592 H.D.Horses:4007 L.D.Horses: Colonel Thackeray, 9th Rl.Dublin Fusiliers, proceeded on leave today.	

1875 Wt. W593/826 1,000,000 4/15 J.B.C. & A. A.D.S.S./Forms/C. 2118.

... War Diaries and Intelligence
...ontained in F. S. Regs., Part II.
...e Staff Manual respectively. Title Pages
...be prepared in manuscript.

WAR DIARY
or
INTELLIGENCE SUMMARY
(Erase heading not required.)

Sheet 3.

Army Form C. 2118

Place	Date	Hour	Summary of Events and Information	Remarks and references to Appendices
WESTOUTRE.	Jan. 1917.			
	24th	9.pm.	Wind N.E., dangerous: hard frost continuous: owing to Pack Train arriving late, reserve rations issued from D.S.C.: 39th Siege Battery, less horses, left Division and joined 8th Corps tonight.	
	25th	9.pm.	Wind N.E., dangerous: hard frost continues: 240.O.R. 1st Entrenching Battalion, left Division today: Officer Commanding, 16th Divisional Train, returned from leave.	
	26th	9.pm.	Wind N.E., dangerous: frost continues: Pack train again delayed: rations issued from reserve: lateness of train due to hard frost freezing injectors of engines.	
	27th	9.pm.	Wind N.E., dangerous: frost continues: pack train again late: rations issued from Reserve: Claims Officerx and A.P.M., proceeded to KEMMEL to 49th Brigade Headquarters on duty.	
	28th	9.pm.	Wind N.E., dangerous: Frost continues with same severity: pack train again late: rations issued from Reserve: train traffic for Officers and men proceeding on leave, stopped in morning: in evening movement of all personnel by train stopped until further notice.	
	29th	9.pm.	Wind,N.E., dangerous: Frost still continues severe: Second Army Commander visited Division: refilling from reserve rations: no change in situation.	
	30th	9.pm.	Wind E.,dangerous: hard frost still continues, but cloudy with snow threatening: leave allotment for this Division for February,..44 places, daily: Lieut-Colonel Sir Antony WELDON, Major KEOGH, and Lieut-Colonel JEFFREYS, proceeded by car to BOULOGNE.	
	31st	9.pm.	Wind N., dangerous up to 8.30.p.m.: then vered to S.W.: frost but not so severe: reinforcements from 24th to 31st inclusive, 4 Officers, 147.O.R.: feeding strength of Division 19385 men, 589 H.D.Horses: 3967. L.D.Horses: no change in situation.	
			C. Knipe Capt for Major-General, Commanding 16th (Irish) Division. 1st Februray, 1917.	

1875 Wt. W593/826 1,000,000 4/15 J.B.C. & A. A.D.S.S./Forms/C. 2118.

W A R   D I A R Y.

FOR MONTH OF FEBRUARY, 1917.

VOLUME 15

UNIT:- "A. & Q." Branch 16th Division

Original

Vol 15

Original

Instructions regarding War Diaries and Intelligence Summaries are contained in F. S. Regs., Part II. and the Staff Manual respectively. Title Pages will be prepared in manuscript.

WAR DIARY

or

~~INTELLIGENCE SUMMARY~~

(Erase heading not required.)

H.Q. 16TH (IRISH) DIV. ("A. & Q." BRANCH.) aw.D/44/15.

Army Form C. 2118

Place	Date	Hour	Summary of Events and Information	Remarks and references to Appendices
	February 1917			
WESTOUTRE	1st	9.am	Wind N.E. and dangerous: frost harder than before: raid on 47th Brigade trenches by enemy repulsed.	
	2nd	9.am.	Wind E. and dangerous: Norwegian officers visited 16th Divisional front: nothing to report.	
	3rd	9.am	Wind N.E. and dangerous: A.A.& Q.M.G. returned from leave last night: concert for French charity at BAILLEUL: Lieut-Col. BELLINGHAM 8th.R.Dublin Fusiliers, left Division to take up appointment as Brig-General, 118th Inf.Brigade: no change in situation:	
	4th	9.am.	Wind N.E. and dangerous: IX Corps Conference at BAILLEUL attended by A.A.& Q.M.G.: Feeding strength of Division, 19445 men: 588 H.D.Horses, and 3995 L.D.Horses: Pack train very late.	
	5th	9.am.	Wind N.E. and dangerous: Feeding strength of Division 19517 men: 584 H.D.Horses and 3797 L.D. horses: D.A.Q.M.G. attended a conference at IX Corps on Road and Traffic Control: Pack train very late:	
	6th	9.am	Wind N.E. and dangerous: 16th Divisional Band gave its first performance at SCHERPENBERG: feeding strength of Division, 19005 men, 584 H.D.Horses and 3857 L.D.Horses: Pack train up to time.	
	7th	9.am.	Wind Slight N.E. and dangerous: some aerial activity (enemy): enemy aeroplane, while flying over LOCRE was shelled, and one "dud" anti-aircraft shell fell in main street, LOCRE, and exploded, killing two horses, which were being ridden and led by a man. The man escaped uninjured. feeding strength of Division 19333 men: 583 H.D.Horses, and 3911 L.D.Horses.	
	8th	9.am	KEMMEL SHELTERS shelled by enemy: three killed and twelve wounded: hutments of two companies badly knocked about: good deal of enemy aerial activity: a fire broke out in shed next to WESTOUTRE Baths: baths saved with difficulty and building next door entirely destroyed: feeding strength of Division 19390 men: 583 H.D.Horses and 3856 L.D.:	
	9th	9.am.	Major-General W.B.HICKIE, C.B., proceeded on 21 days leave: Brig-General G.E.PEREIRA, C.B., C.M.G., D.S.O., assumed command of the Division: feeding strength 19031 men: 584 H.D. and 3854 L.D.Horses:	
	10th	9.am	Wind N.E. and dangerous: 105 Remounts received for the Division: pack train very late and rations did not reach transport lines till after 7.30.p.m: Feeding strength of Division, 19307 men: 584 H.D., and 3849 L.D.Horses.	
	11th	9.am	Wind N.E. and dangerous: slight Thaw: pack train late: feeding strength of Division 19455 men: H.D. 595 and L.D.3851:	
	12th	9.am	Orders received that detached Artillery will return on night 13th/14th February: wind dangerous: steady thaw: feeding strength of Division 19582 men: 585 H.D. and 3861 L.D.Horses:	
	13th	9.am	Detached artillery passed through WESTOUTRE on their way to rejoin 25th Division: wind E. and dangerous: thaw continues: feeding strength of Division 19409 men: 599 H.D., 3881 L.D.Horses.	
	14th	9.am	Wind, N.E.,dangerous: further frost: feeding strength of Division 20208 men: 607 H.D., and 4589 L.D.Horses: 6th Canadian Siege,182nd.Siege,49th Siege Batteries drew rations first time: Rum ration for A.S.C.Coys, discontinued:	

15th (continued):-

1875 Wt. W593/826 1,000,000 4/15 J.B.C. & A. A.D.S.S./Forms/C. 2118.

Army Form C. 2118

Instructions regarding War Diaries and Intelligence Summaries are contained in F. S. Regs., Part II. and the Staff Manual respectively. Title Pages will be prepared in manuscript.

WAR DIARY
or
~~INTELLIGENCE SUMMARY~~
(Erase heading not required.)

Sheet 2.

Place	Date	Hour	Summary of Events and Information	Remarks and references to Appendices
WESTOUTRE.	15th	9.am	Wind N.E. and dangerous: explosion heard at 1.30.a.m. in German lines: cause not yet ascertained: feeding strength of Division: men 20838: Horses, H.D. 597, L.D.4615:	
	16th	9.am	Wind S: a further explosion occurred at 12.50.p.m. cause unknown: said to be a camouflet blown by enemy: D.A.A.& Q.M.G., returned from leave: some aeroplane activity by the enemy: further thaw sets in: thaw restrictions imposed by CORPS: feeding strength of Division: men, 20788: H.D. and L.D.horses 4527:	
	17th	9.am	Wind S: further rise in the temperature and slight fall of rain: followed by mist in the evening Fire at Divisional School, one hut burned down, and one man sleeping in hut burnt to death: feeding strength of Division: men 20446: H.D. 531 and L.D. 4501, horses:	
	18th	9.am	Wind varying from S. to S.W.: Divisional baths commenced working for first time since frost commenced. Feeding strength of Division men 19977: H.D. 361: L.D. 4445:	
	19th	9.am	Wind between S.E. and S: No mail received since 16th: Boulogne closed and leave train stopped running: feeding strength of Division Men 20756: H.D.528: L.D.4414.	
	20th	9.am	Wind S.E: Mail due 18th received: mail of 17th not yet to hand: BOULOGNE re-opened: leave train to start running: feeding strength of Division: men, 20,096: H.D.523: L.D.4501: Information received that whole Belgian population have evacuated KEMMEL except one family.	
	21st	9.am	Wind S.W., and safe: weather mild with slight fog: no sailings from BOULOGNE owing to fog in Channel: further delay in mails: DERRY HUTS shelled by enemy about 1.50.p.m.: one officers' hut destroyed by shell-fire. Feeding strength of Division: men 20942: H.D.541: L.D. 4505: 40 Remounts arrived for Division.	
	22nd	9.am	Wind N.: enemy shelled UPPER KEMMEL SHELTERS: Y.M.C.A.Huts badly damaged: no mail received: feeding strength of Division Men 21185: H.D.541: L.D.4509:	
	23rd	9.am	Wind S.W.: weather very foggy: mail received: feeding strength of Division: men 21193: H.D. 529: L.D.4919:	
	24th	9.am	Wind S.W.: 49th Inf.Bde.H.Q., shelled by enemy about 5.30.p.m.: no damage done: feeding strength of Division Men,20430: H.D.530: L.D.5076:	
	25th	9.am	Wind S.W.: D.A.Q.M.G. returned from leave: feeding strength of Division, men 20472: H.D.580: L.D.4656 horses.	
	26th	9.am	Wind N.W.: Major J.CLEMENTI, I.A., left to be attached to 7th Leinster Regt: Major AUSTIN, Cheshire Regiment, reported for attachment to "Q": feeding strength of Division men, 20580: H.D. 536: L.D.4828.	
	27th	9.am	Wind N.W.: Feeding strength of Division, men 20643: H.D.536: L.D.4837:	
	28th	9.am	Wind N.W.: Feeding strength of Division, men 20481: H.D.535: L.D.4836.	
			Reinforcements received Ist-28th Feb.1917, 49 Officers, 555 Other Ranks.	

[signature] for Brig-General,
Commanding 16th (Irish) Division.

1875 Wt. W593/826 1,000,000 4/15 J.B.C. & A. A.D.S.S./Forms/C. 2118.

W A R D I A R Y

FOR MONTH OF MARCH, 1917.

VOLUME 16

U N I T :- "A.Q." Branch, 16th (Irish) Division

Vol 16

Instructions regarding War Diaries and Intelligence Summaries are contained in F. S. Regs., Part II. and the Staff Manual respectively. Title Pages will be prepared in manuscript.

WAR DIARY
or
~~INTELLIGENCE SUMMARY~~

(Erase heading not required.)

"Q" Branch, 16th (Irish) Division.

Army Form C. 2118

Place	Date	Hour	Summary of Events and Information	Remarks and references to Appendices
	March			
WESTOUTRE	1st	9.am.	Wind, N.N.E.: feeding strength of Division: men 20744: H.D.528: L.D.4841:	
	2nd	9.am.	Wind N.E.: feeding strength of Division: men 20681: H.D.535: L.D.4818:	
	3rd	9.am.	Wind N.E.: feeding strength of Division: men 20680: H.D.535: L.D.4808:	
	4th	9.am.	Wind N.E.: bombardment of enemy line opposite Divisional front during afternoon: feeding strength of Division: men 20671: L.D.4806: H.D.532: slight fall of snow.	
	5th	9.am.	Wind N.W: divisional Commander returned from leave: feeding strength of Division: men 20682: H.D.528: L.D.4805:	
	6th	9.am.	Wind N.W: feeding strength of Division: men 20973: H.D.531: L.D.4810.	
	7th	9.am.	Wind N.E: weather extremely cold and hard frost: boxing tournament held by 49th Bde: A.A.& Q.M.G. attended conference at IX Corps "Q": feeding strength of division: men 20838: H.D.529: L.D.4810: 236 and 255 Siege Batteries rationed for last time today.	
	8th	9.am.	Wind N.E: about 5.p.m. enemy carried out a raid on our front after intense bombardment: five parties each composed about 50 men attempted to enter our trenches between N.30.c., and N.24.a. the three Southern parties were driven back with apparent heavy loss to the enemy: the two Northern parties penetrated as far as the Support line, but were driven out by a counter attack and bombing parties: Six wounded prisoners and several dead were left behind. The raiding parties were probably composed of the STURMTRUPP of 24th Division, XIX Saxon Corps, with a strong party of 133rd I.R. Our casualties were two officers killed and 8 officers wounded. Feeding strength of division: men 20661: H.D., 531: L.D.4890. 25.O.R. killed, 112 O.R.Wounded, 40 O.R. missing.	
	9th	9.am.	At 4.15.a.m., after a heavy bombardment enemy again attempted a raid on our front at N.36.a. In no case did the enemy reach our trenches. Two unwounded prisoners of the 181st I.R. were captured. our casualties 1 o.r. wounded. A.A.& Q.M.G., admitted to hospital. feeding strength of division: men 20558: H.D. 530: L.D. 4802:	
	10th	9.am.	Wind N.W., rise in temperature: feeding strength of division: men 20522: H.D.532: L.D.4801 Major TOMES a/A.A.& Q.M.G., attended conference at IX Corps.	

11th :-

1875 Wt. W593/826 1,000,000 4/15 J.B.C. & A. A.D.S.S./Forms/C. 2118.

Instructions regarding War Diaries and Intelligence Summaries are contained in F. S. Regs., Part II. and the Staff Manual respectively. Title Pages will be prepared in manuscript.

Army Form C. 2118

WAR DIARY

or

~~INTELLIGENCE SUMMARY~~

(Erase heading not required.)

"Q" Branch 16th Div. (Sheet 2.)

Place	Date	Hour	Summary of Events and Information	Remarks and references to Appendices
WESTOUTRE	March 11th	9.am.	Wind S.E. warm: Major AUSTIN and Captain TIPPET left "Q" Branch for attachment elsewhere: news of the fall of BAGDAD received: WAKEFIELD HUTS and LOCRE-DRANOUTRE Road shelled in forenoon.	
	12th	9.pm.	Wind N.W.: rain: Corps Commander visited Division Headqrs: following detachments rationed for last time today on joining X Corps for Railway construction:- 2/R.Ir.Regt 27.o.r.: 7th R/Innisk. Fus 53.o.r.: 7/8th.R.Ir.Fus 26.o.r.: no change in situation.	
	13th	9.pm.	Wind S.E. safe: feeding strength of division: 20368 men: H.D.533: L.D.4833: reinforcements from 1.3.17 to 13.3.17, inclusive, 71 Officers, 255.o.r.	
	14th	9.pm.	Wind N.N.E., dangerous: new disposition of divisional front ordered: previous scheme cancelled: no change in situation:	
	15th	9.pm.	Wind N.N.E., dangerous: 1st Canadian Tunnlg Coy, drew rations with this division for last time today: Lieut-Col. MONCK-MASON returned today from leave from PARIS: no change in situation.	
	16th	9.pm.	Wind S.W., safe: nothing to report.	
	17th	9.pm.	St.Patricks Day: wind S.W., safe: 77th Army Field Artillery Bde drew rations with division for last time: feeding strength of division: 19656 men: H.D.Horses 523: L.D.Horses 4797: Corps Commander visited Divisional ~~xxxx~~ Commander: 2 extra leave places daily for men long in country without leave:	
	18th	9.pm.	Wind S.W., safe: Hdqrs., D.A.C., and Lines this day handed over to 36th Div. LURGAN CAMP and horse lines also handed over to 36th Div.D.A.C. now at WOLFHOEK: Court of Enquiry held at Headqrs Coy Train, on destruction by fire of 2 Armstrong huts: detachment of 1st Entrenching Battn drew 2 days' rations prior to entraining:	
	19th	9.pm.	49th Bde. handed over WAKEFIELD and DONCASTER HUTS at 12 noon: feeding strength of Division 18496 men: H.D.Horses 491: L.D.Horses 3846:	
	20th	9.pm.	Strong gale from N.W.: rain & sleet: A.A.& Q.M.G., 19th Div. visited this office: no change in situation:	
	21st	9.pm.	Wind N.E., dangerous: LOCRE shelled by enemy in the afternoon: 57th Inf.Bde. joined this division today: feeding strength of division: 18571 men: H.D.491: L.D. 3866	

Instructions regarding War Diaries and Intelligence Summaries are contained in F. S. Regs., Part II. and the Staff Manual respectively. Title Pages will be prepared in manuscript.

WAR DIARY

or

~~INTELLIGENCE SUMMARY~~

(Erase heading not required.)

Army Form C. 2118

"Q" Branch, 16th Div. (Sheet 3).

Place	Date	Hour	Summary of Events and Information	Remarks and references to Appendices
WESTOUTRE	March 22nd	9.pm.	Wind N.E., dangerous: 175 Tunnlg Coy.& 77th Army Fd Arty Bde rejoined this division today.	
	23rd	9.pm.	Wind N.N.E., dangerous: feeding strength of division: men 24833: H.D. 654: L.D. 5286	
	24th	9.pm.	Wind N.N.E., dangerous: cabbage plants drawn by S.S.O. from ST OMER: Inspector of Catering visited 47th Bde. Reinforcements from 14th to 24th inclusive, 38 officers, 604 o.r.	
	25th	9.pm.	Wind N.W., dangerous in morning veering to S.E., in afternoon: no change in situation:	
	26th	9.pm.	Wind N.W.,dangerous: O.C.Train proceeded to NOEUX-les-MINES on duty connected with statue, which was to be erected in NOEUX-les-MINES Church, but owing to Church being wrecked by enemy shell fire, statue stored at BRUAY: 82nd Siege Battery joined Division. 16th Div.Administrative Order No. 4 issued today.	Appx.1.
	27th	9.pm.	Wind N.W., dangerous: 77th Army Fd.Arty.Bde.relieved the 180th Bde this night, covering the DIEPENDAAL Sector: feeding strength of division, 24772 men: 631 H.D.: 5340 L.D.:	
	28th	9.pm.	Wind S.W.: 176 Siege Batty joined division today: Inspector of Catering visited 48th Bde today: no change in situation:	
	29th	9.pm.	Wind S.W.: strong and safe: 236th Siege Battery joined division: feeding strength of division 24915 men: H.D. 632: L.D. 5100.	
	30th	9.pm.	Wind S.W., safe: 156th Fd Co.R.E., relieved 155th Fd.Co.R.E., on the right sub-section, VIERSTRAAT Sector: 156th Field Coy.R.E., move to FIETRE;	
	31st	9.pm.	2 16th Division Hdqrs. moved from WESTOUTRE to LOCRE: Wind S.W., safe: the following left the division today:- 77th Army Field Artillery Bde: 57th Infantry Bde: 250th Tunnlg Co.R.E.: 175th Tunnelg Co.R.E: 136th Army Troops R.E.: 1st Entrenchg Btn: 82nd Siege Battery: 176th Siege Batty 236th Siege Battery: 185th Siege Battery: reinforcements from 25th to 31st inclusive, 13 officers, 375 O.R.	

4th April, 1917.

C. Knipe Capt for Major-General,

Commanding 16th (Irish) Division.

1875 Wt. W593/826 1,000,000 4/15 J.B.C. & A. A.D.S.S./Forms/C. 2118.

Tu 1.

SECRET   Copy No. 25

16TH. DIVISION ADMINISTRATIVE ORDER NO.4.

REFERENCE 16TH. DIVISION OPERATION ORDER NO. 89.

1. Re-adjustment of accommodation and Horse Standings will take place, on the dates as shown in the attached table.

2. On 31st. March.

(a) 47th. Infantry Brigade will take over Transport Lines as below :-

4 Battalions.	Lines at :-	
	(M.24.a.7.4.	Vacated by 48th.Inf. Bde.
	(M.24.a.5.3.	" " " "
	(M.23.b.9.1½.	" " 49th. " "
M.G. Company	M.24.d.5.6.	" " 36th. Division.

(b) 49th. Infantry Brigade will hand over Transport Lines as below :-

Lines at :-

M.23.C.6.3.	to	156th. Field Company, R.E.
M.23.C.5.1.	to	157th. Field Company, R.E.
M.23.B.9.1½.	to	47th. Infantry Brigade.

(c) 49th. Infantry Brigade will take over Transport Lines as below :-

Lines at :-

M.23.C.8.6½.	vacated by 48th. Infantry Brigade.
M.23.C.9.7.	" " " " "

(d) Royal Engineers will hand over Transport Lines as under :-

Lines at :-

N.13.C.5.8.	to	19th. Division.
M.12.C.6.2.	"	" "
M.13.C.5.8.	"	" "

(e) 16th. Divisional Train will hand over Lines as under :-

Lines at :-

M.13.B.1.9. to 19th. Division.

/ Para.3. P.T.O.

3. All Area and Billet Stores, as defined in Army Routine Order No. 534 dated 18th. December 1916, will be handed over and Lists signed by both parties forwarded to Divisional Headquarters in due course.

4. All Billets, Hutments and Horse Lines will be handed over clean, and in good order.

5. ACKNOWLEDGE.

Gomes.

"A" & "Q".,
16th. Division.
March 26th.1917.

Major,
for Lieut-Colonel,
A.A. & Q.M.G.,16th. D i v ision.

Issued at 9p.m.

Copies to :-

No. 1. G.O.C.
" 2. 16th. Divl.Art.
" 3. 16th. Div. Engrs.
" 4. 47th. Inf.Bde.
" 5. 48th. Inf.Bde.
" 6. 49th. Inf.Bde.
" 7. 11th.Hants (P).
" 8. 16th.Div. Train.
" 9. A.D.M.S.,16th.Div.
" 10. A.D.V.S.,16th.Div.
" 11. D.A.D.O.S.,16th.Div.
" 12. A.P.M.,16th.Div.
" 13. Camp Commandant.
" 14. A/Town Major,LOCRE.
" 15. French,Mission.
" 16. Belgian Mission.
" 17. 16th. Div.School.
" 18. 16th. Div.Signal Coy.R.E.
" 19. 16th. Div. Coy.
" 20. 16th. Div.Bomb Stores.
" 21. W.O.i/c.Posts.16th.Div.
" 22. 19th. Division "Q")
" 23. 36th. Division "Q") for information.
" 24. 16th. Division "G")
" 25. & 26. War Diary "Q"
" 27. & 28. Filed.

SECRET

TABLE TO ACCOMPANY 16TH. DIVISION ADMINISTRATIVE ORDER NO.4.

Unit.	From.	To.	To move from present location on :-	Remarks.
Divisional H.Q.	WESTOUTRE	LOCRE And LOCRE HOSPICE.	March 31st.1917.	Vide 16th.Divn. Adm. Order No.3. dated 26 - 3 - 17.
112th.Fld.Amb.	WESTOUTRE	BAILLEUL	March 31st.1917.	
47th. Mobile Vet. Section.	M.15.B.3.2.	M.26.B.9½.7.	March 31st.1917.	
11th.Hants (P).	DE ZON Camp.	M.24.A.1.7.	March 31st.1917.	
16th.Div.Band.	SCHERPENBERG	KRABBENHOF FM.	March 27th.1917.	
16th.Div.Bomb Store.	SCHERPENBERG	BRULOOZE,M.24.B.~~2.6~~ A.9.5.	March 31st.1917.	
Salvage Dump.	CANADA CORNER	Old R.E.Dump at M.23.C.6.4½.	March 31st.1917.	
Fld. Coys. R.E. (T'port Lines.	N.13.C.5.8.	M.23.C.6.3.	March 31st.1917.	
(~~Personnel~~)	M.12.C.6.2.	M.23.C.5½.1½.	March 31st.1917.	
Wagon Lines, 180th.Bde.R.F.A.	Present location	About M.21.C.4.8.	April 3rd. 1917.	

WAR DIARY FOR MONTH OF APRIL, 1917.

VOLUME:- 17

UNIT:- "A & Q" Branch, 16th Div. H.Q.

Vol 17

Instructions regarding War Diaries and Intelligence Summaries are contained in F. S. Regs., Part II. and the Staff Manual respectively. Title pages will be prepared in manuscript.

WAR DIARY
or
INTELLIGENCE SUMMARY.
(Erase heading not required.)

Army Form C. 2118.

"A" & "Q" BRANCH, 16th Division Headqrs.

Place	Date	Hour	Summary of Events and Information	Remarks and references to Appendices
LOCRE	APRIL 1st	9pm.	The 47th Inf.Bde., 47th.M.G.Coy., & 47th T.M.Batty relieved the 49th Inf.Bde., 49th M.G.Coy., and 49th T.M.B. 48th Inf.Bde. arrived at TILQUES Training area. Feeding strength of Division: 17842 men: H.D.Horses 492: L.D.Horses 3810: Railhead for Division changed from BOEPENHOEK to HAEGEDOORNE: Refilling Point near ST. JANS CAPEL.	
do.	2nd	do.	No change in situation.	
do.	3rd	do.	No change in situation.	
do.	4th	do.	The 279 Siege Battery attached to 16th Divn for administrative purposes: D.A.Q.M.G. proceeded to 48th Bde at RECQUES: Feeding strength of Division: 14445 men: H.D.Horses 392: L.D.Horses 3493:	
do.	5th	do.	279 Siege Battery left Division.	
do.	6th	do.	No change in situation.	
do.	7th	do.	A.A.& Q.M.G. returned from sick leave.	
do.	8th	do.	Reinforcements from 1.4.17 to 8.4.17, inclusive: 11 Officers and 276 O.R.	
do.	9th	do.	No change in situation.	
do.	10th	do.	D.A.Q.M.G. visited bomb stores in line with Brig-General, 47th Inf. Bde. Feeding strength of Division 12835 men: H.D.Horses 361: L.D.Horses 2787. Army Commander inspected men of the 2nd and 6th Royal Irish Regiment, R.F.A., and R.E., who took part in recent raid.	
do.	11th	do.	IX Corps Commander visited Divisional Headqrs. IX Corps Cyclists attached to 16th Division for administrative purposes.	
do.	12th	do.	16th Divl Administrative Order No. 6 issued (Appx. I)	APPX I.
do.	13th	do.	49th Inf.Bde.Group, less party of 400, 175th Field Coy., R.E., and 113th Field Ambulance, left this area for the RECQUES training area. IX Corps Cyclists and 19th M.M.Gun Battery drew rations with this Division for the last time today, also 49th Bde., less party of 400, drew for last time. Feeding strength of Divn: men 13853: H.D.Horses 393: L.D.Horses 3712:	

Instructions regarding War Diaries and Intelligence Summaries are contained in F. S. Regs., Part II. and the Staff Manual respectively. Title pages will be prepared in manuscript.

WAR DIARY
or
INTELLIGENCE SUMMARY.
(Erase heading not required.)

Sheet 2.

Army Form C. 2118.

Place	Date	Hour	Summary of Events and Information	Remarks and references to Appendices
LOCRE	14th	9pm.	Feeding strength of Division: men 10476: H.D.Horses 305: L.D.Horses 3421:	
do.	15th	do.	16th Divl Administrative Order No. 7 issued (Appendix 2).	APPX 2.
do.	16th	do.	No change in situation. Feeding strength of Division, men 10137: H.D.Horses 305: L.D.Horses 3451	
do.	17th	do.	48th Inf Bde returned to this area from training area. Feeding strength of Division, men 13827: H.D.H rses 407: L.D.Horses 3752:	
do.	18th	do.	One company of 47th Brigade proceeded to CLARE CAMP.	
do.	19th	do.	48th Infantry Brigade relieved the 47th Brigade. Feeding strength of Division, men 13228: H.D.Horses 416: L.D.Horses 33706: 177th Bde. R.F.A., drew with Division for last time today.	
do.	20th	do.	Feeding strength of Division: Men 12284: H.D.Horses 328: L.D.Horses 2925. A.A.& Q.M.G., attended Conference at Corps Headqrs., with reference to Medical administrative arrangements.	
do.	21st	do.	About 6.30.p.m., after $1\frac{1}{2}$ hours shelling, the enemy brought down one of our observation balloons near LOCRE: two observers were seen to descend by Parachutes.	
do.	22nd	do.	180th Brigade, R.F.A., rejoined Division today.	
do.	23rd	do.	16th Divnl Administrative Order No. 8 issued, (Appendix 3). Feeding strength of Division, men 13294: H.D.Horses 362: L.D.Horses 3604.	APPX 3.
do.	24th	do.	Feeding Strength of Division, men 13278: H.D.Horses 350: L.D.Horses 3613:	
do.	25th	do.	Feeding strength of Division, men 13177: H.D.Horses 351: L.D.Horses 3590: 16th Divnl Administrative Order No. 9 issued (Appendix 4).	APPX 4.
do.	26th	do.	Feeding strength of Division: men 13293: H.D.Horses 351: L.D.Horses 3603: Divisional Administrative order No. 10 issued. (Appendix 5).	APPX 5.
do.	27th	do.	Lieut-Col., NATION, A.A.G., G.H.Q., visited the Division today.	

2353 Wt. W2544/1454 700,000 5/15 D. D. & L. A.D.S.S./Forms/C. 2118.

Army Form C. 2118

Instructions regarding War Diaries and Intelligence Summaries are contained in F. S. Regs., Part II. and the Staff Manual respectively. Title Pages will be prepared in manuscript.

WAR DIARY
or
INTELLIGENCE SUMMARY
(Erase heading not required.)

SHEET 3.

Place	Date	Hour	Summary of Events and Information	Remarks and references to Appendices
LOCRE	28th	9pm	Feeding strength of Division, men 13261: H.D.Horses 350: L.D.Horses 3550.	
do.	29th	do.	Divisional Administrative Order No. 11 issued (Appendix 6). The 16th Division is taking over ~~from~~ the 19th Divisional Area.	App+ 6
do.	30th	do.	Taking over from 19th Division started: this will be complete by 2nd May: feeding strength of Division men 13322: H.D.358: L.D.3545: reinforcements from 9.4.17 to 30.4.17, (both inclusive), 52 Officers: 510 O.R.	

1st May, 1917.

[signature] Capt for
Major-General,
Commanding 16th (Irish) Division.

1875 Wt. W593/826 1,000,000 4/15 J.B.C. & A. A.D.S.S./Forms/C. 2118.

I

S E C R E T

Copy No 9

16TH. DIVISION ADMINISTRATIVE ORDER NO.6.

REFERENCE 16TH. DIVISION OPERATION ORDER NO. 96 d/- 11/4/17.

1. Eleven lorries for carriage of Blankets will report to Headquarters, 49th. Inf. Bde. at 7am. on 13th. April.

They are for distribution as under :-

Each Battalion	2
Brigade H.Q.	1.
M.G. Company.	1.
T.M. Battery.	1.

Guides to conduct lorries to Units' Lines will be arranged by the Brigade.

These lorries, on arrival in the RECQUES Area after having been unloaded will report to 48th. Inf. Bde. Headquarters at RECQUES, and will be available for bringing back the baggage of that Brigade to LOCRE Area.

49th. Inf. Bde. will arrange for the despatch of these lorries from ST. OMER Area on 15th. instant, as early as possible, to allow of the baggage of 48th. Inf. Bde. to be loaded in good time for the return journey.

2. Baggage wagons of 144. Coy. A.S.C., 16th. Div. Train will report to Units about 4pm. on 12th. April. Horses will then return to their own lines. They will march on 13th. under the orders of G.O.C., 49th. Inf. Brigade.

3. Supplies will be drawn as under :-

	On.	At.	By.
49th. INF. BDE :-			
	13th.	HAEGEDOORNE.	Supply wagons.
	14th.	WATTEN.	M.T.
	15th.	WATTEN.	Supply wagons.
48th. INF. BDE :-			
	15th.	WATTEN.	Supply wagons.
	16th.	WATTEN.	M.T.
	17th.	HAEGEDOORNE.	Supply wagons.

The Supply Wagons of 49th. Inf. Bde. will march full to HAZEBROUCK Area on 13th; empty to a Refilling Point to be selected by G.O.C., 49th. Inf. Bde. in ST. OMER Area on 14th; and empty to WATTEN on 15th., where they willload and distribute to units the same day.

Supply wagons of 48th. Inf. Bde. will draw supplies from WATTEN and will march full to ST. OMER Area on 15th;

/ empty to Refillong Point - P.T.O.

empty to Refilling Point to be selected by G.O.C., 48th. Inf. Bde. on 16th; and empty to HAEGEDOORNE on 17th., where they will load and distribute to Units the same evening.

Arrangements for drawing by M.T. will be made by G.O's.C. 48th. and 49th. Inf. Bdes. respectively, in conjunction with O's.C. A.S.C. Companies concerned.

The lorries now attached to 48th. Inf. Bde. will be utilized for this purpose.

4. Billeting Areas will be as follows :-

HAZEBROUCK	....	As detailed by Town Major, HAZEBROUCK.
ARQUES. ST.MARTIN AU LAERT	))...	" " " " " ST. OMER.
WIZERNES	....	" " " MAIRE.
HALLINES	....	" " " MAIRE.
RECQUES	....	Billeting Schedule attached.

[signature] for.
Lieut-Colonel.
AA & QMG., 16th. Division.

"A" & "Q".,
16th. Division,
April 11th. 1917.

Issued at 7.30.p.m.

Copies to :-

No. 1. 48th. Inf. Bde.
2. 49th. Inf. Bde.
3. 16th. Div. Train.
4. S.M.T.O., IX.Corps.
5. A.D.M.S., 16th. Div.
6. A.P.M., 16th. Div.
7. "G"., 16th.Div.(for information.)
8.)
9.) War Diary "A" & "Q".
10. Filed.
11. "

"A" Area.

RECQUES. BRIGADE GROUP.

Unit.	Location.	Accommodation. Offrs.	O.R.	Remarks.
Brigade H.Q.	RECQUES	19	250	J.10.d.2.3½.
"A" Battalion.	NORDAUSQUES	1	Company	in village.
	LA PANNE	1	"	J.23.
	LA RECOUSSE	1	"	
	QUEMBERGUE	1	"	J.29.a.
Field Ambulance	J.27.b.			
M.G.Coy.	From J.21.d.9½.3½ To LE FLOUY.			
1 Coy.ASC.	Area bounded by River S.E. TOURNEHEM Station Road N.E. and Railway N.W.			
Field Coy.RE.	J.31.c.8½.8. to S.W.			
"B" Battalion.	TOURNEHEM			
"C" "	ZOUAFQUES	-	800	Good accommodatio
"D" "	MENTQUES	2 Companies.		
	LA RONVILLE	1 Company.		
	INGLINGHEM.	1 Company.		

SECRET 2 Copy No 15

16TH. DIVISION ADMINISTRATIVE ORDER NO.7.

15th.April 1917.

Reference (16th. Div. No. 6908/49(G) dated 13-4-17.
(16th. Div. No. 6908/44(G) dated 12-4-17.

1. BAGGAGE:- Lorries and Busses for baggage and advance parties respectively will report as under :-

177th. BRIGADE, R.F.A.

1 Bus) will report at CHURCH, LOCRE,
4 Lorries) at 6-30a.m. on 18th. April.

180th. BRIGADE, R.F.A.

1 Bus.) will report at H.Q.180th.Bde.R.F.A. at 5p.m.
4 Lorries) on 20th. at NIELLES les BLEQUIN.

Units concerned will arrange for guides to meet Lorries at the hours and places stated above to conduct them to wagon lines.

2. SUPPLIES:- Supplies will be drawn as under :-

177th. BRIGADE, R.F.A.

on 17th.Apl.	from WIPPENHOEK	by	Supply Wagons.
on 18th.Apl.	" "	"	" "
on 19th.Apl.	" HAEGEDOORNE	"	Motor Transport.
on 20th.Apl.	" WATTEN	"	Supply Wagons.

180th. BRIGADE, R.F.A.

on 21st.Apl.	from ST. OMER	by	Motor Transport.
on 22nd.Apl.	" HAEDEDOORNE	"	Motor Transport.
on 23rd.Apl.	" "	"	Supply Wagons.

3. BILLETS:-

177th. BRIGADE, R.F.A.

		Billets arranged by
Night of 18th/19th.	GODEWAERSVELDE	....
" " 19th/20th.	CAMPAGNE	Mairie.
" " 20th/21st.	POLINCOVE	Mairie.

180th. BRIGADE, R.F.A.

Night of 20th/21st.	(NIELLES les BLEQUIN (and AFFRENGUES.	....
Night of 21st/22nd.	WARDRECQUES.	Mairie.
" " 22nd/23rd.	GODEWAERSVELDE	....
" " 23rd/24th.	16th.Div.Area.	....

4. ACKNOWLEDGE.

Grooms Maj
for Lieut-Colonel,
AA & QMG., 16th. Division.

Issued at ....pm.

FOR DISTRIBUTION P.T.O.

DISTRIBUTION OF 16TH. DIVISION ADMINISTRATIVE ORDER No. 7.

Copy No.1.	G.O.C.
" " 2.	"G", 16th.Div.
" " 3.	16th. Divl. Artillery.
" " 4.	16th. Divl. Train.
" " 5.	S.M.T.O., IX. Corps.
" " 6.	S.S.O., 16th. Division.
" " 7.	D.A.D.O.S., 16th. Division.
" " 8.	A.D. M.S., 16th. Division.
" " 9.	A.D.V. S., 16th. Division.
" " 10.	A.P.M., 16th. Division.
" " 11.	Warrant Offr i/c Posts,16th.Div.
" " 12.	IX. CORPS "Q".
" " 13.	16th. Divl. Signal Coy.,R.E.
" " 14.) " " 15.)	War Diary "A" & "Q".
" " 16.) " " 17.)	Filed.

3

SECRET Copy No 8

16TH. DIVISION ADMINISTRATIVE ORDER NO.8.

REFERENCE 16TH. DIVISION OPERATION ORDER No.100 D/- 23-4-17.

April 23rd. 1917.

1. Supplies for 49th. Inf. Brigade will be drawn as follows :-

April 28th. By. M.T. from WATTEN, which will deliver to a Refilling Point in the ARQUES Area, to be arranged by the Brigade.

April 29th. By M.T. from CAESTRE. Lorries will deliver to Supply Wagons in HAZEBROUCK Area, at a Refilling Point to be arranged by the Brigade.

April 30th. By M.T. from CAESTRE, and deliver to 16th. Division Refilling Point.

May 1st. By Supply Wagons from HAEGEDOORNE.

2. Supplies for 47th. Inf. Bde. (less 1 Battalion), will be drawn as follows :-

April 30th. From HAEGEDOORNE, by Supply Wagons and march full to CAESTRE Area.

May 1st. From CAESTRE by Supply Wagons.

143 Coy.A.S.C. will accompany this Brigade.

3. Billets in the CAESTRE Area will be as shown on the Schedule already forwarded to 47th. Inf. Bde. Headquarters.

4. ACKNOWLEDGE.

Headquarters,
"A" & "Q"
16th.Division.

Brown Maj
for. Lieut-Colonel,
A.A. & Q.M.G.,
16th.Division.

Issued at...7...pm.

Copies to :-

No.1. G.O.C.
2. "G", 16th.Div.
3. 47th.Inf.Bde.
4. 49th.Inf.Bde.
5. 16th.Div.Train.
6. S.S.O.,16th.Div.
7. A.P.M.,16th.Div.

No. 8)
9) War Diary.

10)
11) Filed.

3

SECRET Copy No 9

16TH. DIVISION ADMINISTRATIVE ORDER NO.8.

REFERENCE 16TH. DIVISION OPERATION ORDER No.100 D/- 23-4-17.

April 23rd. 1917.

1. Supplies for 49th. Inf. Brigade will be drawn as follows :-

April 28th. By. M.T. from WATTEN, which will deliver to a Refilling Point in the ARQUES Area, to be arranged by the Brigade.

April 29th. By M.T. from CAESTRE. Lorries will deliver to Supply Wagons in HAZEBROUCK Area, at a Refilling Point to be arranged by the Brigade.

April 30th. By M.T. from CAESTRE, and deliver to 16th. Division Refilling Point.

May 1st. By Supply Wagons from HAEGEDOORNE.

2. Supplies for 47th. Inf. Bde. (less 1 Battalion), will be drawn as follows :-

April 30th. From HAEGEDOORNE, by Supply Wagons and march full to CAESTRE Area.

May 1st. From CAESTRE by Supply Wagons.

143 Coy.A.S.C. will accompany this Brigade.

3. Billets in the CAESTRE Area will be as shown on the Schedule already forwarded to 47th. Inf. Bde. Headquarters.

4. ACKNOWLEDGE.

Headquarters,
"A" & "Q"
16th.Division.

[signature] Maj
for Lieut-Colonel,
A.A. & Q.M.G.,
16th.Division.

Issued at....7..pm.

Copies to :-

No.1. G.O.C.
2. "G", 16th.Div.
3. 47th.Inf.Bde.
4. 49th.Inf.Bde.
5. 16th.Div.Train.
6. S.S.O., 16th.Div.
7. A.P.M., 16th.Div.
No. 8)
9) War Diary.
10)
11) Filed.

5

SECRET   Copy No. 15

16TH. DIVISION ADMINISTRATIVE ORDER NO.10.

REFERENCE 16TH. DIVL. ARTILLERY OPERATION ORDER NO.66
d/- 22/4/17.

Reference:- HAZEBROUCK, 5.A. - 1/100,000
Sheet 28 S.W. - 1/20,000

26th.April 1917.

1. BAGGAGE:-

4 lorries for baggage will report at Brigade H.Q., at POLINCOVE Distillery at 5-30p.m. on 2nd. May.

Brigade will arrange for guides to meet lorries at the hour and place stated to conduct them to Wagon lines.

Lorries will return to their Units on May 5th.

2. SUPPLIES:-

Supplies will be drawn as under :-

May 3rd......... from WATTEN, by Motor Transport.
May 4th......... from HAEGEDOORN, by Motor Transport.
May 5th......... from HAEGEDOORN, by Supply Wagons.

3. BILLETS:-

			Billets arranged by
Night of	3rd/4th..	CAMPAGNE.	MAIRIE.
" "	4th/5th..	GODEWAERSVELDE	.....
" "	5th/6th..	16th.Div.Area	Original Wagon Lines.

180th. Bde.,R.F.A. moves to new lines at M.21. Central, on 4th. May.

4. NOTIFICATION OF ADDRESS:-

Map location of Brigade Headquarters will be wired to "Q", 16th. Division daily.

5. ACKNOWLEDGE.

W.F. Austin.
Major,
for Lt-Colonel,
AA & QMG,16th.Division.

Headquarters,
"A" & "Q",
16th.Division.

Issued at...7.0....pm.

Copies to :-

No.1. G.O.C.
2. "G",16th.Div.
3. 16th.D.A.
4. 16th.DivTrain.
5. S.M.T.O.
6. S.S.O.
7. A.D.M.S.
8. D.A.D.O.S.
9. A.D.V.S.
No. 10. A.P.M.
11. W.O.i/c Posts.
12. IX. CORPS "Q"
13. 16th.Div.Sig.Coy.R.E.
14.)
15.)War Diary.
16.)
17.)Filed.

DA & Qrs
Sacas
DA&G
WR
5

SECRET   Copy No. 14

16TH. DIVISION ADMINISTRATIVE ORDER NO.10.

REFERENCE 16TH. DIVL. ARTILLERY OPERATION ORDER NO.66
d/- 22/4/17.

Reference:- HAZEBROUCK, 5.A. - 1/100,000
Sheet 28 S.W. - 1/20,000

26th.April 1917.

1. BAGGAGE:-
4 lorries for baggage will report at Brigade H.Q., at POLINCOVE Distillery at 5-30p.m. on 2nd. May.
Brigade will arrange for guides to meet lorries at the hour and place stated to conduct them to Wagon lines.
Lorries will return to their Units on May 5th.

2. SUPPLIES:-
Supplies will be drawn as under :-

May 3rd......... from WATTEN, by Motor Transport.
May 4th......... from HAEGEDOORN, by Motor Transport.
May 5th......... from HAEGEDOORN, by Supply Wagons.

3. BILLETS:-

		Billets arranged by
Night of 3rd/4th..	CAMPAGNE.	MAIRIE.
" " 4th/5th..	GODEWAERSVELDE	.....
" " 5th/6th..	16th.Div.Area	Original Wagon Lines.

180th. Bde.,R.F.A. moves to new lines at M.21. Central, on 4th. May.

4. NOTIFICATION OF ADDRESS:-

Map location of Brigade Headquarters will be wired to "Q", 16th. Division daily.

5. ACKNOWLEDGE.

W.F. Austin.
Major,
for Lt-Colonel,
AA & QMG,16th.Division.

Headquarters,
"A" & "Q",
16th.Division.

Issued at 7.0 pm.

Copies to :-

No.1. G.O.C.
2. "G",16th.Div.
3. 16th.D.A.
4. 16th.DivTrain.
5. S.M.T.O.
6. S.S.O.
7. A.D.M.S.
8. D.A.D.O.S.
9. A.D.V.S.
No. 10. A.P.M.
11. W.O.i/c Posts.
12. IX. CORPS "Q"
13. 16th.Div.Sig.Coy.R.E.
14.)
15.)War Diary.
16.)
17.)Filed.

6

S E C R E T Copy No. 35

16TH. DIVISION ADMINISTRATIVE ORDER NO.11.

REFERENCE 16TH. DIV. OPERATION ORDER NO.103 DATED 29-4-17.

Map references to Sheet 28.S.W.,1/20,000

29th. April 1917.

1. The 19th. Divisional Area is being taken over, and will be administered by the 16th. Division.

2. WAGON LINES:-

Infantry
49th. Inf. Bde./Transport.. M.17.b.2.3. M.17.c.9.7.
M.17.d.5.9. M.17.c.7.6.
" " " M.G.Company M.17.b.3.1.
" " " Headquartrs M.17.b.3.1.
144 Coy.Div. Train......... M.13.b.8.9.
155 Field Coy.,R.E......... M.18.a.7.9.

3. INSTITUTIONS, LAUNDRIES,ETC:-

Institutions and duties in 19th. Divisional Area will be taken over as follows :-

	No. of OR. required.	Date of Relief.	Time of relief.	Offrs.responsible.
(a)Laundry & Baths, WESTOUTRE.	2 P.B. Wardens	1/5/17	2p.m.	O's. i/c. Laundries concerned.
Bath,LA CLYTTE.	1 P.B. Warden.	2/5/17	11am.	
(b)Divl.Canteens & Recreation Huts	8	30/4/17	6pm.	Camp Cdt.16th. Div.& Senior C.ofE.Chaplain, 19th. Division.
(c)Divl. Bomb Stores	1	30/4/17	9am.	Capt.SHINE,16th Div.& Divl. Bombing Offr., 19th.Divn.
(d)Divl.Salvage Dump.	1	30/4/17	9am.	O's.C.Salvage Coys.concerned
(e) ∅ Traffic Control.		30/4/17	9am.	A.P.M's concerned.
(f)Water Duties.	2 T.U. men.	30/4/17	6pm.	A.D's.M.S. concerned.

(g) French Tramways /P.T.O.

	No.of OR. required.	Date of Relief.	Time of Date Relief.	Offrs.responsible.
(g)Trench Tramways.		30/4/17	6pm.	16th.Div.T.T. Officer.

Ø Forward Traffic Control Posts, night only, will be found by the Brigade in the Line, as under :-

at N.6.a.1.1. ...... 2 men, 6pm. to 6am.
at N.10.b.9.4. ...... 2 men, 6pm. to 6am.

4. ATTACHED UNITS:-

(a) The undermentioned Units are attached for RATIONS from 3rd. May, inclusive :-

Unit.	Strength. Men.	H.D.	L.D.
45th. H.A.Group.	54	-	-
278 Siege Battery.	127	-	-
286 " "	161	-	-
236 " "	126	-	-
285 " "	129	-	-
305 " "	125	-	-
1st.Entrenching Bn.	150	8	6
13th.R.West Surrey) Labour Coy.)	208	4	
136 (A.T.)Coy.R.E.	200	4	25
Y.M.C.A.	2	-	-
250th.Tun. Coy.R.E.	756	8	2
175th. " " "	680	8	2
77th.A.F.A.Bde.R.F.A.	-	-	- At present in Training, out of Divl. Area.

RAILHEAD - HAEGEDOORNE. REFILLING POINT is at M.26.c.6.3.

(b) The undermentioned Units are attached for administration:-

175th. Tun. Coy.R.E. / 250th. " " " / 136th.(A.T.)Coy.R.E.	through C.R.E.,16th.Division.
13th.R.West Surrey Lbr.Coy. / 1st. Entrenching Bn.	through 49th. Infantry Brigade.
77th.A.F.A.Brigade,R.F.A.	through H.R.A.,16th. Division.

5. CAMP WARDENS:-

P.B. or T.U. men as Camp Wardens will be detailed and rationed as under :-

Camp,etc.	Location.	No. of men.	Rationed by.	Rationed from.
Art.Wagon Lines	M.8.central	4	144 Co.A.S.C.	3rd.May,incl.
M.G.Coy.& BdeHQ	M.14. "	2	81st.San.Sec.	3rd.May,incl.
Inf.Bn.Camp.	M.1d.d.9.9.	2	-- do --	-- do --

Inf.Bn,Camp,M.14.b.9.7. /P.T.O.

Camp, etc.	Location.	No. of men.	Rationed by	Rationed from.
Inf.Bn.Camp.	M.14.b.9.7.	2	81st.San.Sec.	3rd.May,incl.
" " "	M.14.b.7.9.	2	-- do --	-- do --
" " "	M.8.d.8.2.	2	-- do --	-- do --
D.H.Q.WESTOUTRE	M.9.c.6.2.	4	-- do --	-- do --
Supply Column	M.15.a.3.1.	2	-- do --	-- do --
1 Sec.D.A.C.	M.16.c.4.9.	2	-- do --	-- do --
Baths & Laundries, WESTOUTRE	M.9.c.2.5.	4	-- do --	-- do --
Mov.Vet.Section	M.15.d.7.3.	2	-- do --	-- do --
CARNARVON Camp.)	M.10.b.8.6.	2	Bn.at CURRAGH Camp.	-- do --
Battery Lines	M.5.c.2.4.	1	-- do --	-- do --
-- do --	M.5.c.3.0.	1	-- do --	-- do --
-- do --	M.11.c.2.6.	1	-- do --	-- do --
-- do --	M.11.c.4.5.	1	-- do --	-- do --
CURRAGH CAMP	M.17.c.3.8.	1	-- do --	-- do --
WESTON.	M.17.a.5.6.	1	-- do --	-- do --
PIONEER CAMP	M.13.c.5.8.	2	) Entrenching Bn	-- do --
-- do --	N.14.a.5.1.	2	) N.13.d.7.8.	-- do --
-- do --	N.7.d.0.4.	2	112th.Field Amb.LA CLYTTE, M.7.c.6.6½.	-- do --

Sub-Area Officers concerned will arrange relief.

List of Camp and Area Stores taken over to be forwarded to Divisional Headquarters.

6. SANITARY SECTION:-

O.C., Divl. Company will detail 6 T.U. men to relieve a similar number of the 19th. Division with the 81st. Sanitary Section at WESTOUTRE. Relief to be completed by 3rd. May, and men rationed by Sanitary Section from that date, inclusive.

7. ARTILLERY WAGON LINES:-

Arrangements for taking over Artillery Wagon Lines will be made by the C.R.A's concerned.

8. ACKNOWLEDGE.

G.A.Webb

Lieut-Colonel,
AA & QMG, 16th. Division.

For distribution P.T.O.

DISTRIBUTION OF 16TH. DIV. ADMINISTRATION ORDER NO.11.

Copy No. 1. G.O.C.
2. 47th. Inf. Bde.
3. 48th. Inf. Bde.
4. 49th. Inf. Bde.
5. 16th. Div.Engrs.
6. 16th. Div. Art.
7. 16th. D.A.C.
8. 16th. Div. Train.
9. D.A.D.O.S.,16th.Div.
10. 47th.Mobile Vet.Sec.
11. A.D.M.S.,16th.Div.
12. A.D.V.S.,16th.Div.
13. S.S.O.16th.Div.
14. A.P.M.,16th.Div.
15. O.i/c.,16th.Div.Ldy.
16. 81st. Sanitary Section.
17. French Mission.
18. Belgian Mission.
19. W.O.i/c. Posts,16th.Div.
20. IX. Corps "Q"
21. IX. Corps H.A.
22. 16th. Div.Camp Commandant.
23. 16th.Div.Trench Tramway Offr.
24. 16th. Sub-Area Offr.
25. 16th. Div. Coy.
26. 19th. Div. "Q".
27. 16th. Div. "G".
28. O.C.,16th.Div.Salvage Coy.
29. 16th. Div.Signal Coy.
30. 1st. Entrenching Bn.
31. 13th.R.West Surrey Lbr.Coy.
32. 136th.(A.T.) Coy.R.E.
33. 250th. Tun. Coy.R.E.
34. 175th. Tun. Coy.R.E.

35.)
36.) War Diary.

37.)
38.) Filed.
39.)

W A R D I A R Y :

-----------oOo----------

VOLUME:- 18

FOR MONTH OF MAY, 1917.

UNIT:- A & Q. Branch 16 Div H. Q (original)

Instructions regarding War Diaries and Intelligence Summaries are contained in F. S. Regs., Part II. and the Staff Manual respectively. Title pages will be prepared in manuscript.

WAR DIARY
or
INTELLIGENCE SUMMARY.
(Erase heading not required.)

Army Form C. 2118.

Place	Date	Hour	Summary of Events and Information	Remarks and references to Appendices
LOCRE	1/5/17.	9pm.	Divisional School drew rations for last time (broken up). Feeding strength of Division men 14131 HD 378 LD. 3583.	
"	2/5/17.	10.30pm.	Feeding strength of Division men 19635 HD 458 LD. 3792 The following units drew with the Division for the first time to-day: 45th H.A. Group — 250th Tunnelling Coy 278th Siege Battery — 175th — " — 286th — " — — 13th R.W.S. (Labour Bn). 285th — " — — 1st Entrenching Bn 236th — " — — 136 A.T. Coy R.E. 305th — " — A "Gas Alarm" was received from "P" at 10.10pm. Strombus horns were heard just previously. Nothing transpired.	
"	3/5/17	9pm.	Feeding strength of Division Men 19960 HD 477 LD 3862.	
"	4/5/17	"	Feeding strength of Division Men 20742, HD. 498, LD. 4549. 305th Siege battery drew for last time to-day 177 Bde R.F.A. drew for first time to-day AA & QMG visited the line with Brig. Gen 48th Bde	

Instructions regarding War Diaries and Intelligence Summaries are contained in F. S. Regs., Part II. and the Staff Manual respectively. Title pages will be prepared in manuscript.

WAR DIARY
or
INTELLIGENCE SUMMARY.
(Erase heading not required.)

Army Form C. 2118.

Place	Date	Hour	Summary of Events and Information	Remarks and references to Appendices
LOCRE	5/5/17	10pm.	Feeding Strength of Division men 22025 HD 531 LD 5453	
			77th Brigade R.F.A. (Army) drew with Division for first time.	
"	6/5/17	"	Feeding strength of Division men 21817 HD 532 LD 5505.	
			Lime Juice issued for first time to units	
"	7/5/17	"	Feeding strength of Division men 22168, HD 542, LD 5513.	
"	8/5/17	"	Feeding strength of Division 22185, HD 528, LD 5502.	
"	9/5/17	"	The 19th Division have come back to the DIPENDAAL Sector & are now taking over from us. ~~R~~ Relief to be complete by 12th inst. We are now once more holding a one Brigade front.	
			Divisional Administrative Order No. 13 issued *	App. 7.
"	10/5/17.	"	Feeding Strength of Division Men 22005, HD. 519, LD. 5506.	
"	11/5/17	"	Feeding strength of Division Men 21870, HD 516, LD. 5483.	
			77th Bde R.F.A, & 47th Inf Bde less 6th Conn R. & 155 Coy RE drew with Division for last time to-day prior to proceeding to training area.	

Instructions regarding War Diaries and Intelligence Summaries are contained in F. S. Regs., Part II. and the Staff Manual respectively. Title pages will be prepared in manuscript.

WAR DIARY
or
INTELLIGENCE SUMMARY.
(Erase heading not required.)

Army Form C. 2118.

Place	Date	Hour	Summary of Events and Information	Remarks and references to Appendices
LOCRE	12/5/17	10pm	Feeding Strength men 18158 HD414 LD4335.	
			225 men of the 7th R.I.R. have been temporarily detached & were rationed by 41st Division from 11-5-17.	
			The ff units were rationed for the last time to-day	
			278th Siege Battery 405th Siege Battery 136th A.T. Coy R.E.	
			286th " 45th H.A.G. 250th Tunn Coy R.E	
			285th " 13 R.W.S Labour Battalion 175th "	
			236th " 1st Entrenching Battalion	
"	13/5/17	"	Feeding Strength of Division men 14801, HD415, LD.4311	
"	14/5/17.		The AA & QMG IX Corps visited the Office to-day.	
			Feeding Strength men 15104, HD.383. LD.4316	
			405th Siege Battery drew with Division first time to-day	
	15/5/17.		Feeding Strength men 16263. HD386, LD.4299	
			123 Brigade Details drew for last time to-day	
			314 Road Construction Company (IX Corps) & No 3 Special Coy RE drew for first time to-day.	

Instructions regarding War Diaries and Intelligence Summaries are contained in F. S. Regs., Part II. and the Staff Manual respectively. Title pages will be prepared in manuscript.

WAR DIARY
or
INTELLIGENCE SUMMARY.
(Erase heading not required.)

Army Form C. 2118.

Place	Date	Hour	Summary of Events and Information	Remarks and references to Appendices
LOCRE	16/5/17	10 pm	The following Administrative Orders have been issued, dated as under and numbered as per margin	
			Administrative Order no 14 — 11/5/17	APP. 8
			" no 15 — 12/5/17	APP. 9
			" no 16. — 13/5/17	APP. 10
			" no 17 — 15/5/17.	APP. 11
			" no 18 — 15/5/17.	APP 12
			Feeding Strength Men 17562. HD. 432 LD. 4496.	
			The 4th Bn Coldstream Guards (Pioneers) + [illegible] O Special Company RE. drew with Division for first time to-day	
"	17/5/17	"	The 6th Conn. Rangers drew with Division for last time to-day.	
			Feeding Strength of Division men 17142. HD 384, LD 4368.	
"	18/5/17	"	The ff units drew with Division for ~~fist~~ first time to-day.	
			24th H.A. Group	
			53rd " —	
			85th " —	

Instructions regarding War Diaries and Intelligence Summaries are contained in F. S. Regs., Part II. and the Staff Manual respectively. Title pages will be prepared in manuscript.

WAR DIARY
or
INTELLIGENCE SUMMARY.
(Erase heading not required.)

Army Form C. 2118.

Place	Date	Hour	Summary of Events and Information	Remarks and references to Appendices
LOCRE	19/5/17	10pm	H. Units drew with Division for the first time today 270th Siege Battery 76th H.A. Group 204th " "	
"	20/5/17	"	Feeding Strength Men 18220 H.D. 501 LD 4439 Following units drew with Division for the first time today 121st Siege Battery 151st Siege Battery 180th Siege Battery 248th Siege Battery 266th do 199th do 121st Heavy Battery 161st do 58th do 126th do 129th do	
"	21/5	"	Feeding Strength of Division - Men 18087. HD 499. LD 4392. No units left or joined the Division today.	
"	22/5	"	Following Units drew rations with this Division to day - 62nd Siege Battery, 33rd Siege Battery, 262 Siege Battery, 23 H.A Group 5th R.M.A. 202nd Siege Battery 203 Siege Battery + 2/1 N Mid Battery	
"	23/5	"	Feeding Strength of Division - Men 20169, HD690, LD 4518. The 239th Siege Battery & 265th Siege Battery drew rations with this Div for the first time today.	

Instructions regarding War Diaries and Intelligence Summaries are contained in F. S. Regs., Part II. and the Staff Manual respectively. Title pages will be prepared in manuscript.

WAR DIARY
or
INTELLIGENCE SUMMARY.
(Erase heading not required.)

Army Form C. 2118.

Place	Date	Hour	Summary of Events and Information	Remarks and references to Appendices
LOCRE	24/5	10pm	Feeding Strength of the Division – Men 20278 H.D. 862, L.D 5366 5th R Horse Artillery drew with this Division for the first time today.	
"	25/5	10pm	Feeding Strength Men 20459, HD 539, LD 5348. The following units refilled last time with the Division today:– 76th HA Group, 129 Heavy Battery, 53 HA Group; 85 HA Group 121 Heavy Battery, 161, 151, 180, 202, 203, 239, 265, 199, 33, 58 62, 121, 126, 204, 248, 266, 405, 24, 255 & 270 Siege Batteries 51st HA Group, 5th RMA 2/1 N Midland Battery & 116 Heavy Battery	
"			The 3rd West India Regiment drew rations with the Division today	
	26/5	10pm	Feeding Strength Men 18083, HD404, LD 5268.	
"	27/5	"	No units left or joined the Division today.	
"	28/5	"	6th East Yorks joined the Division today.	
"	29/5	"	47th Inf Bde left the Training area for ARQUES	
"	30/5	"	47th Inf Bde left ARQUES for WALLON CAPELL	
"	31/5	"	47th Inf Bde left WALLON CAPELL for CLARE CAMP. where it arrived during the afternoon. Divl HQ divided into two Echelons. First Echelon moved to SCHERPENBEG. Second Ech remained in LOCRE.	

H. [illegible] for Maj.-Gen. Comdg 16th Div

2313 Wt W2541/1451 700,000 5/15 D. D. & L. A.D.S.S./Forms/C. 2118.

W A R D I A R Y .

FOR MONTH OF JUNE, 1917.

V O L U M E :- 19

UNIT:- "A & Q" Branch 16th Division

Dup

Instructions regarding War Diaries and Intelligence Summaries are contained in F. S. Regs., Part II. and the Staff Manual respectively. Title Pages will be prepared in manuscript.

WAR DIARY
or
INTELLIGENCE SUMMARY
(Erase heading not required.)

Army Form C. 2118

"A" & "Q" BRANCH, 16th Div.H.Q.

Place	Date	Hour	Summary of Events and Information	Remarks and references to Appendices
	June 1917			
LOCRE.	1st	9.pm	Feeding Strength - men 22642 - H.D. 507 - L.D. 6019. No units left or joined the Division.	
	2nd	9.pm	Rabbits were issued as a ration, for the first time.	
	3rd	do	Situation unchanged.	
	4th	do	219 M.G.Coy., (detachment) joined this Division today.	
	5th	do	218 M.G.Coy., & No. 8 Army Tramway Coy., drew rations with Division for first time today.	
	6th	do	"Q" (2nd Echelon), moved from LOCRE to MONT ROUGE. 4th Coldstream Guards left today.	
MONT ROUGE	7th	do.	The Division attacked the WYTSCHAETE RIDGE. All objectives were taken and consolidated according to plans, pre-arranged. The supply of rations, water, ammunition, and all stores, worked smoothly 33rd Inf.Bde. (11th Division) attached to this Division.	
	8th	do.	Feeding Strength - men 26372 - H.D. 585 - L.D. 6151.	
	9th	do.	Situation unchanged. 33rd Inf.Bde. drew rations with Division for last time.	
	10th	do	Feeding strength - men 21912 - H.D. 494 - L.D. 5910.	
	11th	do.	Divnl H.Q., ("G", "Q"., Artillery R.E., and Signals), moved to LOCRE.	
LOCRE.	12th	do.	Orders received for 16th Division to move into back area: 48th Bde. came out of line and went to CLARE CAMP: Heavy thunderstorm at 4.30.p.m.	
MERRIS	13th	do.	16th Division less Div.Artillery and R.E., moved to back area: 47th Inf.Bde. at METEREN: 48th Inf Bde. at STRAZEELE: Div.Headqrs., and 49th Inf.Bde. at MERRIS.	
	14th	do.	Feeding strength - men 15712 - H.D. 418 - L.D. 3709: Portuguese Railway Construction Coy R.E., attached to Division for rations and administration.	
	15th	do.	Division at MERRIS, resting: nothing to report.	
	16th	do.	No change in situation.	
LOCRE	17th	do.	Division moved out of MERRIS area up to LOCRE: Portuguese Railway Construction Coy drew with Division for last time: A/180th Bde.R.F.A; also drew for last time prior to moving to TILQUES Railhead at BAILLEUL.	
MERRIS	18th	do.	16th Division moved from LOCRE back to MERRIS area in same billets as before.	
	19th	do.	Division in rest in MERRIS area: feeding strength - men 15640 - H.D. 433 - L.D.3512.	
GODEWAERSVELDE	20th	do.	16th Division moved into EECKE area: Div.H.Q. at GODEWAERSVELDE: thunderstorms and rain at intervals.	
	21st	do.	16th Division resting in EECKE area: nothing to report:	
ZEGGERS CAPPEL	22nd	do.	Division moved from EECKE area into VIII Corps Reserve area: Divisional Headquarters at ZEGGERS CAPPEL: 47th Inf.Bde. H.Q., at ERINGHAM: 48th Inf.Bde.H.Q., at RUBROUCK: 49th Inf.Bde.H.Q., at BUYSSCHEURE: A very wet day.	

1875 Wt. W593/826 1,000,000 4/15 J.B.C. & A. A.D.S.S./Forms/C. 2118.

Instructi[illegible] regarding War Diaries and Intelligence Summ[illegible]es are contained in F. S. Regs., Part II. and [illegible] Staff Manual respectively. Title Pages will be prepared in manuscript.

WAR DIARY
or
INTELLIGENCE SUMMARY
(Erase heading not required.)

Army Form C. 2118

Sheet 2. "A" & "Q" 16th Div.

Place	Date	Hour	Summary of Events and Information	Remarks and references to Appendices
	June 1917			
ZEGGERS CAPPEL.	23rd	9.pm	Railhead ARNEKE: No. 4 D.S.C. arrived today to be attached to Division: Headqrs at ARNEKE. Supplies drawn by lorries from Railhea d for first time.	
	24th	9.pm	Nothing to record.	
	25th	do	G.S.O.I and A.A.& Q.M.G., proceeded on leave today.	
	26th	do	Feeding strength of Division - men 12924 - H.D. 362 - L.D. 1220: 16th Division Intelligence Coy formed and attached for rations to 16th Div. Employmeny Company.	
	27th	do	Enemy shelled DUNKERQUE and environs: XV Corps Headqrs hit: feeding strength of Division - men 13446 - H.D.361 - L.D. 1198.	
	28th	do	Nothing to record.	
	29th	do	Situation unchanged.	
	30th	do	49th Inf.Bde. together with 16th Div.Intelligence Coy moved to TATINGHEM for training: Divisional Commander and G.S.O.III proceeded to BOULOGNE.	

[illegible signature] Capt
for Major-General,
Commanding 16th (Irish) Division.

2nd July, 1917.

1875 Wt. W593/826 1,000,000 4/15 J.B.C. & A. A.D.S.S./Forms/C. 2118.

WAR DIARY.

FOR MONTH OF JULY, 1917.

VOLUME :- 20

UNIT :- "A & Q" Branch 16th D.H.Q.

Original

Army Form C. 2118.

Instructions regarding War Diaries and Intelligence Summaries are contained in F. S. Regs., Part II. and the Staff Manual respectively. Title pages will be prepared in manuscript.

WAR DIARY
or
INTELLIGENCE SUMMARY.
(Erase heading not required.)

"A" & "Q" BRANCH,
16th Divisional Headquarters.

Place	Date	Hour	Summary of Events and Information	Remarks and references to Appendices
	July, 1917.			
ZEGGERS CAPPEL.	1st	9.pm	Feeding strength of division: 13265 men: H.D.Horses 353: L.D.1173: D.C.O., to ST JANS CAPPEL re clair against 16th Div.Arty. IX Corps Headqs also visited with reference to revision of recommendations for Honours & Rewards for battle of MESSINES.	
	2nd	9.pm	Divisional Commander & G.S.O.3 returned from BOULOGNE: 2/Lieut.SMITH from 49th Inf.Bde. H.Q., arrived and was attached to "Q" Branch for duty.	
	3rd	9½pm.	Nothing to report.	
	4th	9.pm.	Feeding strength of division: 9935 men: H.D.Horses 271: L.D. 893:	
	5th	9.pm.	Nothing to record.	
	6th	9.pm	G.S.O.II left Division to take up duties as G.S.O.II Second Army.	
	7th	9.pm.	Divisional Commander proceeded to BOULOGNE.	
	8th	9.pm.	G.S.O.I and A.A.& Q.M.G., returned from leave: 48th Inf.Bde. moved from RUBROUCK area to TATINGHEM: 49th Inf.Bde. from TATINGHEM to RUBROUCK.	
	9th	9.pm.	Nothing of importance to record.	
	10th	9.pm.	Divisional Commander inspected 1st R.Munster Fuslrs: feeding strength of Division: 9099 men: H.D.horses 254: L.D.855:	
	11th	9.pm.	D.A.Q.M.G. proceeded on leave: feeding strength of Division 9159 men:	
	12th	9.pm.	47th Inf.Bde. sports held at ZEGGERS CAPPEL.	
	13th	9.pm	No change: nothing to record.	
	14th	9.pm.	No change:	
	15th	9.pm.	Parties from 47th and 48th Inf.Bdes. proceeded in lorries to ST OMER for a special service at the cathedral.	
	16th	9.pm.	feeding strength of division: 8980 men: H.D.horses 239: L.D.horses 864:	
	17th	9.pm.	Nothing to record:	
	18th	9.pm.	Nothing to report:	
	19th	9.pm.	49th Inf.Bde. held their sports at WINNEZEEIE.	
	20th	9.pm.	Feeding strength of Division: men 8718: horses, 247 H.D.: 907 L.D.: 156th Field Coy R.E., drew rations with Division: Col. WATTS, A.D.M.S., 16th Div. to 55th Div: Brev.Col.CUMMINS, C.M.G., took over duties as A.D.M.S.	
	21st	9.pm.	Major AUSTIN returned to Division and took over command of Divisional Employment Company: feeding strength unchanged.	
	22nd	9.pm.	48th.Inf.Bde. moved from ERINGHEM to WINNEZEEIE No. 3 area: 47th.Inf.Bde.transport from TATINGHEM to NOORDPEENE: feeding strength 9118: H.D.247: L.D.1047:	
	23rd	9.pm.	47th.Inf.Bde.transport marched from NORDPEENE to WINNEZEEIE area: 47th.Inf.Bde.troops moved by rail from TATINGHEM to WINNEZEEIE.	

(Sheet 2 :-)

(A7092). Wt. W12839/M1293. 750,000. 1/17. D. D. & L., Ltd. Forms/C.2118/14.

Instructions regarding War Diaries and Intelligence Summaries are contained in F. S. Regs., Part II. and the Staff Manual respectively. Title pages will be prepared in manuscript.

WAR DIARY
or
INTELLIGENCE SUMMARY.

(*Erase heading not required.*)

Army Form C. 2118.

Sheet 2.
"A" & "Q" Branch, 16th Div.H.Q.

Place	Date	Hour	Summary of Events and Information	Remarks and references to Appendices
	July, 1917			
POPERINGHE	24th	9.pm.	Division moved to POPERINGHE from ZEGGERS CAPPEL: feeding strength : men 12602: L.D. 1205: H.D.337:	
	25th	9.pm.	New G.S.O.II arrived: Capt.HOLMES proceeded to 49th Division as D.A.Q.M.G.: No. 4 Supply Column moved from ARNEKE to ABEELE: 47th & 48th Inf.Bdes. moved from WINNEZEELE to WATOU area.	
	26th	9.pm.	Captain HARRISON, Staff Capt., 47th Inf.Bde., proceeded to 19th Division as D.A.Q.M.G.: 49th Inf Bde. moved up into WATOU area.	
	27th	9.pm.	Nothing to record: T/Lt. MASON arrived to take over command of the 49th M.G.Co. Railhead, WIPPENHOEK: feeding strength 12488: H.D.331: L.D.1204:	
	28th	9.pm.	Nothingspecial to report: some inconvenience was caused in the offices owing to a slight dose of sneezing gas arriving apparently from Aeroplane bombs.	
	29th	9.pm.	Feeding strength 12795: H.D.331: L.D.1372:	
	30th	9.pm.	48th Inf.Bde. moved up into VLAMERTINGHE area: 47th & 49th Inf.Bdes. to BRANDHOEK area.	
	31st	9.pm.	7th Leinster Regt., and 1st R.Munster Fuslrs, moved up to forward area to bury cables: ZERO day. 48th Inf.Bde. moved up to Line: 49th Inf.Bde. moved to GOLDFISH CHATEAU area.	

G. Tomms Maj. for
Major-General,
Commanding 16th (Irish) Division.

(A7092). Wt. W12839/M1293. 750,000. 1/17. D. D. & L., Ltd. Forms/C.2118/14.

WAR DIARY.

FOR MONTH OF AUGUST, 1917.

VOLUME 21.........

UNIT "A & Q" 16 Div. Headqrs.

Duplicate

WO 95/1959 121

Instructions regarding War Diaries and Intelligence Summaries are contained in F. S. Regs., Part II. and the Staff Manual respectively. Title pages will be prepared in manuscript.

WAR DIARY
or
INTELLIGENCE SUMMARY.
(Erase heading not required.)

Army Form C. 21

"A" & "Q" Branch
16th (Irish) Division Headqrs.

Place	Date	Hour	Summary of Events and Information	Remarks and references to Appendices
POPERINGHE.	August 1917. 1st	9.pm	Strength 13772:H.D.351: L.D.1404:49th Inf.Bde.moved back to POPERINGHE area: 6th Connaught Rangers & 6th R.Irish Regt moved up to 15th Division to relieve 48th Inf.Bde.	
	2nd	9.pm	Strength 13086:H.D.335:L.D.1346: second magazine for rifles authorised for first time: 47th Inf Bde.relieved 45th Inf.Bde.in the line.	
	3rd	9.pm	49th Inf.Bde.relieved the 46th Inf.Bde.in Support.	
	4th	9.pm	Divnl Headqrs moved ~~from~~ from POPERINGHE to camp at H.7.c.8.5: command of the line taken over by 16yh Division: feeding strength 13215: H.D.336: L.D.1336.	
BRANDHOEK.	5th	9.pm	47th Inf.Bde.relieved by 48th Inf.Bde.in line: feeding strength of division 24716 men: H.D.horses 773:L.D.8459.	
	6th	9.pm	Feeding strength of division 25078 men:H.D.horses 797: L.D.8489: weather dull, but no rain.	
	7th	9.pm	Weather dull,but fine: feeding strength 23892 men: 785 H.D.horses: L.D.8516: heavy gunfire on divisional front at 8.30.p.m.	
	8th	9.pm	No change in situation: nothing to report.	
	9th	9.pm	Weather fine: one shell dropped in Divnl H.Q. camp at 7.30.p.m: others close round: 225 M.G.Coy joined the division: feeding strength 23496 men: H.D.horses 790: L.D. 8556.	
	10th	9.pm	Weather fine,with bright sunshine:ground drying up fast:attack by IInd Corps successful; in gaining the objective required: feeding strength 23106 men: H.D.horses 794: L.D.8512.	
	11th	9.pm	Enemy aeroplanes active during night: heavy bombs dropped,but none in vicinity of H.Q.camp.	
	12th	9.pm	No change: weather fine till 6.30.p.m.	
	13th	9.pm	Weather fine with showers at intervals:feeding strength of division 22651 men: H.D.horses 792: L.D.8558: barrage rations issued to troops.	
	14th	9.pm	Weather fine: feeding strength of division 23636 men: H.D.horses 797: L.D.horses 8477:	
	15th	9.pm	Nothing to report.	
	16th	9.pm.	Division attacked German positions East of YPRES: 2 Officers and 134 O.R. prisoners sent down to Corps cage: heavy casualties in division.	
	17th	9.pm	Weather fine and hot: enemy aircraft very active by day and night: heavy bombs dropped in	
~~WATOU.~~	~~18th~~	~~9.pm~~	neighbourhood of H.Q.camp.	
WATOU	18th	9.pm	16th Division moved out of the line today: Headquarters at WATOU.	
	19th	9.pm	Railhead WIPPENHOEK: feeding strength of division 9925 men:H.D.horses 343: L.D.1477: weather fine: divisional troops and Brigades in billets in WATOU and neighbourhood.	
	20th	9.pm	10th R.Dublin Fuslrs joined division today: feeding strength 10404 men: H.D.horses 339:LD 1571.	
	21st	9.pm	Division started to move to new part of line: 47th.Inf.Bde refilling point at GOMIECOURT: 48th Inf.Bde. at COURCELLE: 49th Inf.Bde. at HALIFAZ CAMP: near ACHIET-le-PETIT.	

22nd:-

(A7092). Wt. W12839/M1293. 750,000. 1/17. D. D. & L., Ltd. Forms/C.2118/14.

Instructions regarding War Diaries and Intelligence Summaries are contained in F. S. Regs., Part II. and the Staff Manual respectively. Title pages will be prepared in manuscript.

WAR DIARY
or
INTELLIGENCE SUMMARY.
(Erase heading not required.)

Army Form C. 2118.

Place	Date	Hour	Summary of Events and Information	Remarks and references to Appendices
ACHIET-le-PETIT	22nd	9.pm	Divisional Headqrs established at ACHIET-le-PETIT: all accommodation of an extemporized nature. feeding strength 11686 men: H.D.horses 364: L.D.1434: railhead at ACHIET-le-GRAND.	
	23rd	9.pm	Amalgamation of 7/8th R.Inniskilling Fusiliers accomplished today.	
	24th	9.pm	Weather fine: feeding strength 12040 men: H.D.horses 378: L.D.1467.	
	25th	9.pm	No change.	
	26th	9.pm	No change.	
	27th	9.pm	Divisional Headqrs moved today in pouring rain to MOYENNEVILLE.	
	28th	9.pm	Railhead BOISLEUX-au-MONT: feeding strength 14287 men: H.D.horses 474: L.D.3787: 16th Divnl Artillery rejoined Division: weather wet and stormy.	
	29th	9.pm	Weather wet and stormy: Corps commander visited Divnl Headqrs: Captain EVANS arrived at Divnl Headqrs to take up duty as D.A.Q.M.G., vice Major C.T.TOMES, to ENGLAND as Instructor at Staff College, CAMBRIDGE.	
	30th	9.pm	No change.	
	31st	9.pm	Major C.T.TOMES, left the division today to take up duty at Staff College, CAMBRIDGE, ENGLAND. feeding strength of division 16105 men: H.D.horses 651: L.D.4123.	

[signature] for
Major-General,
Commanding 16th (Irish) Division.

(A7092). Wt. W12839/M1293. 750,000. 1/17. D. D. & L., Ltd. Forms/C.2118/14.

The following is the statement of casualties to all units in the Division, from 1st to 31st August, 1917, (both dates inclusive).

The figures shewn do not include casualties in attached units during this period:-

O F F I C E R S.			Total.	OTHER RANKS:			Total.	Grand Total.
Killed.	Wounded.	Missing.		Killed.	Wounded.	Missing.		
42	154 (a)	19	215	521	2729 (b)	760	4010	4225.

(a) Includes 22 slightly at duty, and 12 Gassed.

(b) Includes 9 self-inflicted and accidental:
40 slightly at duty.
111 Gassed.

Original.

WAR DIARY.

FOR MONTH OF [redacted] 1917.

VOLUME 22

UNIT "A & Q" Branch 16 Div H.Q.

Vol 22

Instructions regarding War Diaries and Intelligence Summaries are contained in F. S. Regs., Part II. and the Staff Manual respectively. Title pages will be prepared in manuscript.

WAR DIARY
or
INTELLIGENCE SUMMARY.
(Erase heading not required.)

VOLUME XXII

Army Form C. 2118.

"A" & "Q" BRANCH, 16th (IRISH) Division.

Place	Date September 1917	Hour	Summary of Events and Information	Remarks and references to Appendices
MOYENNE-VILLE.	1st	9pm.	Much wind with showers: D.A.A.G. proceeded on leave this day by rail via AMIENS: G.O.S., Divn. to BOULOGNE.	
	2nd	do	Divisional Commander returned from BOULOGNE: feeding strength of division: 16524 men: Horses, H.D. 651: L.D. 3983.	
	3rd	do	Weather fine and calm: Camp Commandant and French Interpreter Officer, to AMIENS to arrange for supplies for canteens: no change in situation.	
	4th	do	49th Inf Bde relieved the 48th Inf Bde in line.	
	5th	do.	Move of Divisional Headquarters to BEHAGNIES postponed: feeding strength of Division: 16028 men: Horses, H.D. 627: L.D. 3806.	
	6th	do.	Weather warm and thundery: no change in situation.	
	7th	do	Selection of brood mares for post-war services: supplies for canteens arrived by lorry from AMIENS.	
	8th	do	Meeting at VI Corps H.Q., of Committee for Winter Sports, Corps Commander presiding: feeding strength of Division: 16213 men: Horses, H.D. 627: L.D. 3787.	
	9th	do	48th Inf Bde reviewed by Divisional Commander in commemoration of the Battle of GUINCHY, on 9th September, 1916.	
	10th	do	D.A.Q.M.G. visited VI Corps Laundry at FREVENT re arrangements for proportion of fuel due from this division: XXXXXXXXXXx 5 F.G.C's M. sat today to try 3 prisoners from 47th Inf Bde and 2 from 49th Inf Bde.	
	11th	do	48th Inf Bde reviewed by VI Corps Commander: feeding strength of division: 15971 men: Horses, H.D. 621: L.D.3762: No. 4 Grazing Company left Division yesterday.	
	12th	do	No change in situation.	
	13th	do	Divisional Commander proceed on 14 days leave to England: D.A.A.G. returned from leave: Brig-Gen G.E.PEREIRA, C.B., C.M.G., D.S.O., assumed temporary command of Division.	
	14th	do	Nothing to report.	
	15th	do	Very successful raid carried out by 50th Division on our left.	
	16th	do	48th Inf Bde relieved the 49th Inf Bde in left section of the line: feeding strength of Division 15999 men: Horses H.D., 619: L.D. 3704.	
	17th	do	VI Corps Headquarters moved today from BIHUCOURT to BRETINCOURT: O.C., 11th Hants Regt (P) and A.D.M.S., returned from leave today.	
	18th	do	Feeding strength of Division, 16056 men: Horses, H.D. 621: L.D.3723.	
BEHAGNIES	19th	do	16th Divisional Headquarters moved from MOYENNEVILLE to BEHAGNIES.	
	20th	do	Weather fine with bright sunshine which has continued for last 7 days: feeding strength of Division 15982 men: Horses, H.D. 728: L.D. 3740.	
	21st	do	No change: nothing to record.	

(continued).

(A7092). Wt. W12839/M1293. 750,000. 1/17. D. D. & L., Ltd. Forms/C.2118/14.

Instructions regarding War Diaries and Intelligence Summaries are contained in F. S. Regs., Part II. and the Staff Manual respectively. Title pages will be prepared in manuscript.

WAR DIARY
or
INTELLIGENCE SUMMARY.
(Erase heading not required.)

Army Form C. 2118.

Place	Date	Hour	Summary of Events and Information	Remarks and references to Appendices
BEHAGNIES	22nd	9pm	Continued fine weather: work on construction of Divisional Headquarter Camp being pushed forward: no change in military situation on Divisional front.	
	23rd	9pm	Weather fine with bright sunshine all day: feeding strength of Division 16519 men: Horses, H.D.635: L.D. 3715.	
	24th	do	Meeting of Sports Committee at VI Corps Headqrs: weather fine with bright sunshine: enemy aeroplanes active over Divisional Headquarters.	
	25th	do	A.A.& Q.M.G., G.S.O.I., and G.S.O.II, returned from short leave to PARIS: weather very warm with bright sunshine all day: two enemy aeroplanes over Divisional Headquarters in course of morning.	
	26th	do	No change: nothing to report.	
	27th	do	Weather continues fine and dry: no change in situation.	
	28th	do	Divisional Commander to G.H.Q. for conference: 49th Inf Bde relieved 48th Inf Bde in the line: fine weather continues:	
	29th	do	No change in situation: weather continues fine with bright sunshine all day:	
	30th	do	Fine weather with bright sunshine all day: feeding strength of Division, 16665 men: horses, H.D. 643: L.D. 3618.	

C. Knope Capt.
for Major-General,
Commanding 16th (Irish) Division.

Original

W A R D I A R Y

FOR MONTH OF OCTOBER, 1917.

UNIT "A. & Q." Branch 16 Division

VOLUME NUMBER 23

Vol 23

Instructions regarding War Diaries and Intelligence Summaries are contained in F. S. Regs., Part II. and the Staff Manual respectively. Title pages will be prepared in manuscript.

WAR DIARY
or
INTELLIGENCE SUMMARY.
(Erase heading not required.)

"A" & "Q" Branch,
16th (Irish) Division.

Army Form C. 2118.

Place	Date	Hour	Summary of Events and Information	Remarks and references to Appendices
BEHAGNIES	October, 1917.			
	1st	9.pm.	Continued fine weather: bright sunshine all day: meeting of Staff Captains & representatives of Divisional Troops held to arrange matters in reference to Winter Sports.	
	2nd	do.	G.C.M. held at ERVILLERS for trial of Capt.D.B.de.A.BORCHERDS, Connaught Rangers: brilliant sunshine all day: feeding strength of division, 16553 men.	
	3rd	do.	No change: weather fine but cloudy.	
	4th	do.	Dull day with rain at intervals and high wind: Divisional Commander confined to his room through accidental fall: feeding strength of Division: men 16583: H.D.Horses 630: LD.Horses 3616.	
	5th	do.	Weather fine with intermittent sunshine.	
	6th	do.	Weather wet all day: feeding strength of Division 16614 men: H.D.634: L.D.3616.	
	7th	do.	No change: winter scale of fuel, comes into force.	
	8th	do.	Weather fine in morning, but wet afternoon: feeding strength 16654 men.	
	9th	do.	No change: feeding strength 16142 men: H.D.624: L.D.3599.	
	10th	do.	Fine all day.	
	11th	do.	No change: feeding strength 15869 men: 624 H.D.: 3599 L.D.	
	12th	do.	Heavy rain in early morning and again in the afternoon: lecture given by Doctor KELMAN to the Division on "America and the war", in Corps Cinema Hall.	
	13th	do.	Weather fine:	
	14th	6.pm.	Weather cold with some rain: Divisional Commander together with American General inspected Trench Mortar Batteries.	
	15th	do.	Weather cold and showery: Divisional Commander accompanied by American General inspected Divisional Train.	
	16th	9.pm	Fine all day: Major-General EDWARDS, U.S.Army, and staff, attached to Division for a period of six days.	
	17th	do.	Continued fine weather.	
	18th	do.	Weather dull and showery: feeding strength 15,034 men: H.D. 689: L.D.3567: representatives of the "REDMOND Memorial Fund", (Messrs. Nicholas BYRNE, and KEOGH, and Doctor ASHE), visited the Division.	
	19th	do.	Fine all day: Messrs BYRNE, KEOGH, and ASHE again visited the Division, and went round trenches in the afternoon, witnessing a Trench Mortar bombardment: feeding strength of Division: 15062 men: H.D.690: L.D.3559: 1st Royal Dublin Fusiliers, joined Division.	
	20th	do.	Weather cloudy but fine: nothing to report.	
	21st	do.	Sunshine all day: successful daylight enterprise carried out by 2nd R. Dublin Fuslrs in Centre Sub-section: 2 prisoners being captured: feeding strength men 15936: H.D.695: L.D.3591.	

P.T.O.:

(A7092). Wt. W12839/M1293. 750,000. 1/17. D. D. & L., Ltd. Forms/C.2118/14.

Instructions regarding War Diaries and Intelligence Summaries are contained in F. S. Regs., Part II. and the Staff Manual respectively. Title pages will be prepared in manuscript.

WAR DIARY
or
INTELLIGENCE SUMMARY.
(Erase heading not required.)

Army Form C. 2118.

Sheet 2.

Place	Date October, 1917.	Hour	Summary of Events and Information	Remarks and references to Appendices
BEHAGNIES.	22nd.	9.pm	Wet morning but fine in afternoon: Divisional Commander presented Medal Ribbons to the 1st Royal Munster Fusiliers: feeding strength men 16296: H.D.701: L.D.3637: 49th Inf.Bde. relieved 48th Inf.Bde. in Left Section.	
	23rd	9.pm.	Heavy rain all day: nothing to report: feeding strength men 16296: H.D.668: L.D.3626.	
	24th	do.	Rain during forenoon: but cleared up in afternoon: no change: feeding strength men 16456: H.D.665: L.D.3625.	
	25th	do.	Fine morning and afternoon, with heavy rain from about 6.p.m. onwards: 77th Army Brigade, RFA. (3 - 18-pdr. Batteries, and B.A.C.), detrained at BOISLEUX-au-MONT, and marched to MERCATEL, on attachment to the Division: feeding strength men 16411: H.D.667: L.D.3627.	
	26th	do.	Squalls and heavy rain all day. Nothing to report: feeding strength men 17050: H.D.666: L.D.4519.	
	27th	do.	Weather fine: frost at night: no change: His Eminence Cardinal BOURNE visited the Division, and attended parades of 2 Btns 48th Inf.Bde., and 2 Btns. 47th Inf.Bde: feeding strength: men, 17229: H.D.669: L.D.4518.	
	28th	do.	Fine all day: conference with Inf.Brigadiers, C.R.A., C.R.E., D.M.G.O., and Staff Officers held by Divisional Commander: otherwise nothing to report: feeding strength, men 16954: H.D., 680: L.D.4458.	
	29th	do.	Successful raid carried out by 49th Inf.Bde., resulting in capture of 3 prisoners.	
	30th	do.	No change: a wet day with much rain: Third Pontoon Park left Division today.	
	31st	do.	Weather brilliantly fine: parties of 29th Div.T.M.B. and 51st Div.T.M.B., joined Division today: feeding strength of Division: men 17809: H.D.588: L.D.4439.	

C. Kimpe Capt
for
Major-General,
Commanding 16th (Irish) Division.

(A7092). Wt. W12839/M1293. 75,080. 1/17. D. D. & L., Ltd. Forms/C.2118/14.

Original.

W A R . D I A R Y

FOR MONTH OF DECEMBER, 1917.

VOLUME :- 25.

U N I T :- "Q" Branch 16th Division

Vol 25

Original

W A R D I A R Y

FOR MONTH OF NOVEMBER, 1917.

x ~~HXXXXXXXX~~
VOLUME : - 24

UNIT :- A & Q Branch 16 D.H.Q

WO 24

Army Form C. 2118.

Instructions regarding War Diaries and Intelligence Summaries are contained in F. S. Regs., Part II. and the Staff Manual respectively. Title pages will be prepared in manuscript.

WAR DIARY
or
INTELLIGENCE SUMMARY.
(Erase heading not required.)

"A" and "Q" BRANCH

16th Division.

Place	Date Nov. 17	Hour	Summary of Events and Information	Remarks and references to Appendices
BEHAGNIES	1st.	9.p.m.	A dull day but no rain: 5th R.H.A.Brigade joined the Division today: feeding strength of Division: Men 18733: H.D.Horses 579: L.D.5082:	
	2nd.		Weather dull & misty: Divisional Commander proceeded to ADNIFER to attend presentation of Medals to 86th Brigade by Divisional Commander of 29th Division.	
	3rd.		A foggy day: Feeding Strength of Division: 18910 men: H.D.horses 611: L.D.5026.	
	4th.		A dull and misty day: 93rd A.F.A. joined Division this day; feeding strength of Division 19718 men: H.D.horses 635: L.D.5737.	
	5th.		No change: nothing to record.	
	6th.		F.G.C.M. sat at ERVILLERS today to try two cases of desertion and three of drunkeness on the part of W.Os. A dull day with rain at frequent intervals.	
	7th.		Weather wet and misty: Feeding strength of Division men 20005: H.D.Horses 635: L.D.5796.	
	8th.		Bright sunshine in morning: rain in evening: feeding strength of Division: men 19772: H.D.Horses 643: L.D.5823.	
	9th.		A wet day: no change.	
	10th.		Conference at Divisional Headquarters at which were present Brigadiers and Senior Divisional Staff: weather dull and threatening.	
	11th.		A dull and cloudy day: feeding strength of Division; men 20135: H.D.horses 643: L.D.5847: Divisional Commander to BOULOGNE for dental treatment.	
	12th.		A bright day after sharp frost during night: no change in situation.	
	13th.		A dull day with some rain: feeding strength of Division: men 20246: H.D.Horses 639: L.D.5701: A party from 29th Division joined 16th T.M.Battery	
	14th.		A fine day with sunshine: feeding strength of Division: men 20246: H.D.Horses 639:L.D. 5701.	
	15th.		Weather fine with bright sunshine: nothing to record.	
	16th.		Weather still fine and bright: 5th R.H.A.Bde. (less B.A.C.) 77th R.F.A.Bde.(less B.A.C.) 93rd A.F.A.Bde. (less B.A.C.) left Division today.	
	17th		Weather fine: feeding strength of Division 18463 men: H.D.horses 607: L.D.4223.	
	18th.		Weather fine: B.A.C. of 5th R.H.A., B.A.C. 77th A.F.A. Bde: B.A.C.93rd Bde.R.F.A. left Division today.	
	19th.		Weather fine: no change.	

(A7092). Wt. W12839/M1293. 750,000. 1/17. D. D. & L., Ltd. Forms/C.2118/14.

Army Form C. 2118.

Instructions regarding War Diaries and Intelligence Summaries are contained in F. S. Regs., Part II. and the Staff Manual respectively. Title pages will be prepared in manuscript.

WAR DIARY
or
INTELLIGENCE SUMMARY.
(Erase heading not required.)

"A" and "Q" BRANCH

16th DIVISION.

Place	Date	Hour	Summary of Events and Information	Remarks and references to Appendices
		Nov '17.		
BEHAGNIES	20th	9 p.m.	Division attacked with success this morning: all objectives gained: feeding strength of Division: men 17938: H.D.horses 595: L.D.3560: Prisoners of War Coy. joined Division for rations: weather wet and stormy.	
	21st.		Weather wet and stormy: enemy counter attacked without success: feeding strength of Division: men 17889: H.D.horses 596: L.D.3561.	
	22nd		Weather wet and misty: clearing of battle field proceeding and dead being buried: feeding strength of Division: men 18132: H.D.horses 584: L.D.3566.	
	23rd.		Brig.Gen. G.E.Pereira, C.B.,C.M.G.,D.S.O. relinquished Command of 47th Bde. today. Minor operation undertaken by 47th Brigade completely successful: 25 prisoners taken: weather fine with intermittent sunshine: 29th T.M.Batteries left Division.	
	24th.		Gale from S.W.: feeding strength of Division: men 18036: H.D.horses 565: L.D.3557.	
	25th.		Violentgale from S.W. with intermittent rain and hail: very cold: no change in situation.	
	26th.		Wind N.W.:rain in evening: 47th and 49th Bde. came out of line today: Corps Commander visited Divisional Commander in afternoon.	
	27th.		No change.	
	28th.		Feeding strength of Division: men 17479: H.D.horses 564: L.D.3537: weather fine.	
	29th.		Weather dull but fine: much movement on road towards the South: feeding strength of Division: men 17479: H.D.horses 564: L.D.3537.	
	30th.		Weather dull but fine: no change in situation: feeding strength of Division: men 17799: H.D.Horses 566: L.D.3517.	

C. Knipe Capt
for Major General,
Commanding 16th (Irish) Division.

Headquarters,
16th Division, 1/12/1917.

(A7092). Wt. W12839/M1293. 750,080. 1/17. D. D. & L., Ltd. Forms/C.2118/14.

SECRET

DUPLICATE.

G. 132

16th Division Q.

Administrative Instructions

SECRET.   16th Division No Q/307/8/5.

16TH DIV. 'G'
No. G132
Date 6.11.17.

G.1.

O.C.,

VI Corps Ammunition Park.

Reference the Ammunition required by the 3 Infantry Brigades of this Division for forthcoming Operations.

Will you please arrange to deliver the following Stores by Light Railway as follows:-

On 6th instant to 48th Infantry Bde: at ROYAL DUMP T.18.d.8.1.

S.A.A. - - - - -	30 Boxes.
Pistol Ammunition - -	4,000 Rounds.
Mills No. 23. - - -	400 Boxes.
1" Very Lights - - -	6 Boxes.
1½" Very Lights (Para. White)	8 Boxes.
Rockets Signal S.O.S.- -	84
Ground Flares. - - -	200

On 7th instant to 47th Infantry Bde: at GUINNESS DUMP. C.2.a.5.8.

S.A.A. - - - - - -	100 Boxes.
Mills No. 23 - - -	1000
Stokes complete rounds -	1000
Flares. - - - - -	4000
Very Lights 1" - - -	1000
Very Lights Green 1"- -	300
Very Lights Red 1" - -	300
"P" Grenades. - - -	300
Smoke Cases - - - -	200
Rockets S.O.S. - - -	100

On 8th instant to 49th Infantry Bde: at ROYAL DUMP. T.18.d.8.1.

S.A.A. - - - - - -	190 Boxes.
Mills Hand. - - - -	4320
Mills Rifle.- - - -	5280
Very Lights White 1"- -	26 Boxes.
Very Lights White 1½" -	3 Boxes.
Rifle Grenades S.O.S. -	156
"P" Bombs. - - - -	1000

Brigades will arrange direct with the Divisional Trench Tramway Officer at ST.LEGER for the number of trucks they require on the Trench Tramway, and it is advisable that they should arrange, if possible, for these to be ear-marked in advance. The necessary fatigue parties will be detailed nightly by the Brigade concerned.

Please inform "Q" Office 16th Division as early as possible the probable hour of the arrival of the train at its destination on each of the above nights so that the Brigade may arrange for the necessary trucks and fatigue parties to be ready to clear the train.

S.G. Evans
Captain.
D.A.Q.M.G.16th Division.

H.Q.16th Division.
5th November.1917.

Copies to:-
47th Infantry Brigade.
48th Infantry Brigade.
49th Infantry Brigade.

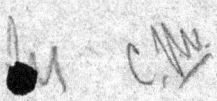

16th Division "G" }
Divl. T.T.O. } For information.

C.W.

G.1.

16TH DIV. 'G'
No G 132
Date 6.11.17

S E C R E T.

47th Infantry Bde.
48th Infantry Bde.
49th Infantry Bde.
16th Div. Artillery.
16th Div. Train.
C.R.E., 16th Divn.
A.D.M.S.
11th Hants. (P).
A.P.M. 16th Divn.

"G"

16th Division No. A.M.1009 - 6-11-1917.

Commencing of the night of 8/9th and continuing for several nights there will be very heavy traffic on the ARRAS - BAPAUME Road.

It is essential that this traffic shall not be blocked by cross traffic.

Ration carts together with other traffic for the line will therefore be East of the ARRAS - BAPAUME Road by 4 p.m. daily.

All other traffic will use tracks as much as possible and will avoid the main road.

The ration carts and other vehicles returning will be allowed to cross the main road under the direction of special posts to be placed in position by the A.P.M.

G.A. Crabbe

Headquarters, "A" & "Q" 16th Divn.

Lieut-Colonel.
A.A. & Q.M.G., 16th Division.

C.T.W.

Dy Sub

G.1.

16TH DIV. 'G'
No G.132
Date 7-11-17.

SECRET:- Copy No. 2

AMENDMENT TO
16th Divisional Administrative Instruction No. 7.

7th November, 1917.

POLICE ARRANGEMENTS:-

The following changes are made in the position of certain Battle Stragglers Posts, and the Advanced Prisoners of War Cage. They will now be situated as below:-

No. 4 Battle Stragglers Post......T.21.d.8.4.
No. 5 Battle Stragglers Post......T.21.a.4.9.
No. 6 Battle Stragglers Post......T.14.b.1.7.
Advanced Prisoners of War Cage....T.28.a.6.5.

Headquarters,
16th Division.

Lieut-Colonel,
A.A.& Q.M.G., 16th Division.

Copies To:-

Copy No. 1....G.O.C.
Copy No. 2...."G" Brch.
Copy No. 3....16th Div.Art.
Copy No. 4....16th Div.Eng.
Copy No. 5....47th Inf.Bde.
Copy No. 6....48th Inf.Bde.
Copy No. 7....49th Inf.Bde.
Copy No. 8....11th Hants (P).
Copy No. 9....A. D. M. S.
Copy No.10....VI Corps "Q".
Copy No. 11...A.P.M., 16th Div.

amended
11-11-17

Q302/13/3
7/11/17

Ref re wire cutters

S E C R E T.

16th Division No. Q 302/13/3

G2

47th Infantry Brigade.
48th Infantry Brigade.
49th Infantry Brigade.
O.C., Divl. Salvage Dump.
C.R.E.
16th Division "G" (For information.)

16TH DIV. 'G'
No 3132
Date 7.11.17

With reference to forthcoming operations.

The following may be drawn from the Divisional Salvage Dump ST. LEGER:-

140 - 2 Gallon Petrol Tins. } Per Brigade.
60 - 4 " " " }

The following may be drawn from the R.E.Dump BOYELLES:-

Picks - - 300 } Per Brigade.
Shovels - 600 }

On 9th instant 6000 Sandbags will be available for each Brigade at R.E.Dump at BOYELLES, but any smaller number that may be required urgently can be drawn at once.

The despatch of 250 YUKON PACKS has been notified and will be issued immediately on arrival, 75 per Brigade.

The question of the issue of a supply of Reserve Rations will be dealt with later.

S. G. Evans
Captain.
D.A.Q.M.G., 16th Division.

H.Q. 16th Division.
7th November, 1917.

H.Q.
16TH DIVISION.
No. 9132
Date 17-11-17.

SECRET

VI. Corps No. SQ/381.

x x x x x
16th. Division.

The following amounts of Smoke, Lachrimatory, and Lethal ammunition will be in possession of Divisions on Z day :-

	AS.	BSK.	BNC.	BCBR.	BPS.	BVN.	BJL.
3rd. Div.	1500	1000	-	746	64	1200	-
16th. Div.	1000	1400	1300	200	100	364	-
34th. Div.	500	500	-	493	14	-	254.

To effect his

"F" Corps Amm. Park will issue to:

3rd. Division.	200	AS.
	200	BSK.
	744	BCBR *
	64	BPS.
16th. Division.	1400	BSK.
	1300	BNC ϕ
	200	BCBR.
	364	BVN.
34th. Division.	400	BSK.
	250	BJL.

* 600 available from Third Army 19th.inst.
ϕ 1300 " " " " " "

34th. Division will transfer to 3rd. Division 300 AS.

"F" Corps Ammn. Park will retain 100 AS in reserve.

17/11/17.

Sd. R.W. ST. L. GETHIN, Lt-Col,
A.Q.M.G., VI. Corps.

---

(2)

"A" & "Q"
16TH
DIVISION.
No. 9/307/8/7

16th. Div. Art.
"G" 16th. Div.

For information.

S.G. Evans
Captain,
D.A.Q.M.G., 16th. Division.

17/11/17.

Army Form C. 2118.

Instructions regarding War Diaries and Intelligence Summaries are contained in F. S. Regs., Part II. and the Staff Manual respectively. Title pages will be prepared in manuscript.

Volume 25.

WAR DIARY
or
INTELLIGENCE SUMMARY.
(Erase heading not required.)

"A" & "Q" Branch,
16th (Irish) Division, Headqrs.,

Place	Date Decbr.	Hour	Summary of Events and Information	Remarks and references to Appendices
BEHAGNIES	1917. 1st	9.pm	Warning order received for Division to move from VI Corps area - feeding strength of Division, 17408 men: horses, H.D.565: L.D.3512: weather dull and cold with strong S.W.wind.	
	2nd	9.pm	A fine bright day with frost: feeding strength of Division: men 17342: horses, H.D.560: L.D. 3491	
LITTLE WOOD near YTRES	3rd	9.pm	Divisional Headqrs moved today from BEHAGNIES to LITTLE WOOD, near YTRES: a bright and frosty day: 47th Inf.Bde. at BEAULENCOURT: 48th Inf.Bde.H.Q. at ROCQUIGNY: 49th Inf.Bde.H.Q., at BARASTRE.	
	4th	9.pm	Divisional Headqrs remained at LITTLE WOOD, Railhead at BAPAUME: orders to take over that part of line, cancelled; fresh orders issued to join VII Corps to relieve 55th Division: weather bright with frost.	
FLAMICOURT	5th	9.pm	Divisional Headqrs moved from LITTLE WOOD to FLAMICOURT, a suburb of PERONNE: railhead at BRIE: 47th Inf.Bde. at BEAULENCOURT: 48th Inf.Bde. at St.EMILIE: 49th Inf.Bde. at TINCOURT: feeding strength of Division: men 14239: horses, H.D.342: L.D.1445: bright sunshine all day with frost at night: 155th,156th,157th Fd.Coys.R.E., and 11th Hants rejoined the Division.	
	6th	9.pm	Railhead at BRIE: 47th Inf.Bde. at HAMEL: 48th Inf.Bde. at St.EMILIE: 49th Inf.Bde. at VILLERS FAUCON: weather still continues fine with bright sunshine all day and frost at night.	
VILLERS FAUCON.	7th	9.pm	Divisional Headqrs moved from FLAMICOURT to VILLERS FAUCON completing relief of 55th Division, and taking over area: Depot Battn transferred from VI to VII Corps at reinforcement camp at GUILLAUCOURT: transfer to take place on 11th instant: Major HEFFERNAN ordered to take up duties as Bde.Major, 48th Inf.Bde, vice Captain BAYFORD, D.S.O., to Depot Battn.	
	8th	9.pm	Railhead at ROISEL: 47th Inf.Bde. at HAMEL: 48th Inf.Bde.at St.EMILIE: 49th Inf.Bde. took over left section of new Divisional front: feeding strength of Division: men 16126: horses, H.D., 453: L.D. 3507: weather dull and warmer: thaw restrictions in force until further notice.	
	9th	9.pm	A wet day: no change in situation: feeding strength of Division, men 16173: horses, H.D.454: L.D.3506.	
	10th	9.pm	Weather fine with bright sunshine: flight of six enemy aircraft over D.H.Q., at 2.p.m. One bomb dropped near incinerator: no damage or casualties: feeding strength of Division, men 18016: horses, H.D., 480: L.D.5584: 65th and 277th Bde. R.F.A., joined Division.	
	11th	9.pm	Seven lorries left for ACHIET-le-PETIT, ERVILLERS, and BOYELLES, to collect and bring back various stores left behind when Division moved from BEHAGNIES: weather dull and very cold with wind from N.E.	
	12th	9.pm	G.S.O.II proceeded on leave after having been recalled when Division moved from BEHAGNIES: weather fine and warmer.	
	13th	9.pm	7th (SIR) R.Irish Regt suffered severe casualties from a shell at ST EMILIE: 22 killed and 41 wounded: observation balloon over VILLERS FAUCON brought down in flames by enemy aeroplane: weather fine, with low clouds.	

(A7092). Wt. W12839/M1293. 75 ,0 0. 1/17. D. D. & L., Ltd. Forms/C.2118/14.

Sheet 2 :- (contd)

Army Form C. 2118.

Instructions regarding War Diaries and Intelligence Summaries are contained in F. S. Regs., Part II. and the Staff Manual respectively. Title pages will be prepared in manuscript.

WAR DIARY
or
INTELLIGENCE SUMMARY.
(*Erase heading not required.*)

SHEET 2:

Place	Date	Hour	Summary of Events and Information	Remarks and references to Appendices
	Dec'r, 1917			
VILLERS FAUCON.	14th	9.pm	D.M.G.O. and A.D.M.S., proceeded on leave: damp drizzle all day: feeding strength of Division men 17402: horses, H.D.513: L.D.5351: 47th and 49th Inf.Bde. Headqrs at St.EMILIE shelled about 7.30.p.m., and at intervals during night.	
	15th	9.pm	A fine day with bright sunshine: enemy artillery active: no change.	
	16th	9.pm	A dull cold day with bright ~~snowfall~~ sunshine: 47th and 49th Inf.Bde.Headqrs moved out of St.EMILIE into dug-outs prepared in Railway cutting, close by.	
	17th	9.pm	Heavy fall of snow during night: wind from N.E.: feeding strength of Division: men 18852: horses, H.D.476: L.D.6106.	
	18th	9.pm	Very cold with wind from N.E: traffic congested on account of snow drifts: 47th M.G.Coy relieved by 48th M.G.Coy and 49th M.G.Coy: 47th M.G.Coy to Divisional Reserve at TINCOURT: 48th Inf.Bde. less M.G.Coy, relieved 49th Inf.Bde.,less M.G.Coy, in left section of line on night of 17th/18th.	
	19th	9.pm	Hard frost with wind from N.W.: no change.	
	20th	9.pm	Frost continues with fog: feeding strength of Division: men 18639: horses, H.D.340: L.D.6086: Fifth Army Commander visited Divisional Commander today: 65th A.F.A.Bde, left Division today.	
	21st	9.pm	Very cold: dull with wind from N.E.: frost continues: neutralizing shoot by our artillery at 6.15.p.m.	
	22nd	9.pm	A fine bright day, with hard frost: no change in situation.	
	23rd	9.pm	Frost still continues: 16th Div.Arty. joined Division today: feeding strength, men, 19388: horses H.D.512: L.D.5994:	
	24th	9.pm	Wind from S.E.: frost shews signs of breaking: VII Corps Commander visited Divisional Commander today: 49th Inf.Bde.(less M.G.Coy), relieved 47th Inf.Bde. in right section during night 23rd/ 24th,	
	25th	9.pm	Thaw during night: wind S.W.: dinners to N.C.O's and men of Divisional Headqrs Staff: situation quiet: further heavy fall of snow in evening.	
	26th	9.pm	Wind N.W. with snow: no change in situation.	
	27th	9.pm	Wind N.E. herd frost continues: feeding strength men 19521: H.D. 530: L.D.5374.	
	28th	9.pm	Frost still continues: wind N.E: no change.	
	29th	9.pm	Rations did not come up: iron rations consumed: frost still continues: wind N.E.:	
	30th	9.pm	Wind N.W., slight thaw: F.G.C.M. convened to sit at D.H.Q., for trial of two O.R. of Dublin Fusiliers, was postponed .	
	31st	9.pm	Frost after slight thaw: feeding strength of Division. men 19221: horses, H.D.494: L.D.5333:	

16th D.H.Q.,

2nd Jan.1918.

for G. Knipe Capt
Major-General,
Commanding 16th (Irish) Division.

A7092 Wt. W2900/M1293 75,000 1/17. D. D. & L., Ltd. Forms/C.2118/14.

W.O. 26

Original

WAR DIARY,

FOR MONTH OF JANUARY, 1918.

VOLUME :- 26.

UNIT :- "A. & Q." Brch. 16th D.H.Q.

Instructions regarding War Diaries and Intelligence Summaries are contained in F. S. Regs., Part II. and the Staff Manual respectively. Title pages will be prepared in manuscript.

Army Form C. 2118.

WAR DIARY

or

[redacted]

(Erase heading not required.)

"A" & "Q" Branch,
16th (Irish) Division Headquarters,
VOLUME 26.

Place	Date Jany. 1918	Hour	Summary of Events and Information	Remarks and references to Appendices
VILLERS FAUCON.	1st	9.pm	Wind S.E: Slight thaw, changing to frost again when wind veered to N.E., in afternoon: feeding strength of Division: Men, 19238: Horses, H.D., 494: L.D.5346: 48th Mobile Workshop joined Division today.	
"	2nd	"	Wind N.: hard frost with bright sunshine: 48th Machine Gun Coy relieved 47th M.G.Coy. in left section of line: latter to TINCOURT: garrison guard of MARQUAIX attached to Division today: Divisional Commander proceeded on leave today: Brig-Gen.LEVESON-GOWER, C.M.G., D.S.O., assumed temporary command of the Division: Divisional Commander receives K.C.B.	
"	3rd	"	Hard frost with wind from N.E.: no change.	
"	4th	"	Hard frost, but wind veered to S.E.: bright sunshine: no change in situation.	
"	5th	"	Wind S.E: frost continues feeding strength of Division, 19,005 men: H.D., 490: L.D.5313.	
"	6th	"	Wind S.W.: frost continues: enemy aircraft bombed ROISEL and neighbourhood during night: many horses killed and wounded.	
"	7th	"	Rapid thaw with rain: wind S.W.: frost again in evening and during night with wind from N.: feeding strength of Division, men, 19074: Horses, H.D.482: L.D.5306.	
"	8th	"	Gale from N.N.W., with driving snow and frost.	
"	9th	"	Hard frost continued with wind and snow from N.N.W.L in evening wind veered to W., with rain and rapid thaw: 277th Bde. A.F.A., less B.A.C., left Division today.	
"	10th	"	Thaw continues with rain during night: feeding strength of Division, men 18048: Horses, H.D., 463: L.D. 4464.	
"	11th	"	Thaw continues: wind W.N.W.: A.A.& Q.M.G. returned from leave today: 49th Bde. relieved 47th Bde. in left section of line during night.	
"	12th	"	D.A.A.G., proceeded on leave: F.G.C.M. assembled at H.Q., of 11th Hants Regt to try three men of 217th Employment Company for drunkenness, and one man of 1st R.Muns.Fus for Conduct to the Preju-dice., etc: wind W.N.W.: slight frost in evening with snow.	
"	13th	"	Wind N.W.: brilliant sunshine: no change in situation.	
"	14th	"	Feeding strength of Division 17740 men: Horses, H.D. 472: L.D.4803.	
"	15th	"	Wind S.W., blowing a gale: F.G.C.M.assembled at Div.H.Q., for trial of one man of 7th Leinster Regt and one man attached R.A.M.C.	
"	16th	"	Gale in morning from S.W. with heavy rain at intervals: no change in situation.	
"	17th	"	Move of 16th Div.H.Q. to new camp near TINCOURT which was to have taken place today, postponed until the 19th: heavy rain in morning with strong wind from S.W.: thaw restrictions in force.	
"	18th	"	Wind S.W. with rain: mild: feeding strength of Division, Men 17555: Horses, H.D. 481: L.D.4732.	
"	19th	"	Weather fine and mild with wind from S.W.: Divisional Machine Gun Coy arrived today and was billeted in VILLERS FAUCON.	
"	20th	"	No change in situation: weather mild with wind from S.W.	

(A7092). Wt W12839/M1293. 75 ,0 0. 1/17. D. D. & L., Ltd. Forms/C.2118/14.

(continued):-

Instructions regarding War Diaries and Intelligence Summaries are contained in F. S. Regs., Part II. and the Staff Manual respectively. Title pages will be prepared in manuscript.

WAR DIARY
or
INTELLIGENCE SUMMARY.
(Erase heading not required.)

Sheet -2-.

Army Form C. 2118.

Place	Jany. 1918	Hour	Summary of Events and Information	Remarks and references to Appendices
VILLERS FAUSON	21st	9.pm.	Wind S.W.: mild: feeding strength of Division men 18273: Horses, H.D., 479: L.D.4822.	
J.17.b.8.8. (sheet 62c.) near TINCOURT.	22nd	9.pm.	Wind S.W: Divisional Headquarters moved today to new camp near TINCOURT. F.G.C.M. assembled at Headquarters, 11th Hants Regt (P) for trial of three prisoners: one for desertion: two for absence without leave.	
TINCOURT.	23rd	"	Feeding strength of Division: men 18180: Horses, H.D., 477: L.D.4708.	
"	24th	"	Weather wet and very damp.	
"	25th	"	Weather very bright and fine.	
"	26th	"	Instructions received re re-organization of Infantry Brigades: Major-General Sir W.B.HICKIE, K.C.B., returned from leave.	
"	27th	"	Weather fine.	
"	28th	"	Further instructions received re re-organization of Infantry Brigades: 2nd R.Munster Fuslrs and 2nd Leinster Regiment to join 16th Division: 8/9th and 10th Royal Dublin Fuslrs, 6th Royal Irish Regiment, 7th Leinster Regiment, and 7/8th R.Irish Fuslrs, to be broken up.	
"	29th	"	Up to date, six Gum-boot drying rooms have been erected in front line area.	
"	30th	"	Feeding strength of Division: men 17945: Horses, H.D. 472: L.D., 4612: Issue of rations, Bread 75%., biscuit 25%: slight frost.	
"	31st	"	No change.	

1st Feb., 1918.

[signature] Major-General,
Commanding 16th (Irish) Division.

~~Original~~ Duplicate

W A R   D I A R Y .

FOR MONTH OF FEBRUARY, 1918.

VOLUME:- 24

UNIT:- A & Q Branch 16th D.H.Q.

Instructions regarding War Diaries and Intelligence Summaries are contained in F. S. Regs., Part II. and the Staff Manual respectively. Title pages will be prepared in manuscript.

WAR DIARY

or

~~INTELLIGENCE SUMMARY.~~

(Erase heading not required.)

"A" & "Q" Branch,
16th (Irish) Division.
Volume 27.

Army Form C. 2118.

Reference Sheet 62.C.

Place	Date	Hour	Summary of Events and Information	Remarks and references to Appendices
Terrace Camp, near TINCOURT, J.17.b.8.8.	Feb. 1918 1st	9pm.	The 2nd Leinster Regt arrived in the 16th Division from 24th Division, and were billeted in TINCOURT: weather cold, but fine.	
	2nd	"	Further instructions issued re re-organization of Inf.Bdes: 2nd Leinster Regt marched to SAULCOURT and joined 47th Inf.Bde: on withdrawal of 21st Div. from the line, the administrative area of this Division was extended northwards, and 110th Inf.Bde., came under our orders.	
	3rd	"	The 2nd R. Munster Fusrs joined this Division from 1st Division, and marched to LONGAVESNES, where they came under the orders of the 48th Inf.Bde.	
	4th	"	Weather fine: further orders issued on re-organization.	
	5th	"	A. F.G.C.M. assembled at Div.H.Q., for trial of 3849 Pte.T.DILLON, 1st R.M.Fus: 13767 Pte. COURTNEY, 8/9th R.Dublin Fusrs: 19192 Pte.D.VICKERY, 2nd R.Dublin Fusrs: 22277 Pte. C.SEDDON, 1st R.Dublin Fusrs.	
	6th	"	One company of Italians, strength 3 Officers 306 O.R., arrived, and came under the orders of Division for administration. 5 Offcrs 100 O.R. joined 11th Hants Regt (P) from 14th Hants Regt, 39th Div.	
	7th	"	Presentation of medal ribbons by G.O.C., Fifth Army: feeding strength, men 19997: Horses, H.D. 519: L.D.4854: chopping of hay commenced for Infantry under Divisional arrangements.	
	8th	"	Weather mild and dry:	
	9th	"	12 Offcrs 240 O.R. proceeded by Bus to join 1st Battn Royal Irish Fusiliers, and 11 Offcrs and 245 O.R. proceeded by Bus to join 9th Battn Royal Irish Fusiliers, 36th Div, from 7/8th Royal Irish Fusiliers on their disbandment: Battn H.Q., remained intact. 13 Offcrs 286 O.R. proceeded to 2nd R.Irish Regt., and 16 Offcrs 298 O.R., proceeded to 7th (SIH) R.Irish Regt from 6th Royal Irish Regt., on disbandment: Battn H.Q., remained intact.	
	10th	"	10 Offcrs 200 O.R. proceeded to 1st R.Dublin Fusrs and a similar number to the 2nd R.Dublin Fusrs on the disbandment of 8/9th R.Dublin Fusrs: remainder of Battn remained intact.	
	11th	"	Remainder of 8/9th R.Dublin Fusrs marched to HAMEL from LONGAVESNES.	
	12th	"	Transport of 10th R.Dublin Fusrs marched to HERVILLY on transfer to the 24th Division: 4 G.S. wagons belonging to 7/8th R.Irish Fusrs sent to Army Salvage Section for work: a F.G.C.M. assembled at Div H.Q., for trial of 9210 Sergt.J.WHELAN, 1st R.Dublin Fusrs: 8199 Pte. E. CARTER, 7th (SIH) R.Irish Regt: 4363 Pte. McCARTHY, and 10828 Pte. GOODINES, 2nd Leins.Rgt.	
			Sheet 2 :-	

Army Form C. 2118.

Instructions regarding War Diaries and Intelligence Summaries are contained in F. S. Regs., Part II. and the Staff Manual respectively. Title pages will be prepared in manuscript.

WAR DIARY

or

~~INTELLIGENCE SUMMARY.~~

(*Erase heading not required.*)

Sheet 2.

Place	Date	Hour	Summary of Events and Information	Remarks and references to Appendices
Terrace Camp near TINCOURT. J.17.b.8.8.	Feb. 1918. 13th	9.pm	Transport of 7th Leins.Rgt marched to PERONNE en route to Fourth Army, 1st Div., to which it was being transferred: 10th R.Dublin Fusrs marched to BARLU where they came under the orders of O.C., VII Corps Reinforcement Depot: they are to work under A.D.R.T., on railways: all battn stores and equipment were handed in to Ordnance before unit proceeded to BARLU.	
	14th	9.pm	15 Offcrs 300 O.R. proceeded to 2nd Leins.Rgt on disbandment of 7th Leins.Regt.	
	15th	"	No change: weather became much colder.	
	16th	"	Details of 8/9th R.Dublin Fusrs moved to SOREL: feeding strength, men 18989: Horses, H.D. 453 L.D.4719	
	17th	"	Details of 6th R.Irish Regt, 7/8th R.Irish Fusrs, and 7th Leins.Rgt moved back to BARLU and came under the orders of O.C., 10th R.Dublin Fusrs.	
	18th	"	No change.	
	19th	"	Enemy's trenches successfully raided at A.7(62.B), by "Z" Coy., 1st R.Munster Fusrs: five prisoners taken belonging to 11th Bav.R.I.R., 9th Bav.Res.Divn.	
	20th	"	)	
	21st	"	)No change.	
	22nd	"	)	
	23rd	"	Major-General Sir C.P.A.HULL, K.C.B., assumed command of the 16th Division, vice Brig-General F.W.RAMSAY, C.M.G., D.S.O., wo re-assumed command of the 48th Inf.Brigade.	
	24th	"	)	
	25th	"	)	
	26th	"	)No change.	
	27th	"	)	
	28th	"	Orders received from VII Corps cancelling relief of 16th Div. by 21st Div, which had previously been ordered to take place between night 28th Feb / 1st March, and 6.a.m., 3rd March. During the night 28th Feb/1st Mar., the 110th Inf.Bde. 21st Div. relieved the 49th Inf.Bde. in the left section: on relief the left section 16th Div.Front, became the right section 21st Div.Front. On relief the 49th Inf.Bde. came into Divisional Reserve at VILLERS FAUCON.	

[signature] Major-General,
Commanding 16th (Irish) Division.

A7092 Wt. W128 9/M1293. 750,000. 1/17. D. D & L. Ltd. Forms/C2118/14.

16th Division Administrative.

A. & Q.

16th DIVISION

M A R C H 1 9 1 8

Appendices attached:-

Administrative notes on operations.

19

Administrative Branch

16th Div H.Q.

Original

Vol 28

11

Army Form C. 2118.

WAR DIARY
or
INTELLIGENCE SUMMARY.
(Erase heading not required.)

Instructions regarding War Diaries and Intelligence Summaries are contained in F. S. Regs., Part II. and the Staff Manual respectively. Title pages will be prepared in manuscript.

Place	Date	Hour March	Summary of Events and Information	Remarks and references to Appendices
TINCOURT		1st	No change	
do		2nd	No change. Very quiet day. Q Conference held at Corps H.Q.S.	
do		3rd	No change	
do	4th		49th Inf Bde relieved 47th Inf Bde in Right Section of Div. Front 47th Inf Bde moved into Corps Reserve Bde H.Q. & 2 Bns VILLERS FAUCON. 1 Bn ST. EMILIE	
do	5th		At 2.55 am enemy raided one of our posts S.W. of GILLEMONT FARM 2 men reported missing	
do	6th		No change	
do	7th		Enemy attempted to raid MULE Trench but were repulsed leaving 2 prisoners	

A5834 Wt. W4973/M687 750,000 8/16 D. D. & L. Ltd. Forms/C.2118/13.

Army Form C. 2118.

Instructions regarding War Diaries and Intelligence Summaries are contained in F. S. Regs., Part II. and the Staff Manual respectively. Title pages will be prepared in manuscript.

WAR DIARY
or
INTELLIGENCE SUMMARY.

(Erase heading not required.)

Place	Date	Hour	Summary of Events and Information	Remarks and references to Appendices
TINCOURT	8th		No change	
do	9th		No change	
do	10th		No change	
do	11th		No change	
do	12th		No change	
do	13th		No change	
do	14th		2nd Roy Munster Fus raided KILDARE POST capturing 3 prisoners	
do	15th		No change	
do	16th		No change: At 6.50 am owing to an S.O.S. signal 2nd Leinsters were ordered to embus from TINCOURT & move to VILLERS FAUCON; this was carried out without hitch	
do	17th		No change	

A5834 Wt. W4973/M687 750,000 8/16 D. D. & L. Ltd. Forms/C.2118/13.

Army Form C. 2118.

Instructions regarding War Diaries and Intelligence Summaries are contained in F. S. Regs., Part II. and the Staff Manual respectively. Title pages will be prepared in manuscript.

WAR DIARY
or
INTELLIGENCE SUMMARY.
(*Erase heading not required.*)

Place	Date	Hour	Summary of Events and Information	Remarks and references to Appendices
TINCOURT	18th		No change: a small raid on CHAFFINCH LANE resulted in the capture of 2 prisoners, one of whom died on way back	
do	19th		No change	
do	20th		No change	
do	21st		At 4.30 AM. the enemy opened a heavy barrage & at 9 am attacked heavily reaching the BROWN LINE by 1.30 pm. During night 21/22nd ammunition was dumped at selected sites on GREEN LINE.	
do	22nd		HQ's 47th Inf Bde were established at VILLERS FAUCON. HQs 48th & 49th Inf Bdes in vicinity of Div. HQs TINCOURT. At 12.50 am the elements of the Div moved to the GREEN LINE. During the afternoon Div. HQ (Advanced Echelon) moved to J 17 central 2nd Echelon & transports retired to DOINGT	

A5834 Wt. W4973/M687 750,000 8/16 D. D. & L. Ltd. Forms/C.2118/13.

Instructions regarding War Diaries and Intelligence Summaries are contained in F. S. Regs., Part II. and the Staff Manual respectively. Title pages will be prepared in manuscript.

WAR DIARY
or
INTELLIGENCE SUMMARY.
(Erase heading not required.)

Army Form C. 2118.

Place	Date	Hour	Summary of Events and Information	Remarks and references to Appendices
J 1 / Central	22nd (Cont).	9pm	Div H.Q's moved to DOINGT, Train & transport to PERONNE	
DOINGT	23rd	6.35 am	Div withdrew to Line DOINGT - AIZIECOURT - E edge BOIS-DE-VAUX	
		9.30 am	Div H.Qs moved to BIACHES about H30 d 2.7 & thence to CAPPY	
		10.30 pm	Div. was relieved by 39th Div	
CAPPY.	24th		Reorganisation for the greater part of the day	
			Div. HQs moved to MORLANCOURT	
			Brig Gen. Gregorie DSO. returned from leave & resumed command of 47th Inf. Bde	
MORLANCOURT	25th	4am	The Div. was transferred to XIX Corps: Div H.Q. moved to LAMOTTE-EN-SANTERRE	

A5834 Wt. W4973/M687 750,000 8/16 D. D. & L. Ltd. Forms/C.2118/13.

Army Form C. 2118.

Instructions regarding War Diaries and Intelligence Summaries are contained in F. S. Regs., Part II. and the Staff Manual respectively. Title pages will be prepared in manuscript.

WAR DIARY
or
INTELLIGENCE SUMMARY.
(Erase heading not required.)

Place	Date	Hour	Summary of Events and Information	Remarks and references to Appendices
LAMOTTE - EN - SANTERRE	25th		Approximate Casualties from 21st - 24th March inclusive.	

		Officers	O.Rs.
47th Inf Bde	6th Connaughts	15	450
	2nd Leinsters	24	400
	1st R. Munsters	20	450
		59	1300
48th Inf Bde	2nd R. Munsters	27	550
	1st R. Dublins	24	600
	2nd R. Dublins	25	640
		76	1790
49th Inf Bde	2nd R. Irish	18	450
	7th (S.I.H) R. Irish	17	650
	7/8 R. Innis Fusiliers	18	500
		53	1600

	Officers	O.R.s.
11th Hants (P)	3	150
Grand Total	191	4840
16th M.G. Bn	12	500

59

(A7092). Wt W12839/M1293 75 ,0 0. 1/17. D. D. & L., Ltd. Forms/C.2118/14.

Instructions regarding War Diaries and Intelligence Summaries are contained in F. S. Regs., Part II. and the Staff Manual respectively. Title pages will be prepared in manuscript.

WAR DIARY
or
INTELLIGENCE SUMMARY.
(Erase heading not required.)

Army Form C. 2118.

Place	Date	Hour	Summary of Events and Information	Remarks and references to Appendices
LA MOTTE -EN- SANTERRE	26th		Div. H.Qs moved to HAMEL.	
			2nd Echelon & Div. Train retired to PETIT-BLANGY.	
HAMEL			Surplus Transport of Bns & all men of Employment Coy who were in any way unfit to march were sent off under Lt. CRILLY Transport Officer of 7/- ? Irish Fus. to march to ABBEVILLE	
			Transport of Bdes located near HAMEL	
HAMEL	27th		Fighting on line PROYART-FROISSY & withdrawal to line in front of HAMEL	
FOUILLOY			Div. H.Q's shelled out of HAMEL & moved to ~~FROIS~~ FUILLOY where they were located in College.	
FOUILLOY	28th		Reorganization of Div into one composite force known as 16 Div Infantry.	
			All stragglers & tired men from the line were collected in AUBIGNY where a soup kitchen Clean Socks & medical attendance were installed under the direction of Lt. REDMOND.	

(A7092). Wt. W12839/M1293. 75,000. 1/17. D. D. & L., Ltd. Forms/C.2118/14.

Army Form C. 2118.

Instructions regarding War Diaries and Intelligence Summaries are contained in F. S. Regs., Part II. and the Staff Manual respectively. Title pages will be prepared in manuscript.

WAR DIARY
or
INTELLIGENCE SUMMARY.

(Erase heading not required.)

Place	Date	Hour	Summary of Events and Information	Remarks and references to Appendices
FUILLOY	29th		For the purpose of feeding the Div Inf in line, two S A A wagons of D A C were kept at advanced Div H Qs, as soon as anyone called for S A A these wagons delivered & two more were sent from S A A section to replace.	
			A dump of ammunition was formed in HAMEL	
			A reserve store of 1000 rations was kept at Div H Q's, as the Div frequently had to feed members of CAREYS FORCE, this reserve store was of the greatest utility.	
FUILLOY	30th		Repulse of hostile attack on HAMEL.	
			All requirements of ammunition & supplies were promptly met.	
FUILLOY	31st		No change.	

[signature]
for Major-General
Commanding 16th Division

(A7092). Wt. W12839/M1293. 75,000. 1/17. D. D. & L., Ltd. Forms/C.2118/14.

Copy to "G" for information.

SECRET

16th Div.No.Q.M.4.

W.M.R. 16TH DIV. G
No G.146
Date 13.5.18

XI CORPS.
XIII CORPS.

ADMINISTRATIVE NOTES ON RECENT OPERATIONS EAST OF AMIENS.

1. The following notes are forwarded in response to your request; they make no pretence of being exhaustive, but bring to notice certain points which experience proved to be worthy of attention.

2. GENERAL. It is clear that in the case of the area occupied by 16th Division the following administrative services had been brought dangerously near the front, with the object of saving transport, and making things convenient for formations and units. (The distances were about 5,500 to 6,500 yards).

Divl. Ammunition R.P.	Fuel Dump,
Transport Lines,	Chaff-Cutting Shed,
Quartermaster's Stores	Refilling Point.

3. During mobile operations it was found of the very greatest value to have a "Q" Staff Officer permanently back in the neighbourhood of the Infantry Transport and Divisional Train, with definite power to act on his own authority within clearly defined limits.

4. AMMUNITION SUPPLY. The Ammunition Refilling Point was continuously barraged from the commencement of the battle on March 21st and rendered unusable, a number of bays being exploded by shellfire: no shortage of ammunition occurred however on this account. Otherwise the arrangements for the supply of ammunition worked satisfactorily throughout, and give no grounds for comment.

5. SUPPLY. It was proved that it is a matter of urgent necessity, immediately mobile operations are likely, that Mechanical Transport, or at any rate, ample lorries for supply purposes, should be put directly under the Division. Under the conditions mentioned, detailing through the S.M.T.O. immediately becomes unworkable.

6. When drawing by horse transport the dumping of the extra days ration becomes a source of danger, and it seems advisable that when there is any chance of a sudden change to mobile conditions, either drawing should take place by motor transport, or that arrangements should be made for the extra days ration to be kept at the lines of the M.T.Company.

7. It was found essential that sufficient lorries should be earmarked for supply, to enable all the rations of the Division to be

carried in one trip; the second trip usually proves impracticable.

8. It was found absolutely necessary to maintain a reserve of preserved rations of about 1,000; if this is not done, constant complications arise owing to the advent of stragglers, reinforcements, etc. Arrangements for carrying this reserve should be thought out beforehand, and be ready before the operations begin.

A travelling Soup Kitchen would have proved of the utmost value in refreshing exhausted men, and building up their vitality to again go back to the line.

9. TRANSPORT. The advantage of having very close touch between the Train and the First Line Transport became very marked, and it was generally found best to have their lines within about a mile of each other. The Small Arm Section of the D.A.C. was as a rule parked with the first line Transport and the arrangement worked most satisfactorily. In the case of the 18th Division, all Companies of the Train were kept together throughout the operations and this proved an advantage.

10. In parking the lorries it should be carefully considered in which direction the lorries should be facing, as, in case of a retirement being ordered at short notice, the turning of a convoy of lorries is very disorganising to traffic for some little time; this case arose on one occasion.

In the case of Horse Transport their lines should, if possible, be placed on the side of the road which enables them to pull off in the direction in which they are most likely to march without crossing the stream of traffic.

11. WATER. It would have proved a great advantage had water supply points been marked on the 1/40,000 Maps. There was in practice considerable difficulty in finding the best water supply in strange country without undue delay. Light wire rope for use with wells would have been useful as part of the equipment of a Field Company.

12. MEDICAL. It was found that the touch between motor ambulance convoys and field ambulances was defective, which caused the long distances which usually existed between Casualty Clearing Stations and Main Dressing Stations to be an embarrassment to Divisional ambulances, which were badly overworked.

13. PROVOST ARRANGEMENTS. Under the conditions which existed at the end of March, the Divisional Police were altogether insufficient to cope with the many problems which arose, particularly that of straggling.

Directly mobile operations seem imminent, it would appear advisable that the Policing of all important villages and towns should be taken in hand in good time by the Corps or Army concerned, with a very strong force of Military Police. Experience proves that it would be difficult to provide too many men for the needs of the situation which arises when the civil population are evacuating their houses, and the problems of straggling, looting, and traffic control, often under shell-fire or aerial attack, become acute. As a rule the arrangements for rationing stragglers' collecting posts by Corps were inadequate, and this Division was many times requested to provide large numbers of rations, at a moment's notice, for men who were otherwise unprovided for.

14. ROYAL ENGINEERS. The Field Companies consider that a certain quantity of instantaneous fuse should be added to their equipment.

During the rapid movements Field Companies very much felt the want of a Field Kitchen.

H.Q. 16th Divn. Major-General,

12th May, 1918. Commanding 16th (Irish) Division.

7

Instructions regarding War Diaries and Intelligence Summaries are contained in F. S. Regs., Part II. and the Staff Manual respectively. Title pages will be prepared in manuscript.

Army Form C. 2118.

Vol 29

WAR DIARY or INTELLIGENCE SUMMARY.

HQ Administrative Branch, 16th Div HQ.

(Erase heading not required.)

ORIGINAL

29

Place	Date April	Hour	Summary of Events and Information	Remarks and references to Appendices
FUILLOY	1st		Div. H.Q's 1st Echelon in Convent FUILLOY: "B" Echelon at PETIT-BLANGY. Composite Bde made up of troops of 48th 49th Inf Bde and stragglers from other Units and Divs at HAMEL. Transport, Div. Train & D.A.C. Section at PETIT-BLANGY. 47th Inf Bde H.Q's moved to HAMELET. Soup kitchen started in AUBIGNY. All stragglers coming down from line, were collected at the school AUBIGNY by Lt Adc R.S. REDMOND, given hot soup, clean socks & had their feet attended to & were then moved to a billet to have a good nights rest. All requirements of Composite Bdes in ammunition were promptly met. 300 additional rations were sent up at a moments notice for personnel of "CAREY'S" Force.	
do.	2nd		No change in situation: Supplies and ammunition all delivered with out trouble.	

(A7092). Wt. W12839/M1293. 750,000. 1/17. D. D. & L., Ltd. Forms/C.2118/14.

Instructions regarding War Diaries and Intelligence Summaries are contained in F. S. Regs., Part II. and the Staff Manual respectively. Title pages will be prepared in manuscript.

WAR DIARY
or
INTELLIGENCE SUMMARY.
(Erase heading not required.)

Army Form C. 2118.

Place	Date	Hour	Summary of Events and Information	Remarks and references to Appendices
FUILLOY	3rd		No change in situation. During the afternoon & night the Div. was relieved by the 14th Div. The Bdes as relieved marching to PETIT-BLANCY were the 47th & half 49th Inf Bdes embussed at 7 p.m and the 48th & half 49th Inf Bdes embussed at 12 midnight. Debussing Point SALEUX were the whole Div. was billeted. Approximate strength of Div. (less Artillery) 3241.	
SALEUX	4th		The Division moved by tactical Train to CERISY Area The First train left SALEUX at 3 p.m The Second train was due to leave SALEUX at 6 pm but owing to a breakdown on the line due to shelling did not leave till 3 AM. Detraining Station BLANCY. All troops proceeding to entraining point were provided with hot soup before leaving station. The transport of the Div. moved by march route to CERISY Area halting for the [illegible] night at ALLERY. The 19th Entrenching Bn joined the Division. On Completion of move Div. was distributed as follows Div. H.Q's: CERISY. 47th Inf Bde Group: BOUILLANCOURT - TRANSLAY - FRAMICOURT Area 48th Inf Bde Group: RAMBURELLES - RAMBURES Area 49th Inf Bde Group: VISMES AU VAL - TOURS EN VIMEU Area. 11th HANTS FRESNES TILLELOY Area Transport: ALLERY.	

(A7092). Wt. W12839/M1293. 75,0 0. 1/17. D. D. & L., Ltd. Forms/C.2118/14.

Instructions regarding War Diaries and Intelligence Summaries are contained in F. S. Regs., Part II. and the Staff Manual respectively. Title pages will be prepared in manuscript.

WAR DIARY
or
INTELLIGENCE SUMMARY.
(Erase heading not required.)

Army Form C. 2118.

Place	Date	Hour	Summary of Events and Information	Remarks and references to Appendices
CERISY	5th		No change: The 19th Entrenching Bn were disbanded the personnel being sent to the 2nd Munsters. Transport of 19th Entrenching Bn was utilized to make up deficiencies throughout the Div the surplus being sent to ABBEVILLE	
do	6th		No change: Units refitting	
do	7th		No change: Units bathed	
do	8th		No change: The M.G. Bn were ordered to proceed to CAMIERS for reposting to other Bns. Transport of M.G. Bn ordered to ABBEVILLE	
do	9th		The Div moved by March Route to GAMACHES Area (155 & 157 Coys R.E being left behind for work)	
GAMACHES		10am	On completion of move Units were located as follows: Div H.Qs: GAMACHES: 47th Inf Bde Group "A" Area H.Q's AULT 48th Inf Bde Group "C" Area: H.Qs FEUQUIERES 155 Coy. R.E DARGNIES 49th Inf Bde Group: "B" Area H.Qs TULLY 11th Hants OUST-MAREST	

Army Form C. 2118.

WAR DIARY
or
INTELLIGENCE SUMMARY.
(Erase heading not required.)

Instructions regarding War Diaries and Intelligence Summaries are contained in F. S. Regs., Part II. and the Staff Manual respectively. Title pages will be prepared in manuscript.

Place	Date April	Hour	Summary of Events and Information	Remarks and references to Appendices
GAMACHES	10th		Units of Div. (less Arty. M.G. Bn. 156 + 157 Coy R.E.) moved by train to 1st Army Area.	
			Entraining Stations WOINCOURT and EU.	
			Detraining Stations WISERNES and ARQUES.	
			First train left EU. 2.19 am 10th inst.	
			Last train left WOINCOURT. 1.04 am 11th inst.	
		9.30 am	Div. H Qs closed at GAMACHES.	
			Feeding strength Men 7716 Horses H.D. 355 L.D 1309.	
FAUQUEMBERGUES		3.10 pm	Div. H.Qs opened at FAUQUEMBERGUES and came under orders of XIII Corps, 1st Army	
do	11th		Div in billets as follows –	
			47th Inf Bde. THIEMBRONNE Area – Bde H.Qs THIEMBRONNE	
			48th Inf Bde – CAMPAGNE-LES-BOULONNAIS Area – Bde H.Qs CAMPAGNE-LES-BOULONNAIS	
			49th Inf Bde – ELNES Area – Bde H.Qs ELNES	
			11th Hants (P) AVROULT – 155 Coy R.E. HERVARRE Chateau.	
			16th Div Train WAVRANS	
			Railhead LOTTINGHEM. Feeding strength Men 6670. Horses: H.D 326 L.D. 922	

(A7092). Wt. W12839/M1293. 75,0.0. 1/17. D. D. & L., Ltd. Forms/C.2118/14.

Instructions regarding War Diaries and Intelligence Summaries are contained in F. S. Regs., Part II. and the Staff Manual respectively. Title pages will be prepared in manuscript.

WAR DIARY
or
INTELLIGENCE SUMMARY.
(Erase heading not required.)

Army Form C. 2118.

Place	Date	Hour	Summary of Events and Information	Remarks and references to Appendices
FAUQUEMBERGUES	12th		In billets - Lt-Col G.A. WEBB D.S.O. AA+QMG left to assume duties of A.Q.M.G. IX Corps. Lt-Col W.B. RENNIE M.C. assumed duties of AA+QMG. Major GREENWOOD M.C. assumed duties of D.A.A.G. from Staff Capt. 1st Army. Work of re-organization and refitting proceeds. Feeding strength Men 6460. Horses H.D. 320. L.D. 928.	
do	13th		In billets - Feeding strength Men 7147. Horses H.D. 328. L.D. 884.	
do	14th		Units of three Bdes. formed into a Composite Bde group & moved to THEROUANNE Area. H.Q's Composite Inf. Bde. UPEN D'AVAL: H.Q's 47th Inf Bde: REMILLY-WIRQUIN: H.Q's 49th Inf Bde: ELNES: 1st Portuguese Inf Bde. joined the Division: H.Q's at BOMY. Feeding strength: Men 9487 Horses: H.D. 330. L.D. 1305.	
do	15th		16th Div. (less Art. & M.G. Bn) and 1st Portuguese Inf Bde moved to STEENBECQUE - BOESEGHEM - ISBERGUES Area. Div. H.Q's AIRE. H.Q's Composite Bde. BOESEGHEM: 47th Inf Bde H.Q's REMILLY and 49th Inf Bde H.Q's DELETTE: 1st Portuguese Inf Bde H.Qs ISBERGUES. Feeding Strength: Men 10527: Horses H.D. 326: L.D. 954.	

Army Form C. 2118.

WAR DIARY
or
INTELLIGENCE SUMMARY.
(Erase heading not required.)

Instructions regarding War Diaries and Intelligence Summaries are contained in F. S. Regs., Part II. and the Staff Manual respectively. Title pages will be prepared in manuscript.

Place	Date	Hour	Summary of Events and Information	Remarks and references to Appendices
AIRE.	16th.		Div. re-organized into 4 Bns: (2nd Roy. Irish Reg: 2nd Leinster Reg: 1/2 Roy. Dublin Fus: 1/2 Roy. Munster Fus:) and six Training Staffs (H.Q's 7th Roy. Irish Reg. S.I.H: 5th Connaught Rangers: 7/8 Roy. Inniskilling Fus: 2nd Roy. Munster Fus: 2nd Roy. Dublin Fus: 11th Hants (P)) each of 10 officers and 55 O.R's. Railhead BLARINGHEM. Train H.Q's moved to AIRE. Feeding Strength: Men 11033: Horses: H.D. 313. L.D. 1113.	
do.	17th		H.Q's 49th Inf. Bde moved to BOESEGHEM. H.Qs 48th Inf. Bde moved to DELETTE Feeding Strength: Men 12503 Horses: H.D 322: L.D. 1309. Portugese Field Coy. joined the Div and were billeted in ISBERGUES.	
do.	18th		H.Q's 48th Inf. Bde. moved to ELNES Feeding Strength Men: 13625. Horses: H.D. 335: L.D. 1324.	
do	19th.		No change: Feeding Strength: Men 10320 Horses: H.D. 327: L.D. 1151.	

(A7092). Wt. W12839/M1293. 75,0.0. 1/17. D. D. & L., Ltd. Forms/C.2118/14.

Army Form C. 2118.

Instructions regarding War Diaries and Intelligence Summaries are contained in F. S. Regs., Part II. and the Staff Manual respectively. Title pages will be prepared in manuscript.

WAR DIARY
or
INTELLIGENCE SUMMARY.
(Erase heading not required.)

Place	Date	Hour	Summary of Events and Information	Remarks and references to Appendices
AIRE	20th.		Lieut (T/Capt) W. E. Muir M.C. assumed duties of G.S.O. III vice Capt. G. T. Shaw M.C. 1st Roy. Munster Fus. (i.e 1/2 Roy Munster Fus. less Bn. H.Qs of 2nd Roy. Munster Fus.) proceeded to join the 57th Div. proceeding by Lorry. Feeding Strength 12432 Men: Horses: H.D. 304: L.D. 1281.	
do.	21st		No change. Feeding Strength: Men 10395: Horses H.D 305: L.D. 1352.	
do.	22nd		No change: Feeding Strength: Men 9368: Horses H.D. 318: L.D. 1324. Div. Troupe re-opened in SALLE des Concerts.	
do.	23rd.		2nd Bn. Roy. Irish Reg. proceeded by Lorry to join 63rd Div. 2nd Bn. The Leinster Reg. proceeded by March Route to join 29th Div. 2 Coys. Portugese Pioneers joined 1st Portugese Inf. Bde and proceeded to billets in STEENBECQUE. Feeding Strength: Men 10450. Horses H.D 350: L.D 1212.	

(A7092). Wt W12839/M1293 75,000. 1/17. D. D. & L., Ltd. Forms/C.2118/14.

Instructions regarding War Diaries and Intelligence Summaries are contained in F. S. Regs., Part II. and the Staff Manual respectively. Title pages will be prepared in manuscript.

WAR DIARY
or
INTELLIGENCE SUMMARY.
(Erase heading not required.)

Army Form C. 2118.

Place	Date	Hour	Summary of Events and Information	Remarks and references to Appendices
AIRE	24th		No change: Feeding Strength: Men 7330: Horses H.D. 227: L.D. 853.	
do.	25th		H.Qs & Training Staffs administered by 47th & 48th Inf Bdes moved to BLEQUIN – VAUDRINGHEM – LEDDINGHEM Area. Gala performance by Div. Troupe. Feeding Strength Men 8509: Horses H.D. 189. L.D. 813.	
do.	26th.		1st Roy. Dublin Fus. proceeded by march route to join 29th Div. Personnel of 2 Batteries Portugese H.A joined 1st Portugese Inf. Bde and were billeted in STEENBECQUE. Feeding Strength Men 8542: Horses: H.D. 225. L.D. 861.	
do.	27th.		No change: Feeding Strength: Men 7272: Horses: H.D. 210. L.D. 803.	

(A7092). Wt W12839/M1293. 75,0 0. 1/17. D. D. & L., Ltd. Forms/C.2118/14.

Instructions regarding War Diaries and Intelligence Summaries are contained in F. S. Regs., Part II. and the Staff Manual respectively. Title pages will be prepared in manuscript.

WAR DIARY
or
INTELLIGENCE SUMMARY.
(Erase heading not required.)

Army Form C. 2118.

Place	Date	Hour	Summary of Events and Information	Remarks and references to Appendices
AIRE	28th		No change: Feeding Strength: Men 7316: Horses H.D. 210 L.D. 800.	
do	29th		156th and 157th Field Coys R.E. rejoined the Div. from attachment to Fourth Army. They detrained at THIENNES & proceeded to billets at PECQUER and ISBERGUES respectively. Feeding Strength Men: 7278: Horses H.D. 187: L.D. 747.	
do.	30th		No change: Feeding Strength 7642 Horses H.D. 225: L.D. 865.	
			28/5/18	

H E Sett Smith Lt
for Major Gen.
Commandg 16th Div

Army Form C. 2118.

Instructions regarding War Diaries and Intelligence Summaries are contained in F. S. Regs., Part II. and the Staff Manual respectively. Title pages will be prepared in manuscript.

Administrative Branch WAR DIARY or INTELLIGENCE SUMMARY.

16th Division (Erase heading not required.)

Original

Vol 30

Place	Date May	Hour	Summary of Events and Information	Remarks and references to Appendices
AIRE.	1st		H.Q's and Training Staffs of 7th Roy. Irish Reg. (S.I.H) and 7/8th Roy Inniskilling Fus. moved to PECQUER.	
			Feeding Strength: Men 7628 : Horses: H.D. 187 L.D. 880.	
			40 officers and 1559 O.R arrived as reinforcements detraining BLAIRINGHEM 9 p.m. and proceeding by march route to billets in PECQUER Area.	
do.	2nd		~~No change~~. H.Q's 11th Hants and Training Staff moved from LA ROUPIE to BLECQUIN Area where it came under administration of 47th Inf. Bde.	
			Surplus personnel of 11th Hants moved by rail from AIRE to base depot.	
			Feeding strength: Men. 7914 Horses H.D. 247. L.D. 1053.	
do	3rd		No change: Feeding Strength Men. 9175: Horses H.D. 226. L.D. 1051.	

(A7092). Wt W12839/M1293. 75 ,0.0. 1/17. D. D. & L., Ltd. Forms/C.2118/14.

Army Form C. 2118.

Instructions regarding War Diaries and Intelligence Summaries are contained in F. S. Regs., Part II. and the Staff Manual respectively. Title pages will be prepared in manuscript.

WAR DIARY
or
INTELLIGENCE SUMMARY.
(Erase heading not required.)

Place	Date	Hour	Summary of Events and Information	Remarks and references to Appendices
AIRE	4th		Major-general Sir C.T.A. HULL KCB. left to assume Command of 56th Div. Brigadier-general F.R. RAMSAY CMG. D.S.O assumed Temporary Command of 16 Div. Feeding Strength Men 7451: Horses: H.D. 191: L.D. 940.	
do.	5th		No change: Capt: Sir F.H. RIPLEY Bart 3rd Argyll & Sutherland Highlanders assumed duties of A.P.M. Feeding Strength: Men: 8907 Horses: H.D. 204 L.D. 1069.	
do.	6th		Brig-general Leveson-Gower DSO left for England for six months tour of duty at home. Brig-General Nash DSO assumed command of 49th Inf. Bde. Major MONT M.C. (G.S.O 2) Major Evans M.C. (DAQMG) Capt Stitt (Staff Capt 49th Inf Bde) joined 52 Div. for temporary duty Feeding Strength Men: 9236: Horses H.D. 199 L.D. 971.	
do	7th		No change: Feeding Strength Men 9118: Horses H.D. 202. L.D. 914.	
do	8th		No change: Feeding Strength Men 9505: Horses H.D. 201 L.D. 1016.	

D. D. & L., London, E.C.
(A8094) Wt. W1771/M2931 750,000 5/17 Sch. 52 Forms/C2118/14

Instructions regarding War Diaries and Intelligence Summaries are contained in F. S. Regs., Part II. and the Staff Manual respectively. Title pages will be prepared in manuscript.

WAR DIARY
or
INTELLIGENCE SUMMARY.
(Erase heading not required.)

Army Form C. 2118.

Place	Date	Hour	Summary of Events and Information	Remarks and references to Appendices
AIRE	9th		No change. 48th Inf. Bde. held a very successful horse show at VAUDRINGHEM. Feeding Strength: Men 9095 Horses H.D. 203 L.D. 954	
do	10th		Major General A. B. RITCHIE CMG assumed command of 16th DIV. Feeding Strength: Men 9256 Horses H.D 204 L.D 978	
do	11th		112 Fld Ambulance left to join 77th Div. U.S. Army Feeding Strength: Men 9202 Horses H.D. 192 L.D 970.	
do	12th		Major Evans returned from attachment to 52nd Division. Div. Troupe gave a performance at 2nd Army School LUMBRES Feeding Strength: Men 9345 Horses H.D. 198 L.D. 950.	
do	13th		Conference of Div. Salvage officers at Cops Q. 48th Inf Bde. moved to BECOURT Feeding Strength: Men 8947 Horses H.D. 179 L.D. 931.	
do	14th		No change: Men 8945 Horses H.D. 176 L.D 970.	
do	15th		47th Inf. Bde + 48th Inf Bde with their respective training staffs proceeded to DESVRES by march route. 41st Inf Bde (14th Div) relieved 49th Inf. Bde + took over administration of all ... Reinforcements in the Area. On relief 49th Inf. Bde proceeded by march to DOHEM. 155 Coy. R.E. proceeded to DESVRES by Lorry Feeding Strength: Men 8949; Horses H.D. 174. L.D. 969.	

(A7092). Wt W12839/M1293. 75 ,0 0. 1/17. D. D. & L., Ltd. Forms/C.2118/14.

Instructions regarding War Diaries and Intelligence Summaries are contained in F. S. Regs., Part II. and the Staff Manual respectively. Title pages will be prepared in manuscript.

WAR DIARY
or
INTELLIGENCE SUMMARY.
(*Erase heading not required.*)

Army Form C. 2118.

Place	Date	Hour	Summary of Events and Information	Remarks and references to Appendices
AIRE	16th		The Div were relieved by the 14th Division	
SAMER		10am	On Completion of relief the Div HQ moved to SAMER. C.R.E. remained in AIRE to hand over work.	
			49th Inf. Bde. moved to BLEQUIN.	
			Train H.Q's moved to WIERRE-AU-BOIS	
			Feeding Strength Men 8756 Horses H.D. 179. L.D. 952.	
do	17th		No change in Locations of Units.	
			Railhead was changed to DESVRES. Refilling Points BLEQUIN & LE CROCQ.	
			Feeding Strength: Men 2496. Horses H.D. 230. L.D. 614	
do	18th		47th Inf Bde moved to PARANTY.	
			49th Inf. Bde moved to SAMER	
			One Section 155th Coy. R.E. moved to SAMER.	
			2 Marquees & 150 tents C.S.L. were procured & erected in a field by the Station to form a concentration Camp. Cookhouses were put up & latrines dug.	
		3pm.	2nd Bn. 59. I.R. U.S.A arrived, detraining SAMER. Troops marched to Concentration Camp where they were provided with a hot meal & the band discoursed music. At 6.30pm the Bn moved off & proceeded by March Route to MENNEVILLE where they billetted.	
		7pm	3rd Bn. 59. I.R. U.S.A. detrained, proceeded to Concentration Camp for night.	
			Feeding Strength Men 2694 Horses H.D 242. L.D. 707.	

(A7092). Wt W12839/M1293. 75 ,o.o. 1/17. D. D. & L., Ltd. Forms/C.2118/14.

Instructions regarding War Diaries and Intelligence Summaries are contained in F. S. Regs., Part II. and the Staff Manual respectively. Title pages will be prepared in manuscript.

WAR DIARY
or
INTELLIGENCE SUMMARY.
(Erase heading not required.)

Army Form C. 2118.

Place	Date	Hour	Summary of Events and Information	Remarks and references to Appendices
SAMER	19th		47th Inf Bde moved to PARANTY	
			48th Inf Bde moved to QUESTRECQUES CHATEAU	
			49th Inf Bde moved to FRENCQ.	
		11AM.	12th M.G. Bn U.S.A detrained at SAMER: Marched to Concentration Camp where they had dinner. A Canteen was opened in Camp & the Band gave selections throughout their stay	
		3pm	The 12th M.G. Bn marched to billets in LE TURNE.	
			12 Lorries & 14 G.S. Wagons were supplied by M.T. Coy & Train respectively and were parked in Squeeze & by Rly. Station & were used for conveying ordnance Stores & personnel baggage to Units of U.S.A which as they arrived. By 7pm all stores were cleared from Railhead	
			Feeding Strength Men 6369. Horses H.D 760: L.D 729	
do	20th	3pm.	The following Units of U.S.A arrived SAMER: 4th American Divisional H.Q.S and 1st Bn. 59th Inf Reg: 59th I.R. Reg. H.Q.S: 8th Inf Bde H.Q.S: After being rested in Concentration Camp they marched to Billets as under:	
			8th Inf Bde H.Q.S to LE BRUNQUET	
			59th Inf Reg H.Q.S to DESVRES	
			1st Bn 59th I.R to DESVRES	
			4th American Div. H.Q.S were located in SAMER.	
			Feeding Strength Men 9515: Horses H.D 435 L.D. 1602	

(A7092). Wt W12839/M1293 75 ,0 0. 1/17. D. D. & L., Ltd. Forms/C.2118/14.

Army Form C. 2118.

Instructions regarding War Diaries and Intelligence Summaries are contained in F. S. Regs., Part II. and the Staff Manual respectively. Title pages will be prepared in manuscript.

WAR DIARY
or
INTELLIGENCE SUMMARY.
(Erase heading not required.)

Place	Date	Hour	Summary of Events and Information	Remarks and references to Appendices
SAMER	21st		4th Engineer Reg. U.S.A detrained SAMER 4.30 pm: All officers & men were provided with tea at Concentration Camp. at 5.30pm the Reg. marched to billets in HAUT PICOT – NIEMBOURG – HALINGHEN.	
			All ~~surplus~~ 1st Line transport of 2nd R.M.F & 2 R.D.F with exception of Baggage Wagons, 1 Mess Cart, 1 Water Cart, 7 Riders, were handed over to 2nd & 3rd Bns of 59 I.R. U.S.A respectively	
			6 Motor Cars having arrived were handed over to 4th American Div	
			Feeding Strength: Men 7247: Horses H.D. 301 L.D. 1459.	
do	22nd		No change: Transport complete turnouts for 4th American Div. H.Q's: 8th Inf Bde. H.Q's; 59th Reg. H.Q's	
			1st Bn I.R. 59th Inf. Reg. 12th M.G. Bns arrived from A.H.D. ABBEVILLE & were distributed by Div. Train to Units concerned.	
			13 M.T. Lorries were handed over to American Div. & were parked in Square	
			Feeding Strength: Men 9380: Horses H.D. 389: L.D. 1673	
do	23rd		No change: Feeding Strength: Men 10170: Horses H.D: 412: L.D. 1763	
do.	24th		No change: Feeding Strength: Men 10270 Horses H.D. 311: L.D. 1756	

(A7092). Wt. W12839/M1293. 75,0.0. 1/17. D. D. & L., Ltd. Forms/C.2118/14.

Instructions regarding War Diaries and Intelligence Summaries are contained in F. S. Regs., Part II. and the Staff Manual respectively. Title pages will be prepared in manuscript.

WAR DIARY
or
INTELLIGENCE SUMMARY.
(Erase heading not required.)

Army Form C. 2118.

Place	Date	Hour	Summary of Events and Information	Remarks and references to Appendices
SAMER	25th		No change. Transport Complete Turn outs arrived from Adv. Horse Transport Depot ABBEVILLE for 4th Reg. American Engineers, this was concentrated in a Camp just outside SAMER while being checked preparatory to handing over. Feeding Strength Men 9491: Horses H.D. 976: L.D. 899	
do	26th		No change. Chinese Labour Coy gave a fête in Concentration Camp at which various members of Div. Troops contributed items, invitations were sent to all local inhabitants & troops in area. Feeding Strength: Men 9457: Horses H.D. 412: L.D. 1224.	
do	27th		No change. Transport Comple Turn out was handed over to 4th Reg. American Engineers. 2 Platoons of H.A.C. arrived in Area to give Demonstrations to American Troops as to how a platoon should work Feeding Strength: Men 9460 Horses H.D. 407 L.D. 1207	

(A7092). Wt. W12839/M1293. 750,000. 1/17. D. D. & L., Ltd. Forms/C.2118/14.

Instructions regarding War Diaries and Intelligence Summaries are contained in F. S. Regs., Part II. and the Staff Manual respectively. Title pages will be prepared in manuscript.

WAR DIARY
or
INTELLIGENCE SUMMARY.
(Erase heading not required.)

Army Form C. 2118.

Place	Date	Hour	Summary of Events and Information	Remarks and references to Appendices
SAMER	28th		2nd Bn 56th Inf Reg arrived by train from CALAIS at 3.30pm. After being given tea at Concentration Camp they marched to billets in HESDIGNEUL in 4th Inf. Bde Area	
		7pm	The 10th M.G. Bn & 2 Coys 3rd Bn 56th Inf Reg arrived by train from CALAIS. They were accommodate for the night in Concentration Camp	
			An officers Club was opened in Concentration Camp for all officers of British or U.S.A Army to procure meals	
			Feeding Strength: Men 9894 Horses H.D. 389 L.D. 1234	
do	29th		The 10th M.G. Bn marched to billets at FRENCQ at 8.30pm	
			The 2 Coys 3rd Bn 56th Inf. Reg. U.S.A. marched to billets in HESDIGNEUL	
			Feeding Strength: Men 11648 Horses H.D. 388 L.D. 1218	
			5 Transports complete arrived from CUCQ Camp & were concentrated in POOL CAMP	
do	30th		2nd Bn. 39th I. Reg. U.S.A. detrained SAMER 12.30pm after having dinner at Concentration Camp they marched to DOUDEAUVILLE	
			3rd Bn 39th I. Reg. U.S.A. detrained SAMER 4.30pm after having teas at Concentration Camp marched to BEZINGHEM.	

(A7092). Wt. W12839/M1293. 750,000. 1/17. D. D. & L., Ltd. Forms/C.2118/14.

Instructions regarding War Diaries and Intelligence Summaries are contained in F. S. Regs., Part II. and the Staff Manual respectively. Title pages will be prepared in manuscript.

WAR DIARY
or
INTELLIGENCE SUMMARY.
(Erase heading not required.)

Army Form C. 2118.

Place	Date	Hour	Summary of Events and Information	Remarks and references to Appendices
SAMER	30th (cont)		1st Bn. 58th I.R. U.S.A arrived SAMER Station 7pm & were accommodated for the night in Concentration Camp. 135 & 136 Field Ambulances joined the Division Feeding Strength Men 11269 Horses H D 434 L D 1259	
SAMER	31st		1st Bn 58th I.R. U.S.A marched to HESDIN L'ABBAYE at 8.30 am. HQs 2nd R.M.F. & training staff moved by lorry to RECQUINGHEM on transfer to 31st Div. H Q's 2nd R.D.F. & training staff moved by lorry to RECQUINGHEM on transfer to 31st Div Both these Bns are to be made up to strength 2/10th Kings (Liverpool Regt) were transferred from 47th to 48th Inf Bdes & moved to CHATEAU L'ENFER 20th Middlesex Reg. were transferred from 40th Div. to 16th Div & moved by lorry to DESVRES & came under orders of G.O.C 48th Inf. Bde Feeding Strength Men: 15127 Horses H.D. 494 L.D. 1446	

A. Hull [illegible]
for Major Gen
Comdg 16th Divn

(A7092). Wt W12839/M1293 75,0.0. 1/17. D. D. & L., Ltd. Forms/C.2118/14.

Instructions regarding War Diaries and Intelligence Summaries are contained in F. S. Regs., Part II. and the Staff Manual respectively. Title pages will be prepared in manuscript.

WAR DIARY
or
INTELLIGENCE SUMMARY.
(Erase heading not required.)

16 DIV A
JUNE

Army Form C. 2118.

Place	Date JUNE	Hour	Summary of Events and Information	Remarks and references to Appendices
SAMER	1st		11th M.G. Bn U.S.A arrived SAMER 4 pm & after 1½ hours interval for tea moved by road to FRENCQ Area H.Q's 7th Inf. Bde. U.S.A. also arrived by same train. The Divisional Troupe proceeded by lorry to II American Corps H.Q. FRUGES where they gave a performance. Feeding Strength. Men 15971 Horses H.D. 552 L.D. 2057	
SAMER	2nd		No change Feeding Strength: Men 15626 Horses H.D. 518 L.D. 1655	
do	3rd		H.Q. 4th American Train & M.P. H.Q. 39th Inf. Reg & 59th Inf. Reg arrived from HAVRE at 1 pm; 1st Bn 47th Inf. Reg U.S.A arrived from CALAIS at 1.30 pm; 2nd Bn 47th Inf. Reg arrived from CALAIS 3.30 pm. ~~All~~ Bns marched to PARENTY Area coming under orders of 47th Inf Bde 3rd Bn 47th Inf. Reg & M.G. Coy arrived SAMER 6.15 pm & were accommodated for the night in rest camp	

(A7092). Wt W12839/M1293. 75 ,o.o. 1/17. D. D. & L., Ltd. Forms/C.2118/14.

Instructions regarding War Diaries and Intelligence Summaries are contained in F. S. Regs., Part II. and the Staff Manual respectively. Title pages will be prepared in manuscript.

WAR DIARY
or
INTELLIGENCE SUMMARY.
(Erase heading not required.)

Army Form C. 2118.

Place	Date	Hour	Summary of Events and Information	Remarks and references to Appendices
SAMER	3rd (cont)		Training Staffs of 4th Lincolns, 2/5th Notts & Derby, 5th North Staffords, 5th Oxford & Bucks Light Infantry, 9th K.R.R.s and 9th R. Bde also 157 Coy R.E. arrived & were accommodated in BLEQUIN Area. H.Q.s 49th Inf Bde moved to CHATEAU at QUILEN. Feeding Strength Men 16666, Horses H.D. 549 L.D. 1575	
SAMER	4th		No change. Feeding Strength Men: 20919. Horses: H.D. 542 L.D. 1660.	
SAMER	5th		No change. Feeding Strength Men. 20661: Horses H.D. 547: L.D. 1683	
SAMER	6th		Casuals of 4th American Div arrived SAMER 7.30 am. The Div Commander 80th American Div. Major General CRONKITE & staff arrived from BOULOGNE by car & proceeded to billets in CAMPAGNE-LES-BOULONNAIS. Billeting party of 1st Bn 318 I.R.U.S.A arrived by train & proceeded to WICQUINGHEM. Feeding Strength Men: 20530 Horses H.D 558 L.D. 1686	

(A7092). Wt. W12839/M1293. 75,0.0. 1/17. D. D. & L., Ltd. Forms/C.2118/14.

Instructions regarding War Diaries and Intelligence Summaries are contained in F. S. Regs., Part II. and the Staff Manual respectively. Title pages will be prepared in manuscript.

WAR DIARY
or
INTELLIGENCE SUMMARY.
(Erase heading not required.)

Army Form C. 2118.

Place	Date	Hour	Summary of Events and Information	Remarks and references to Appendices
SAMER	7th		H.Q's 80th American Div arrived from CALAIS at 6 pm. They were accommodated for the night in Rest Camp.	
			1st Bn 318th Inf. Reg U.S.A also arrived at same hour & were kept for the night at Rest Camp	
			VII Corps School moved to this area & took up their position in Prisoners of War Camp BOIS DE EPIRCHE	
			Feeding Strength Men 21113. Horses H.D. 588 L.D. 1919	
do	8th		1st Bn 318th Inf Reg. moved at 8.30 am to Rest Camp at ENQUIN	
			1st Bn 320th Inf Reg arrived SAMER 2 pm. & moved to CARLY	
			2nd Bn 320th Inf Reg arrived SAMER 6 30 pm & stayed the night in Rest Camp	
			315th M.G. Bn arrived SAMER 4 pm & moved to VERLINCTHUN	
			320th M.G. Coy arrived SAMER 6.30 pm & moved to HUBERSENT	
			160th Inf. Bde HQ's were billeted for night in SAMER	
			Feeding Strength Men 22298: Horses H.D. 588. L.D 1906.	
do	9th		2nd Bn 320th Inf Reg. marched to QUESTRECQUES	
			315th M.G. Bn moved to FRENCQ	
			1st Bn 318th Inf Reg moved to CORMONT: 160th Inf. Bde moved to LE BRUNQUET	

(A7092). Wt W12839/M1293 75,0 0. 1/17. D. D. & L., Ltd. Forms/C.2118/14.

Instructions regarding War Diaries and Intelligence Summaries are contained in F. S. Regs., Part II. and the Staff Manual respectively. Title pages will be prepared in manuscript.

Army Form C. 2118.

WAR DIARY
or
INTELLIGENCE SUMMARY.

(Erase heading not required.)

Place	Date	Hour	Summary of Events and Information	Remarks and references to Appendices
SAMER	9th (Contd)		1st Bn 319th Inf Reg. U.S.A arrived SAMER 2 pm & marched to DESVRES	
			2nd Bn. 319th Inf. Reg. U.S.A arrived SAMER 4 pm & marched to MENNEVILLE	
			M.G. Coy moved to HUBERSENT	
			3rd Bn 319th Inf Reg arrived SAMER 6 30 pm & remained night in Rest Camp	
			The 4th American Div. less Div. H Qs moved from this Area on having completion of being administered by 16 Div & proceeding to take up new duties.	
			One Coy 14th Div. Train arrived SAMER & proceeded to WIERRE-AU-BOIS coming under orders of O.C 16 Div Train	
			Feeding Strength Men 26886 Horses H.D 530 L.D 1960	
	10th		3rd Bn 319th Inf Reg. moved to COURSET.	
			3rd Bn 318th Inf Reg arrived SAMER at 1.30 pm & moved to ENQUIANHAUT. 318th M.G. Coy moved to	HUBERSENT.
			2nd Bn & Reg. H Q S 316th Inf Reg arrived 7.30 pm. 2nd H.Q.S moved to BERNIEULLES. Bn remained night in Rest Camp: 49th Inf. Bd. H.Qs moved to FRENCQ	
			Feeding Strength Men 27985 Horses H.D 660 L.D 1966	

(A7092) Wt W12839/M1293 75,0.0. 1/17. D. D. & L., Ltd. Forms/C.2118/14.

Instructions regarding War Diaries and Intelligence Summaries are contained in F. S. Regs., Part II. and the Staff Manual respectively. Title pages will be prepared in manuscript.

WAR DIARY
or
INTELLIGENCE SUMMARY.
(Erase heading not required.)

Army Form C. 2118.

Place	Date	Hour	Summary of Events and Information	Remarks and references to Appendices
SAMER	11th.		2nd Bn 316th Inf. Reg. U.S.A. moved to BOUT-de-HAUT, leaving Rest Camp 9 am. Div. Concert party gave a performance at G.H.Q at which the C in C was present. Feeding Strength Men: 17158 Horses H.D. 248: L.D. 813	
do.	12th.		No change: one Coy of 14th Div. Train joined the Div. to-day Feeding Strength: Men 15973 Horses H.D. 326: L.D. 865.	
do	13th.		No change Feeding Strength: Men 16036: Horses H.D. 399. L.D. 834.	
do	14th		No change.	
do	15th		No change.	

A5834 Wt. W4973/M687 750,000 8/16 D. D. & L. Ltd. Forms/C.2118/13.

Vol 30

HQ A&Q 16 D

Army Form C. 2118.

WAR DIARY
or
INTELLIGENCE SUMMARY.
(Erase heading not required.)

Instructions regarding War Diaries and Intelligence Summaries are contained in F. S. Regs., Part II. and the Staff Manual respectively. Title pages will be prepared in manuscript.

June Vol 31

Place	Date	Hour	Summary of Events and Information	Remarks and references to Appendices
SAMER	16th		Billeting parties of 317 Inf. Reg arrived & proceeded to their areas 159th Inf Bde HQS arrived & proceeded to PARENTY. 1st Bn 317th Inf Reg proceeded to HODICQ 2nd Bn 317 Inf Reg — BEZINGHEM 3rd Bn 317 Inf Reg — CRANDAL. HQ Coy DOUDEAUVILLE M.G. Coy HUBERSENT Supply Coy DOUDEAUVILLE	
SAMER	17th		305th Engineer Reg & Train arrived SAMER & proceeded to billets as follows 1st Bn: WIDEHEM 2 Bn HALINGHEM & HAUT PICOT. H.Q. Train & M.P proceeded to DALLE. At 8.30 pm Div HQS, 3 Inf Bde HQS 7th Roy Dublin Fus Training Staff & 11th Hants (P) Training Staff entrained at SAMER for BOULOGNE en route for ENGLAND	H. Esq. [illegible] Lt
BOULOGNE	18th		Div. HQs: 3 Inf Bde HQs. Training Staffs 7th Roy. Dublin Fus & 11th HANTS (P) embarked for ENGLAND 2 pm: The Div. Band played the ship out of harbour & gave selections on the voyage.	

A7092) Wt. W12S 9/M1293 750,000. 1/17. D. D & L. Ltd. Forms/C2118/14.

Instructions regarding War Diaries and Intelligence Summaries are contained in F. S. Regs., Part II. and the Staff Manual respectively. Title pages will be prepared in manuscript.

WAR DIARY HQ 16 Division A+Q

~~INTELLIGENCE SUMMARY.~~

(Erase heading not required.)

{JULY 1918 / AUGUST}

Army Form C. 2118.

(1)

WO 32/3

Place	Date	Hour	Summary of Events and Information	Remarks and references to Appendices
BOULOGNE	30th, 31st, AUGUST 1st, 2nd		Disembarkation and arrival of Division in SAMER Area in accordance with table attached.	Appendix I
SAMER			Feeding Strength Men 10148 Horses H.D. 288 L.D 1509	
	3rd		Division in Billets in SAMER Area - Training D.H.Q at SAMER.	Ref. CALAIS SHEET 13 1/100,000
	4th		No change	
	5th		11th Hants moved from MENTY to Billets in BERNIEULLES	
	6th		No Change	
	7th		No Change	
	8th		No Change	
	9th		No Change Feeding Strength Men 11332 Horses H.D 371 L.D 1418	

D. D. & L., London, E.C.
(A10266) Wt W5300/P713 750,000 2/18 Sch. 52 Forms/C2118/16.

Instructions regarding War Diaries and Intelligence Summaries are contained in F. S. Regs., Part II. and the Staff Manual respectively. Title pages will be prepared in manuscript.

WAR DIARY
or
INTELLIGENCE SUMMARY.
(Erase heading not required.)

August 1918

Army Form C. 2118.

(2)

Place	Date	Hour	Summary of Events and Information	Remarks and references to Appendices
SAMER	10th		No Change	
do	11th		14 LEICESTERSHIRE REGT changed billets from DOEAUDEAUVILLE to ENGUINHAUT THOBEAUVILLE and LE VIEILHAUME	
do	12th		No Change	
do	13th		No Change	
do	14th		156 FD COY RE rejoined Division from FIFTH ARMY – Billeted in LACRES	
do	15th		No Change. Feeding Strength men 11573 Horses HD 311 LD 1421	
do	16th		No Change.	
do	17th		Orders received for move of Division to 1st Corps Area. Supply arrangements for 47 Inf Bde Group to be as detailed in 16 Divl No A 409 attached – Move to be by Lorry.	Appendix II
			Administrative Instructions Nos 1 & 2 issued with Location list in new Area	Appendices III & IV
			Supply arrangements for 49 Inf Bde Group issued and attached – Instructions No 3	Appendix V
			Supply arrangements for 16 DAG Group issued – Instructions No 4	Appendix VI
do	18th		Advance party 47 Bde Group moves to 1st Divl Area	
			Transport of same Bde Group by March Route	
			Supply arrangements for 48 Infy Bde Group No 5 issued	Appendix VII

D. D. & L., London, E.C.
(A10266) Wt W5300/P713 750,000 2/18 Sch. 52 Forms/C2118/16.

Army Form C. 2118.

WAR DIARY
or
INTELLIGENCE SUMMARY.
(Erase heading not required.)

AUGUST 1918

(3)

Instructions regarding War Diaries and Intelligence Summaries are contained in F. S. Regs., Part II. and the Staff Manual respectively. Title pages will be prepared in manuscript.

Place	Date	Hour	Summary of Events and Information	Remarks and references to Appendices
SAMER	19th		DHQ moved to MONCHY CAYEUX	Ref LENS 11 1/100 000
			47 Infy Bde Group Personnel moved by bus to NOEUX LES MINES Area	
MONCHY CAYEUX	20th		49 Infy Bde Group Personnel moved by bus to DIEVAL area	
	21st		47 Infy Bde went into line	
			49 Infy Bde moved to NOEUX LES MINES Area	
			48 Bde Group moved to QUILEN Area	
	22nd		49 Infy Bde Group went into line CAMBRIN Sector	
			48 Infy Bde Group moved to NOEUX LES MINES Area	
			DHQ moved to RUITZ (R25C42)	
RUITZ	23rd		Nothing to report. Feeding Strength Men 11459 Horses H D 327 L D 1484	
	24th		Area thoroughly reconnoitred. Billets ~~stand~~ taken over, Transport lines inspected with	
	25th		a view to improvement. Accommodation inspected & all administrative details	
	26th		gone into. Divl Reception Camp BOIS D'OLHAIN opened & all drafts	
	27th		despatched there. Personnel Railhead CAMBLAIN RICOUART	
			SUPPLY RAILHEAD BARLIN	

D. D. & L., London, E.C.
(A10266) Wt W5300/P713 750,000 2/18 Sch. 52 Forms/C2118/16.

Instructions regarding War Diaries and Intelligence Summaries are contained in F. S. Regs., Part II. and the Staff Manual respectively. Title pages will be prepared in manuscript.

WAR DIARY
or
INTELLIGENCE SUMMARY.
(Erase heading not required.)

Army Form C. 2118.

August 1918 (4)

Place	Date	Hour	Summary of Events and Information	Remarks and references to Appendices
RUITZ	28th		Administrative arrangements of area continued.	
K25C42	29th		5th R.I. Fusiliers arrived and accommodated in Reception Camp.	
	30th		Amalgamation of 5th R.I. Fusiliers with 11th R.I. Fusiliers commenced.	
	31st		Amalgamation above referred to completed – Surplus personnel sent to Reception Camp for despatch to Base.	
			Fighting Strength 31st August attached	Appendix VIII
			Feeding Strength Men 12493 Horses HD 335 LD 1512.	

R N Greenwood Major DAAG
for Major General
Commanding 16th Division

D. D. & L., London, E.C.
(A10266) Wt W5300/P713 750,000 2/18 Sch. 52 Forms/C2118/16.

SECRET.

Table of Moves and Entrainment of 16th Division.

APPENDIX I

Date.	Formation or Unit.	Arrive Boulogne.	Depart Boulogne.	Arrive Samer.	Arrive Desvres.	Remarks.
Tuesday. 30.7.18	47th Inf. Bde Transpt. No 3 Sec, D.A.C. Stores of T.M. Battys.				7. A.M. 1. P.M.	Proceed to Parenty Area Proceed to Le Breuil.
	47th Inf. Brigade Personnel.	1.30. P.M. 8. P.M.				Proceed to Ostrohove Camp
Wednesday 31/7/18.	16th D.H.Q. Stores. 48 Inf. Bde. Transpt. Train Transport.				7. A.M. 1. P.M.	To be brought by Lorry to Samer Proceed to Desvres Area To join Divisional Train
	16th D.H.Q. 48th Inf. Bde. Personnel. 217th Emplmt. Coy.	11. A.M. 5. P.M.				To be brought by Lorry to Samer Proceed to Ostrohove Camp
	47th Inf. Brigade Personnel.		3.55. P.M. 5.55. P.M.		5.12. P.M. 7.12. P.M.	Proceed to billets in Parenty Area.
Thursday 1.8.18.	49th Inf. Bde. Transpt. 11th Hants (P) "				7. A.M. 1. P.M.	Proceed to Frenco Area Proceed to Menty Area.
	49th Inf. Bde Personnl. 11th Hants (P) " Medium T.M. Btys. "	11. A.M. 5. P.M.				Proceed to Ostrohove Camp
	48th Inf. Bde. Personnl. 217th Emplymt. Coy.		8.55. A.M. 10.55. A.M.	9.39. A.M. 11.39. A.M.		Proceed to billets in Desvres Area Proceed to billets in Samer.
Friday. 2.8.18.	49th Inf. Bde. Personnl. 11th Hants (P) " Medium T.M.B. "		8.55. A.M. 10.55. A.M. 11.55. A.M.	9.39. A.M. 11.39. A.M. 12.39. P.M.		Proceed to billets in Frenco Area Proceed to billets in Menty Area Proceed to billets Le Breuil

APPENDIX II

Office

SECRET. 16th Div.No.A.409.

Supply Arrangements for Move of 47th Infantry Brigade Group, consisting of :-
47th Infantry Bde.H.Q.
14th Leicester Regt.
18th Welsh Regt.
9th Royal Hrs.
47th Light T.M.Bty.
156th Field Coy.R.E.
77th Field Ambulance.
143rd Coy.A.S.C.
H.Q. & 2 Companies, M.G.Bn.

On August 18th there will be double refilling for all units of the Group.

This will enable the portion proceeding by buss to carry with them in the buses rations for consumption on the 19th and 20th.

Similarly the Transport will start on the evening of the 18th, carrying forage and rations for consumption on the remainder of the 18th plus the whole of the 19th and 20th.

On the 19th inst. lorries will draw from DESVRES and dump one day's supplies at or near the Church at ANVIN.

The exact spot will be selected by the Supply Officer, 47th Infantry Brigade who, with his Supply Details will travel on the lorries, and this Officer will arrange for guides (should they be necessary) to await the Horse Transport at AVION Church from 7.30 pm. on the 19th.

These Supplies (which arefor consumption on the 21st) will be picked up by the Supply Section on the evening of the 19th, and delivered to units on arrival in the forward area on the evening of the 20th.

On the 20th inst. lorries will draw from DESVRES supplies for consumption on the 22nd and will dump them at a Refilling Point in the forward area, which will be selected by O.C. Train and notified to all concerned.

W.B. Rennie

16th Division 'Q'.
17-8-18. HF.

Lieut-Colonel,
A.A.& Q.M.G., 16th Division.

Copies to:-

4 47th Inf.Bde.	2 A.D.M.S.
4 48th " "	/ D.A.D.V.S.
4 49th " "	/ D.A.D.O.S.
11th Hunts.(P).	/ A.P.M.
16th M.G.Bn.	/ French Mission.
C.R.E.	/ D.G.O.
S.A.A.Sec.	/ Camp Comdt.
Div.Train.	/ Employt.Coy.
M.T.Coy.	/ Area Comdt.SAMER.
"G".	/ 1st Division (for infmn.)

Distributed with DO 239 17/8/18 WR

DAAG

DAQMG

DUPLICATE.

APPENDIX III

S E C R E T :

No. 1

ADMINISTRATIVE INSTRUCTIONS TO ACCOMPANY
16th DIVISION ORDER No. 239.

-------------- oOo --------------

With reference to 16th Division Order No. 239 of today's date. Location lists of units in the Division on arrival in the new area, and certain administrative notes on the new area, will be issued to all concerned as early as possible.

1. GENERAL:-

The following arrangements have been made for the move.

Each Brigade Group Transport will march on the afternoon of the day preceding embussment, and will rejoin the personnel travelling by bus, on the evening of the day following embussment.

The transport will march in the cool of the morning and again in the evening to save the animals from the midday heat.

Lewis guns and Magazines will be carried with the gun teams in the busses, and this will set free a portion of the Lewis gun limbers for other baggage.

2. SUPPLY:-

Supply arrangements will be notified to all concerned for each Brigade group, separately.

Supply Railhead will be BARLIN, on and from the 21st inst.

Preserved rations will be issued during the move, as far as possible.

Any fresh meat taken on the men will be cooked the day previously.

A sufficient number of camp kettles will be taken with the embussing portion of the personnel.

3. WATER:-

Water carts are being lent as follows by I Corps for the convenience of units until the arrival of their transport. Brigades will be responsible for meeting the carts and distributing them as necessary:- 47th Inf.Bde. will lend four water carts to 48th Inf.Bde. and 11th Hants on the 22nd inst., until their transports arrive:-

Aug.19th..4 carts at RUITZ Church at 1.0.p.m., for 47th Group.
Aug.20th..4 carts at DIEVAL Church at 1.0.pm., for 49th Group.

The carts for the DIEVAL area will rejoin the units of 49th Inf.Bde. in the BARLIN area by route march on the 21st inst., under orders of 49th Inf.Bde. Notification will be sent to Divisional Headqrs., when carts are no longer required.

4. TRANSPORT:-

Extra transport will be provided on the scale shown below:-
Lorries will report as follows:-

	Time:	Date:	Place:
4 Lorries	5.0.a.m.	19.8.18.	47th Inf.Bde.H.Q.
4 Lorries	7.0.a.m.	20.8.18.	49th Inf.Bde.H.Q.
1 Lorry	7.0.a.m.	20.8.18.	H.Q.M.G.Btn., CORMONT.
4 Lorries	5.0.a.m.	22.8.18.	48th Inf.Bde.H.Q.
1 Lorry	6.0.p.m.	21.8.18.	11th Hants c/o Area Cmdt. BOUDREAUVILLE.

P. T. O.:-

Each Brigade will provide guides to (cont'd):-

4. TRANSPORT (cont'd):-

Each Brigade will provide guides to direct the lorries to the various Battalions.

The five lorries on the 20th inst. will remain with the units and resume their march on the 21st. In all instances lorries will be released from duty immediately units arrive in the forward area. O.C. 16th M.T.Coy., will issue orders to the drivers in advance for their subsequent movements. In no case may a unit use a lorry for a second journey.

5. SANITATION:-

Particular attention will be paid to leaving all billets, billeting areas, and transport lines in a scrupulously clean condition, and any shallow trench latrines, will be filled in.

6. AREA STORES:-

Any moveable area stores will be handed in to Area Commandants or their representatives, in order to avoid thefts by the inhabitants. Tents will be left standing under the charge of Area Commandants. A stringent order has been issued through the French Civil Authorities with a view to preventing theft or damage to any Government property. Particularly rifle ranges, bayonet courses, etc. Formations and units will take any steps in their power to assist in this matter before leaving the area.

7. MISCELLANEOUS:-

The Division will take over, on arrival, a sufficient supply of petrol tins as trench stores, and units should be reminded that they need sand-bags to send up rations as soon as battalions go into the line.

The bus convoy on the 19th will consist of 89 busses in front and 32 lorries in rear. Busses hold 25, lorries 20. In forming up, six vehicles occupy 80 yards of road.

W.B. Rennie

Lieut-Col.,
A.A.& Q.M.G., 16th Division.

Headquarters,
16th Division,
17th August, 1918,
HT.

Copies to:-

16th Div.Art.(3)	16th Div.Train (5)
16th Div.Engrs.(4)	16th M.T.Coy.
16th Div.Sig.Co.	A.P.M.
47th Inf.Bde.(5)	D.A.D.V.S.
48th Inf.Bde.(5)	D.A.D.O.S.
49th Inf.Bde.(5)	D.G.O.
11th Hants.	Camp Comdt.
16th M.G.Bn.	217th Empt.Coy.
D.T.M.O.	1st Corps.
No.3 Sect.D.A.C.	XXII Corps.(2)
A.D.M.S. (4)	1st Division.
"G".	War Diaries (3).

REFERENCE ADMINISTRATIVE INSTRUCTIONS TO ACCOMPANY
16TH.DIVISIONAL ORDERS NO.239.

LOCATION LIST OF THE 16TH.DIVISION ON ARRIVAL IN NEW AREA.

UNIT.	LOCATION.	WAGON LINES.
H.Q.16TH.DIVISION.	RUITZ. K.25.c. 4.2.	With Unit.
16th.Div.Signal Company	RUITZ. K.25.c. 4.2.	K.27.b. 5.5.
A.D.M.S.	RUITZ. K.25.c. 4.2.	-
A.P.M.	RUITZ. K.25.c. 4.2.	BARLIN.
C.R.E.	RUITZ. K.25.c. 4.2.	With Unit.
S.C.F.,D.C.G's Dept.	RUITZ. K.25.c. 4.2.	-
Reserve Infy.Brigade Area.		
Brigade Headquarters.	BARLIN.	K.31.c.
One Battalion.	BARLIN.	K.31.c.
One Battalion.	K.23.	K.31.c.
One Battalion.	K.23.	K.31.c.
Trench Mortar Battery.	K.23.	-
Right Infantry Brigade.		
Brigade Headquarters.	ANNEQUIN FOSSE.	K.18.b. 9.7.
One Battalion.	IN THE LINE.	K.18.b. 9.7.
One Battalion.	IN THE LINE.	K.18.b. 9.7.
One Battalion.	IN THE LINE.	K.18.b. 9.7.
Trench Mortar Battery	IN THE LINE.	-
Left Infantry Brigade.		
Brigade Headquarters.	CHATEAU DES PRES.	K.18.b. 7.7.
One Battalion.	IN THE LINE.	K.18.b. 7.7.
One Battalion.	IN THE LINE.	K.18.b. 7.7.
One Battalion.	IN THE LINE.	K.18.b. 7.7.
Trench Mortar Battery.	IN THE LINE.	-
11th.Hampshire Regt(P)	SAILLY LABOURSE.	BARLIN. K.27.c. 6.1.
16th.Bn.Machine Gun Corps.	BARLIN.	BARLIN. K.33.a. 8.8.
One Field Company.	SAILLY LABOURSE.	MAISNIL LES RUITZ.J.36.b. 1.3
One Field Company.	ANNEQUIN NORTH.	MAISNIL LES RUITZ.J.36.b. 1.3
One Field Company.	TOURBIERES.	MAISNIL LES RUITZ.J.36.b. 1.3
One Field Ambulance.	BARLIN.	K.20.a. 5.5.
One Field Ambulance.	RUITZ.	K.20.a. 5.5.
One Field Ambulance.	RUITZ.	K.20.a. 5.5.
16th.Divisional Train H.Q.	RUITZ.	K.20.a. 5.5.
One Company Train.	RUITZ.	K.20.a. 5.5.
One Company Train.	K.31.c.	K.20.a. 5.5.
One Company.Train.	MAISNIL LES RUITZ.	K.20.a. 5.5.
Reserve Bde.Refilling Point.	K.31.c. Central.	
Right Brigade " "	K.33.c. 4.3.	
Left Brigade " "	K.33.b. 2.4.	
16th.Div.Troops " "	K.33.c. Central.	
16th.Divl. M.T.Company.	Q.2.d. 9.1.	
D.A.D.V.S.	BARLIN.	
47th.Mobile Veterinary Sect.	BARLIN.	
D.A.D.O.S.	BARLIN.	
217th.Employment Coy.	BARLIN.	
Supply Railhead.	BARLIN.	

Divl.Salvage Officer and Company	L.3.c.3.3.
Divl.Canteens & Canteen Officer.	BARLIN.
Personnel Railhead.	CALONNE RICOUART.
Divl.Reception Camp.	BOIS D'OLHAIN, Q.8. Central.
S.C.F. P.C's Dept.	BARLIN.
French Mission.	CHATEAU RUITZ.
S.A.A.Section D.A.C.	MAISNIL LES RUITZ.

D.T.M.C. Under orders of C.R.A. 1st Division.

R A Greenwood
Major.
D.A.A.G. 16th. Division.

H.Q. 16th.Division.
17th.August.1918.

Same distribution as ADMINISTRATIVE INSTRUCTIONS, 16th.Division No.1 dated 17th.August.1918.

DUPLICATE

Appendix IV

S E C R E T.

ADMINISTRATIVE INSTRUCTION No. 2.

The following are a few administrative details in connection with the new area. This information is not intended in any way to be complete, and fuller details will be obtained by Brigades on relief.

SUPPLIES.

Railhead - BARLIN.
Reloading is carried out by Train Wagons.
The usual system of refilling is for the Train Wagons to draw from the Broad Guage and deliver to the Eight Railway on which the rations are sent up to Units.
REFILLING POINTS:-

1st Inf.Bde.	-	K.31.c.Central.
2nd -do-	-	K.33.c.4.6.
3rd -do-	-	K.33.b.2.4.

irrespective of whether the Brigade is in or out.
Railhead for personnel is CALONNE RICOUART.

RESERVE RATIONS AND WATER.

(a) Right Inf. Bde.		-	4780 rations.
(b) Left -do-		-	5100 rations.
(c) Reserve -do-	NOEUX Locality		4000 rations.

WATER.

Each Infantry Brigade in the line - 500 gallons.
The above is calculated on a basis of 1 day's supply per man.

LOCALITIES.

CAMBRIN. 250 gallons in petrol cans, plus 1000 gallons in tanks.
ANNEQUIN. 200 gallons -do- 1000 gallons -do-

S.A.A. & GRENADES.

Corps Dump is at HESDIGNEUL.
Divisional Dump is at BALLY BUNION.
S.A.A., Grenades, etc. are sent up from Divisional Dump by Light Railway to :-

Right Brigade Dump.

No.1. Chemists Shop, CAMBRIN.	-	A.19.d.8.2.
No.2. VERMELLES.	-	G.8.c.5.9.

Left Brigade Dump.

No.1. HARLEY STREET.	-	A.20.d.35.15.
No.2. NEW DUMP.	-	F.22.d.5.7.

All requirements will be submitted to Divisional Headquarters, who will order the ammunition to be delivered to Brigade Dumps by the advanced Echelon of D.A.C., which is established at BALLY BUNION Dump. The Light Railway will be used as far as possible.

SUPPLY OF R.E. STORES.

No.	Name.	Location.	Map Ref.	On authority of.
1.	Corps Yard.	MINX.	K.5.b.central.	C.R.Es.
2.	Main Divl. Dump.	SAILLY LABOURSE.	L.3.b.4.9.	-do-

Area No.	Area.	Responsibility for clearing.
A. Right Brigade Sector.	East of Broad Guage Railway running thro' F.29.a.	Brigade in the line.
B. Left Brigade Sector.	F.29.b. - L.XX 5.b. - L.6.a.- L.6.b. - L.12.a.	-do-
C. Divisional Area West of the above line.		Divl. Salvage Company.

LIGHT RAILWAYS.

Light Railways are used for transport of Supplies and for reliefs. For left Brigade and for left Battalion of right Brigade trains for personnel are run as far as ANNEQUIN. For right Battalion of right Brigade they are run to VERMELLES. Troops usually entrain and detrain at BARLIN and LA BOURSE, but other stations can be utilised as required.

Application for trucks is made to C.L.R.O., Office at MINX, K.6.a.

TRENCH TRAMWAYS.

There is a system of Trench Tramways forward of CAMBRIN and VERMELLES. R.T.O's at these points control traffic and rolling stock on this system.

REINFORCEMENTS.

Reinforcements (except Artillery) and all personnel returning from leave and courses are sent to CALONNE RICOUART. On arrival they are accommodated for the night at Canadian Corps Railhead Depot, where there is an Officers' Club and a Y.M.C.A. Hut.

On the following morning they proceed by ~~route~~ march route to the Divisional Reception Camp, BOIS D'OLHAIN. (Q.8.Central.)

Transport for Officers' kits and men's packs is provided daily.

Reinforcements are retained at the Divl. Reception Camp until they have passed the necessary test in anti-gas precautions, when they are despatched to their Units.

Artillery Reinforcements are sent from the First Army Artillery Reinforcement Camp according to the requirements of the Divl. Artillery under arrangements made by I Corps.

BATHS.

Location.	Capacity.	Apply to.
ANNEQUIN.F23.d.9.1.	400 per diem.	Brigade in line.
NOEUX LES MINES.K.18.b.6.4.	680 per diem.	Town Major.
BARLIN.K.33.a.9.4.	500 -do-	Div.Baths Officer.
FOSSE.No.7. K.31.c.	1800 -do-	-do- (thro' Town Major, BARLIN.)

The charge for baths at FOSSE No.7 is 8 centimes a head, which is paid through the Imprest a/c of the Town Major, BARLIN. Units forward receipts for money paid for bathing to the Divisional Baths Officer.

Delousing plants exist at all the above baths except at FOSSE 7.

LAUNDRIES. Clothing is washed under Army arrangements.

SUPPLY OF CLEAN CLOTHING.

Corps Clean Clothing Depot. RUITZ.
Divl. -do- D.A.D.O.S. Stores. BARLIN.

O.C., Divisional Baths draws clean clothes from RUITZ and arranges for the delivery of the clothing to the Divisional Clean Clothing Store and Baths.

S.G. Evans
Major,
D.A.Q.M.G., 16th Divn. for
A.A. & Q.M.G., 16th Divn.

H.Q., 16th Division.
17th Aug., 1918.

SECRET.

AMENDMENT TO LOCATION LIST ISSUED ON 17-8-18, TO ACCOMPANY 16TH DIVISIONAL ORDER No.239.

With reference to LOCATION LIST published with 16th Divl. Orders No.239.

The headings "Right Infantry Brigade" and "Left Infantry Brigade" should be reversed.

R.N. Greenwood

Major,
D.A.A.G., 16th Division.

H.Q.16th Division,
19-8-18. HF.

Same distribution as ADMINISTRATIVE INSTRUCTIONS, 16th Division No.1, dated 17-8-18.

DISTRIBUTION.

47th Infantry Bde.
48th Infantry Bde.
49th Infantry Bde.
11th Hants Regt. (P).
16th Div.M.G.Bn.
16th Div.Sig.Coy.
16th Div.Train.
C.R.E.
General Staff.
S.S.O.
16th Div.M.T. Coy.
16th Div.Salvage Officer.
Div.Employ. Coy.
Camp Comdt.

APPENDIX V

S E C R E T .

16TH.DIVISION ADMINISTRATIVE INSTRUCTION. No.3.

SUPPLY ARRANGEMENTS FOR MOVE OF 49TH.BRIGADE GROUP.

Brigade Group consisting of
- 49th.Infantry Brigade Headquarters.
- 6th.Somerset Light Infantry.
- 18th.Gloucester Regiment.
- 34th.London Regiment.
- 49th.Light Trench Mortar Battery.
- 157th.Field Company.R.E.
- 144th.Company. A.S.C.
- Two Companies Machine Gun Battalion.

There will be double Refilling for all units of this Group on the 19th.instant.

This will enable the portion proceeding by bus to c rry with them in the buses on the 20th. rations for consumption on 20th. and 21st. instant. Similarly the Transport will start on the evening of the 19th. instant carrying forage and rations for consumption on the remainder of the 19th. plus the whole of the 20th. and 21st.

Lorries will draw from DESVRES on the 20th.instant and dump one day's supplies at ANVIN(for consumption 22nd.) at or near the Church. The spot being the same as used by the 47th.Brigade - Supply Officer 49th.Brigade and his Supply Details will travel in these lorries and this Officer will arrange for guides(if necessary)to await horse transport at ANVIN Church from 7.30 p.m. on 20th.instant.

These supplies(which are for consumption on 22nd.)will be picked up by the Supply Section on the evening of 20th.instant and delivered to units on arrival in the new area on the evening of 21st.

Guides from all units of the Group will await the Transport at RUITZ Church from 7.30 p.m. on the 21st.instant.

Lorries will draw from BARLIN on the 21st. instant rations for consumption 23rd. and dump at Refilling Point in forward area in accordance with orders which will be issued by O.C.Train.

ARRANGEMENTS FOR S.A.A.SECTION D.A.C.

19th.August. Refill twice(rations for consumption 20th. and 21st)

20th.August. Rations for consumption 22nd. instant will be drawn by lorry from DESVRES with 49th.Brigade Group and dumped at ANVIN with those for 49th.Brigade Group. Supply wagons will pick these up and deliver to units on the evening of 21st.instant in their bivouac.

21st.August. Rations for consumption 23rd instant will be drawn by lorry from BARLIN and dumped at the 49th.Brigade Refilling Point in the forward area.

O.C.Train will arrange for transport of Supplies from Refilling Point to S.A.A.Section transport lines.

W.B. Rennie

H.Q.16th.Division. Lieut.Colonel.
17.8.18. A.A.&.Q.M.G. 16th. Division.

P T.O.

Copies to:-
49th.Infy.Bde.(5)
Machine Gun Battn.(2)
C.R.E. (2)
Divl.Train (3)
Divl.M.T.Coy. (2)
A.D.M.S.
D.A.D.V.S.
D.A.D.O.S.
A.P.M.
French Mission.
Camp Commandant.

Appendix VI

16th DIVISION ADMINISTRATIVE INSTRUCTIONS No. 4.

S E C R E T :

SUPPLY ARRANGEMENTS FOR MOVE OF 16th DIVISIONAL HEADQUARTERS GROUP, CONSISTING of :-

Divisional Headquarters.
Headquarters, 16th Divisional Engineers.
16th Divisional Signal Company.
217th (Div) Employment Company.
Divisional Signal School.
Headquarters, 16th Div.Train
47th Mobile Veterinary Section.
French Mission.

1. The following will NOT move with Divisional Headquarters, but will follow a few days later :-
(a) A.O.D.personnel less D.A.D.O.S.,
(b) Canteen Personnel.

2. 18th instant: Double refilling (rations for consumption 19th and 20th insts.)

3. 19th instant: supplies drawn by lorry from DESVRES, with those of 47th Brigade Group and dumped with the latter at ANVIN. (see this office No. A.409 of today's date).
Supply wagons will refill from this dump on the evening of the 20th instant, Camp Commandant getting into touch with 16th Division Supply Officer on duty at ANVIN.

4. 20th August...Rations for consumption 22nd instant, will be drawn by lorry from DESVRES with those of the 49th Brigade Group, and again dumped at ANVIN.

5. 21st August...Rations for consumption 23rd instant will be drawn by lorry from BARLIN and dumped on 49th Brigade Refilling Point, and will be drawn in the ordinary way on the evening of 22nd instant, after arrival of D.H.Q. in the forward area.

6. Details of Embussment and start of the horse transport will be arranged by Camp Commandant.

W.B. Rennie
Lieut-Col.,
A.A.& Q.M.G., 16th Divn.

16th D.H.Q.,
17th Aug., 1918.
HW.

DISTRIBUTION:-

Camp Commdt....(2)	D. A. D. O. S.,
C. R. E., 16th Div.	16th Div.Train (3)
16th Signal Coy.	47th Mob.Vet.Sec.
217th Employ.Coy.	French Mission.
D. A. D. V. S.	"G" (for inf).

SECRET. No.5.

Appendix VII

16th DIVISION ADMINISTRATIVE INSTRUCTIONS.

SUPPLY ARRANGEMENTS FOR 48TH INFANTRY BRIGADE GROUP, CONSISTING OF :-

48th Infantry Bde.Headquarters.
22nd Northumberland Fusiliers.
18th Scottish Rifles.
11th R.Irish Fusiliers.
48th Light T.M.Battery.
155th Field Coy.R.E.
145th Company A.S.C.
11th Hants.Regt.(P).
112th Field Ambulance.

20th Aug. Two days rations and forage for this group will be drawn from DESVRES and dumped at present Refilling Point.

21st Aug. Double refilling for consumption 22nd and 23rd. This will enable personnel to embus with two days rations; similarly, Transport will start on evening of 21st with rations and forage for consumption on 22nd and 23rd.

22nd Aug. Supplies for consumption on 24th will be drawn from BARLIN and will be dumped at Refilling Point in new area. Supply Officer and Supply Details of 48th Infantry Brigade will embus on 22nd August with 48th Infantry Brigade and take over supplies on arrival at Refilling Point in new area.

23rd Aug. Transport for this Group on arrival in forward area on 23rd will pick up supplies for consumption 24th and deliver to units, under arrangements being made by O.C.Train.

Guides from all Units will await transport at RUITZ Church from 7.30 p.m. on the 23rd inst.
The same rendezvous will be convenient for guides to meet the lorries allotted to 48th Brigade and 11th Hants.Regt.etc. for extra baggage.

W. B. Rennie

H.Q.16th Division,
18-8-18. HF.

Lieut-Colonel,
A.A.& Q.M.G. 16th Division.

Distribution:-

48th Inf.Bde.	(5)	D.A.D.V.S.
11th Hants.	(2)	D.A.D.O.S.
C.R.E.	(2)	A.P.M.
M.T.Coy.		French Mission.
A.D.M.S.	(2)	"G" (for information).
Div.Train.	(3)	

First Army Pro Forma No. 3—*continued.*

DETAILS OF OFFICERS "TAKEN ON" OR "STRUCK OFF" STRENGTH.

UNIT.	Rank.	Name.	Initials.	Remarks.
18th Welsh Regiment.	2/Lt.	WOLSEY.	E.	Wounded 24.8.18
	2/Lt.	HOLMES.	E.	Wounded 24.8.18
	2/Lt.T	THOMAS.	S.H.	Wounded 24.8.18
9th.Roual Highrs.	Capt.	SLEIGH.	G.R.	To Base Depot Unfit.
	2/Lt.	MENZIES.	J.N.	47th.Bde Intell.Offcr
	Capt.	PROUDFOOT.	F.	joined 28.8.18.
18th.Scottish Rif.	Capt.	CRAIGIE.	J.H.	Rejoined from Aldershot
	2/Lt.	HART.	W.	48th.Bde.Intell Offcr.
5th.R.Irish Fus.	Capt.	STEVENTON.	P.W.	From 11th.R.Irish Fus.
	Lieut.	SANDILANDS?	P.I.R.	do.
	Lieut.	AND RSON.	E.	do.
	Lieut.	REYNELL.	H.B.	do.
	Lieut.	JOURDAIN.	F.W.S.	do.
	2/Lt.	LEWIS.	W.R.	do.
	Lieut.	CREIGHTON.	J.L.	To Base 28.8.18
	2/Lt.	MOSS.	H.W.	do.
	2/Lt.	JAMES.	A.A.	do.
	2/Lt.	ARLETT.	N.J.	Str.off on amalgamation
	2/Lt.	HOURIHANE.	G.O.B.	Transfd to Indian Army.
6th.Somerset L.I.	2/Lt.	BRIDGMAN.	R.G.	Joined 25.8.18
	2/Lt.	HAYNES.	G.V.	do.
	2/Lt.	WILLS.	F.J.	do.
	2/Lt.	CARTER.	G.de L.	do.
	2/Lt.	FINNEGAN.	A.J.	29.8.18.
	2/Lt.	ELLIS.	J.R.	29.8.18
	Lieut.	HAYHURST.	A.E.	Wounded 24.8.18.
18th.Gloucester Regt.	2/Lt.	HODGES.	T.H.	Joined 29.8.18.
34th.London Regt.	Lieut.	BOND.	W.H.	49th.Bde.Intell.Offr.
11th.Hants Regt(P)	2/Lt.	TAYLOR.	F.H.	Rejd from"D" I.B.D.18/8

Appendix VIII

First Army Pro Forma No. 3.

16TH. DIVISION. A.22/1.

Strength Return made up to 12 noon Saturday, 31st. August. 1918.

UNIT.	A. Strength Return excluding attached.		B. Not present with the unit and not at the disposal of C.O. (included in Column A).		A. *minus* B. Available Fighting Strength (including personnel of Battalion Transport and Quartermaster's Stores).	
	Officers.	O.R.	Officers.	O.R.	Officers.	O.R.
47th. Infantry Brigade.						
14th. Leic. Regt.	42	885	9	40	33	845
18th. Welsh Regt.	38	877	9	78	29	799
9th. Royal Highrs.	38	850	10	70	28	780
T O T A L :-	118	2612	28	188	90	2424
48th. Infantry Brigade:-						
22nd. N'land Fus.	39	865	9	78	30	787
18th. Sco. Rifles.	38	738	5	59	33	680
5th. R. Irish Fus.	41	905	14	314	27	591.
T O T A L :-	118	2509	28	451	90	2058.
49th. Infantry Brigade.						
6th. Somerset L.I.	45	835	11	79	34	756
18th. Glos. Regt.	41	715	14	56	27	659
34th. London Regt.	40	838	10	55	30	783.
T O T A L :-	126	2388	35	190	91	2198.
11th. Hants. Bn. (P).	40	718	6	29	34	689
GRAND TOTAL.	402	8227	97	858	305	7369.
16th. Mach. Gun Battn.	48	884	-	5	48	879
TOTALS ...						

(signed) R.N.GREENWOOD. Major. D.A.A.G.
for Major General.
Commanding 16th. Division.

Headquarters.
16th. Division.
31st. August. 1918.

PRINTED IN FRANCE BY ARMY PRINTING AND STATIONERY SERVICES. PRESS A—4/18—6095D—3,000.

Original

Instructions regarding War Diaries and Intelligence Summaries are contained in F. S. Regs., Part II. and the Staff Manual respectively. Title pages will be prepared in manuscript.

WAR DIARY
or
~~INTELLIGENCE SUMMARY.~~
(Erase heading not required.)

16 Division A+Q

Army Form C. 2118.

SEPTEMBER

"A" & "Q" 16TH DIVISION. No.........

Place	Date	Hour	Summary of Events and Information	Remarks and references to Appendices
RUITZ K25C42	1st		In view of reported enemy withdrawal administrative arrangements in case of an advance were considered – Administrative instructions No 6 were published (attached)	Sh LENS 11 1/100,000 Appendix I
			Feeding Strength Men 12125 Horses HD 329 LD 1435.	
			Casualties:– Officers Killed Nil Wounded Nil Missing Nil Other Ranks Killed 2 Wounded 11 Missing 1	
	2nd		Brigades made necessary arrangements for supplies and ammunition in case of advance.	
			Casualties Officers Killed Nil Wounded Nil Missing Nil Other Ranks Killed 3 Wounded 3 Missing –	
	3rd		Casualties Officers Killed Nil Wounded Nil Missing Nil Other Ranks Killed 1 Wounded 8 Missing 1	
	4th		Casualties Officers Killed Nil Wounded 3 Missing Nil Other Ranks Killed Nil Wounded 3 Missing –	
	5th		Wagon Transport lines inspected & canteens.	
			Arrangements made for material for roads etc to be sent up in case of advance.	
			Casualties Officers Killed Nil Wounded Nil Missing Nil Other Ranks Killed 4 Wounded 9 Missing –	
			Notification received that 16 Divisional Artillery are rejoining. Administrative instruction No 7 published and attached.	Appendix II

D. D. & L., London, E.C.
(A10266) Wt W5300/P713 750,000 2/18 Sch. 52 Forms/C2118/16.

Instructions regarding War Diaries and Intelligence Summaries are contained in F. S. Regs., Part II. and the Staff Manual respectively. Title pages will be prepared in manuscript.

WAR DIARY
~~or~~
~~INTELLIGENCE SUMMARY~~.
(Erase heading not required.)

Army Form C. 2118.

SEPTEMBER 1918

Place	Date	Hour	Summary of Events and Information	Remarks and references to Appendices
RUITZ	6th		Work on Transport Lines - Horse standings progressing & well in hand.	Ref
K25 c 4.2			47 & 49 Inf Bde pushed forward in view of Enemy withdrawal - Frenade stores moved forward	LENS 11
			48 Bde Hq moved from BARLIN to SAILLY LABOURSE	1/100,000
			1st GLOUCESTERS ~~[illegible]~~ moved to CAMBRIN LOCALITY 1st LEICESTERS to ANNEQUIN locality	
			5 R I Fusiliers to NOEUX LES MINES	
			Casualties to NOON Officers Killed NIL Wounded 4 Missing 1 Other Ranks Killed 3 Wounded 101 Missing 11	
			Feeding Strength Men 11973 ~~[illegible]~~ Horses HD 332 ~~[illegible]~~ LD 1471 ~~[illegible]~~	
do	7th		AA & QMG inspected Transport ~~and~~ with DADVS also work on horse standings.	
			Fighting Strength for 6th Noon 7th attached	Appendix III
			Casualties to NOON Officers Killed NIL. Wounded 3 ~~[illegible]~~. Missing NIL Other Ranks Killed 7 Wounded 91. Missing 3	
do	8th		Casualties to NOON Officers Killed NIL Wounded 1 Missing NIL Other Ranks Killed NIL Wounded 2 Missing NIL	
do	9th		Disposition of unit & Arts attached	Appendix IV
			Feeding Strength Men 14151 Horses HD 430 LD 3223	
			Casualties to noon Officers Wounded 2 Other ranks Wounded 91 Missing 1	
do	10th		Casualties to noon Other Ranks Wounded 67	
			DAPMG ~~[illegible]~~ I Group re probable change of Divisional Area. [illegible] reconnoitred new villages for accommodation	
			If change takes place we shall have a great deal of horse accommodation [illegible]	

D. D. & L., London, E.C.
(A10266) Wt W5300/P713 750,000 2/18 Sch. 52 Forms/C2118/16.

Instructions regarding War Diaries and Intelligence Summaries are contained in F. S. Regs., Part II. and the Staff Manual respectively. Title pages will be prepared in manuscript.

WAR DIARY
or
INTELLIGENCE SUMMARY.
(Erase heading not required.)

SEPTEMBER 1918

Army Form C. 2118.

Place	Date	Hour	Summary of Events and Information	Remarks and references to Appendices
RUITZ K 25 c 4 2	11th		Casualties ~~Killed~~ Officers Wounded 4 Other ranks 3 Killed 12 Wounded 35 Missing 2.	
"	12th		[illegible]	
			Casualties Officers killed 1 wounded 3. Other ranks killed 11 wounded 46	
"	13th		Casualties Officers killed 1 other ranks killed 3 wounded 6 Feeding strength of Division men 13724. H.D. 437. L.D. 3209.	
"	14th		Casualties other ranks killed 2 Officers wounded 2 Other ranks wounded 47 mostly gas.	
"	15th		Casualties other ranks killed 8 wounded 105 missing 16 Officers wounded 4. (mostly gas wounds). Feeding Strength of Divn men 13424. H.D. 435. L.D. 3201.	
"	16th		Casualties killed other ranks 2 wounded Officers 5 other ranks 14	
"	17th		Casualties killed other ranks 2 wounded Officers 3 other ranks 65 (mostly gas wounds) 48th Infantry Bde relieved the 49th Bde in the line.	

D. D. & L., London, E.C.
(A10266) Wt W5300/P713 750,000 2/18 Sch. 52 Forms/C2118/16.

Instructions regarding War Diaries and Intelligence Summaries are contained in F. S. Regs., Part II. and the Staff Manual respectively. Title pages will be prepared in manuscript.

WAR DIARY
or
INTELLIGENCE SUMMARY.
(Erase heading not required.)

Army Form C. 2118.

Place	Date	Hour	Summary of Events and Information	Remarks and references to Appendices
RUITZ K25 C 4.2	18th		Casualties killed other ranks 3 wounded 94 missing 13 (wounded mostly gas) 5th R. Irish Fusiliers moved to ANNEQUIN. Feeding strength of Divn men 13438 H.Q. ~~409~~ L.D. 3354.	
"	19th		Casualties killed other ranks 3 wounded officers 2 O.R. 87 missing 14	
"	20th		Casualties killed other ranks 2 wounded other ranks 27	
"	21st		Casualties killed other ranks 1 wounded other rank 4 Feeding strength of Divn men 13391. H.Q. 416. L.D. 3319.	
"	22nd		Casualties killed other ranks 1 wounded officers 1 other ranks 8	
DROUVIN	23rd		Casualties killed other ranks 1 wounded other ranks 6. Divisional Headquarters moved to DROUVIN see APPENDIX V.	Appendix V
"	24th		Casualties wounded officers 1 other ranks 4 Feeding strength of Divn men 12879. H.Q. 416. L.D. 3322.	
"	25th		Casualties wounded other ranks 1	

D. D. & L., London, E.C.
(A10266) Wt W5300/P713 750,000 2/18 Sch. 52 Forms/C2118/16.

Instructions regarding War Diaries and Intelligence Summaries are contained in F. S. Regs., Part II. and the Staff Manual respectively. Title pages will be prepared in manuscript.

WAR DIARY
or
INTELLIGENCE SUMMARY.
(*Erase heading not required.*)

Army Form C. 2118.

Place	Date	Hour	Summary of Events and Information	Remarks and references to Appendices
DROUVIN	26		A/AA & QMG visited 47th Bde Headquarters. DA QMG inspected the transport of the Welsh & Leicester Regts. Casualties 1 O.R. wounded. D.A. & Q.M.G. & D.A.A.G. 1st Corps called. Administrative instructions no 8 issued	Appendix VI
"	27		A/AA & QMG visited Corps Headquarters. Casualties Nil. Feeding strength of Divn men 13549: H 4435: / B 3326:	
"	28		Casualties Wounded OR 3. Fighting strength of Divn at noon today attached. Salvage organization in Divn area issued today	Appendix VII Appendix VIII
"	29		Casualties O.R. Killed 1 Wounded 8 missing 1	
"	30		Casualties Killed O.R. 3 Wounded OR 13 missing OR 1	

H.Q.
16 Divn.

R. Greenwood [signature]
Major for
Major Gen.
Commdg 16 Divn

D. D. & L., London, E.C.
(A10266) Wt W5300/P713 750,000 2/18 Sch. 52 Forms/C2118/16.

SECRET. No.6.

NOTES ON ADMINISTRATION IN THE EVENT OF AN ADVANCE.

App. I

1. The following notes are intended as guides only, as the circumstances whihh would attend an Advance cannot be forseen.
The notes are purposely kept as brief as possible, as it is realised that voluminous instructions on such a subject defeat their own object.
The guiding principles are that everything must be sacrificed to keeping communication with the advance troops as free as possible, and supplying them with everything they require.

2. Instructions in more detail have been issued to the following :- C.R.A., C.R.E., Div.Train, Postal Service, D.A.D.O.S., D.P.M., Salvage Officer.
Corps Standing Orders contain much that bears on this subject which should be studied by all concerned.

3. Any suggested alterations or anticipated difficulties should be communicated to these Headquarters as soon as possible.

Section 1. TRENCH MORTAR BATTERIES.

Heavy and Medium Trench Mortar Batteries unless ordered to move with the Division, will collect their Mortars in a convenient dump under a guard, and the personnel will concentrate at MAZINGARBE under the orders of the D.T.M.O., applying for accommodation to Town Major.
They will be administered by the Administrative Commandant, First Corps Area, who will have his Headquarters at NOEUX-LES-MINES.
Supplies will be drawn from a Supply Dump at BARLIN Railhead, unless sufficient rations are available from local reserve ration dumps. Applications for Transport should be made to Town Major.
Any Stokes Batteries ordered to remain behind will be dealt with in a similar manner.

Section 2. SUPPLIES and ORDNANCE.

(i). The Railhead for both will probably be at BARLIN, NOEUX-LES-MINES or LABOURSE.
The Field Supply Depot or dump at BARLIN Railhead will be the stand-by for all those requiring rations which are not provided for otherwise.
(ii). One Ordnance lorry will serve each Brigade, and one the Divisional Troops. Ordnance stores will be distributed with Supplies. More detailed instructions are being issued to D.A.D.O.S.

Section 3. TRAFFIC CIRCUITS.

The circuits for Lorries will be notified direct to M.T.Coys. by Corps and repeated to Divisions.

Section 4. AMMUNITION.

(i). The guiding principle will be that all echelons will be filled up again at the earliest possible moment after they have been drawn upon.

(ii). An advanced ammunition railhead will be opened as soon as the situation admits, and this position will be notified to all concerned.

(iii). Immediately any orders for an advance are issued, the S.A.A. Section of the D.A.C. will automatically come directly under the orders of 16th Division H.Q.

(iv). Directly an advance appears imminent, ammunition dumps will be reduced as far as possible, to minimise the quantity which will be left behind and require collection.

(v). Corps Standing Orders Section 11, paras. 5 and 5a. should be closely studied by all concerned.
Fuller instructions are being issued to Divisional Artillery.

P.T.O.

Section 5. DIVISIONAL RECEPTION CAMP.

This will stand fast until it receives orders to move from the Division.

Section 6. ADMINISTRATIVE COMMANDANT, I CORPS AREA.

This Officer (Col.F.J.W.CAULFEILD) will establish his office at NOEUX-LES-MINES, and will administer all units left behind. Such units will arrange to send an orderly to report at this officer for orders at 11.0 a.m. and 7.0 p.m. daily.

Units without transport will apply to the nearest Town Major for assistance in the form of hired civilian wagons.

Section 7. WATER.

(i) In case of an advance it is quite possible that the enemy may poison drinking water. Neither boiling nor chlorinating has any effect on water containing metallic poisons.

Each Medical Officer with the Battalion is provided with means for testing the water for poisons, and this should be done before any troops are permitted to drink.

(ii) Unit Commanders will be held responsible that the above instruction is rigidly adhered to, and if necessary guards must be mounted, or means of getting at the water removed.

(iii) As soon as the state of the water is ascertained, notice-board will be erected as follows:- "POISONED", "UNFIT FOR DRINKING", "FIT FOR DRINKING" as the case may be. Sentries must be maintained over sources known to have been poisoned so long as troops are in the neighbourhood, or until the source is purified or closed down.

(iv) Should poison be found, the M.O. will forward a sample through the nearest Field Ambulance, stating (a) Source (well, tank, etc). (b) Exact location, (c) poison found by rapid test (d) date and hour of collection) (e) signature and unit of M.O.

(v) It may be taken that it is impossible to poison a stream with a good flow of water.

(vi) In case other tests are inconvenient, a German prisoner if available may be ordered to drink not less than a pint of any suspected water. If no symptons are observed within an hour it may be assumed that the water does not contain any serious quantity of poison.

(vii) Units should provide themselves with long ropes and buckets to draw water from deep wells, as the enemy is likely to destroy the original ropes and buckets.

(viii) The memorandum "Cleansing and disinfection of wells in area taken over from the enemy" issued with G.R.O.2230 of 7-4-17 should be studied.

Section No.8. R.E.STORES.

(i) On an advance, R.E.Stores will be collected at Company and Divisional R.E.Dumps, the former being collected at the latter as opportunity permits.

(ii) C.R.E. will detail one Regimental Sergeant Major and two Sappers at the Divisional Dump, one Sapper at each Company Dump.

The Field Engineer will supply civilian labour and transport if possible to assist at these dumps. Fuller instructions are being handed to C.R.E.

Section 9. DETACHED PERSONNEL.

Every effort will be made to collect all detached personnel whose employment ceases or is suspended in the event of an advance: e.g. N.C.Os and men attached to Tunnelling Companies, as soon as mining ceases, and those employed with First Army Purchase Board.

Section 10. GAS APPLIANCES.

(i) In the event of an advance box respirators will be worn in the XXXX alert position.

(ii) The Divisional Reserve of box respirators will be stored in the first instance and brought forward as opportunity occurs.

(iii) Experience has shown that it is important for units to take forward gas rattles and gongs. If this cannot be done at once it may be done by close co-operation of Divl.Gas Officer and Salvage Officer.

(iv) Strombus Horns will be moved forward as soon as possible after a definite line is established.

Section 11. POSTAL ARRANGEMENTS.

Mails will be delivered with supplies. Detailed instructions are being sent to the W.O. i/c. of the Postal Services.

Section 12. SALVAGE.

(i) The Salvage personnel will remain behind under the general administration of the Area Administrative Commandant.

(ii) For purposes of Salvage the Divisional area will be divided into three sub-areas, the first two of which will correspond with the areas of the Right and Left Brigade in the Line respectively. The third sub-area will embrace the whole of the remainder of the Divisional Area.

(iii) In case of advance, extra personnel will be found as follows :- Each Brigade 1 Officer, each Infantry Battalion 1 trained man for dealing with grenades and explosives left in the trench area. This personnel will report to the Divl.Salvage Officer, SAILLY-LABOURSE immediately an advance takes place, each officer collecting the men from all Battalions of his Brigade.

(iv) In all collection of salvage Light Railways will be utilized as much as possible.

(v) A scheme for the collection of stores will be issued separately.

(vi) The Divisional Salvage Officer will make special efforts to salve and collect all petrol tins for use of troops of the Division. These will be sent forward to Divisional H.Q. as opportunity permits.

Section 13. PROVOST BRANCH.

Traffic Control will be established in the regained territority as soon as possible, under the direction of the D.A.P.M.

Whilst actually on the move Divisions will control traffic with the M.M.P.

Modifications to the scheme of Straggler Posts will be arranged by Corps A.P.M.

D.A.P.M. will make every effort to police places likely to be looted as soon as captured.

More detailed instructions are being forwarded to D.A.P.M., to whom instructions for control of civilians are also being forwarded.

P.T.O.

Section 14. BOOBY TRAPS & ENEMY RUSES.

All troops should be warned against the above, which are likely to be adopted on a large scale.

Captured dug-outs should not be entered until they have been inspected by the special parties referred to in the instructions on the subject from "G" Branch.

Gas booby traps are likely to be used in dug-outs, and special attention should be paid to roads when first passed over, with a view to discovering probable mines designed to explode when weights are passed over them.

Freshly turned earth on or near a road should be the subject of special investigation. Such mines are easy to remove and are inocuous so long as no pressure is applied to the top.

Section 15. RESPONSIBILITY FOR THE ISSUE OF THESE NOTES TO UNITS.

The responsibility of XXXXXX seeing that all units concerned are made acquainted with any portion of these notes which affect them rests with the formations or departments administering them.

Lieut-Colonel,
A.A. & Q.M.G., 16th Division.

H.Q. 16th Divn.
1st Sept. 1918.

Distribution :-

Div.Arty.	12	Copies
S.A.A. S.D. .C.	1	"
47th Inf.Bde.	12	"
48th Inf.Bde.	12	"
49th Inf.Bde.	12	"
11th Hants.	8	"
C.R.E.	7	"
M.G.Bn.	6	"
Sig.Coy.	8	"
Div.Train.	8	"
A.D.M.S.	7	"
M.T.Coy.	3	"
D.A.D.V.S.	2	"
D.A.D.O.S.	1	"
A.P.M.	1	"
Posts.	1	"
French Mission	1	"
Salvage Officer	1	"
Div.Gas Offr.	1	"
Employmt.Coy.	1	"
Camp Comdt.	1	"
Snr.Chap.D.C.G.	1	"
Snr.Chap. P.C.	1	"
"G" (for infmn)	2	

APPENDIX II

S E C R E T.

16TH DIVISION ADMINISTRATIVE INSTRUCTIONS, NO.7.

1. 16th Divisional Artillery is rejoining the 16th Division and will be administered by them for all purposes from noon 7th instant.

2. 16th Divl.Artillery is relieving 84th and 147th Army Brigades R.F.A. in the line and these Brigades will come under the Command of XXII Corps at noon on the 9th instant after relief.

3. 16th Divl.Artillery with the Sections M.T.Company attached thereto and 142nd Coy. A.S.C. will be rationed for consumption 9th instant and onwards by 16th Division. Strength 2,060 ALL RANKS, 1720 ANIMALS.

4. 84th and 147th Army Brigades R.F.A. will be rationed by XXII Corps for consumption 11th instant and onwards.

5. The Sections of 16th M.T.Coy. on arrival will park at Q.2.d. (Sheet 44.B.)

6 Railhead for 16.D.A. BARLIN from 6th (inc)

W.B. Rennie

H.Q. 16th Division,
5th Sept. 1918.

Lieut-Colonel,
A.A. & Q.M.G., 16th Division.

Distribution :-

"G".
16th Div.Art. (3)
Div.Signal Coy.
47th Inf.Bde.
48th Inf.Bde.
49th Inf.Bde.
Div.Train (2).
M.T.Coy.
A.D.M.S.
D.A.D.V.S.
D.A.D.O.S.
D.A.P.M.
Div.Reception Camp.
Postal Services.
French Mission.
D.G.O.
217th Employment Coy.
S.C.F., D.C.G's Dept.
S.C.F., P.C's Dept.
Area Comdt, RUITZ.
Area Comdt, BARLIN.
O.C., Railhead Depot.

APPENDIX III A.22/1.

First Army Pro Forma No. 3.

16th. DIVISION.

Strength Return made up to 12 noon Saturday, 7th. September. 1918.

UNIT.	A. Strength Return excluding attached.		B. Not present with the unit and not at the disposal of C.O. (included in Column A).		A. *minus* B. Available Fighting Strength (including personnel of Battalion Transport and Quartermaster's Stores).	
	Officers.	O.R.	Officers.	O.R.	Officers.	O.R.
47th. INFANTRY BRIGADE.						
14th. Leicester Regt	40	876	9	70	31	806
18th. Welsh Regt.	38	868	14	104	24	764
9th. R. Highlanders.	38	753	10	82	28	671
TOTAL.	116	2497	33	256	83	2241
48TH. INFANTRY BRIGADE.						
22nd. N'land Fus.	36	799	18	155	28	744
18th. Scottish Rif:	38	722	16	76	32	646
5th. R. Irish Fus.	42	932	16	315	26	617
TOTAL.	116	2453	30	446	86	2007
49TH. INFANTRY BRIGADE.						
6th. Somerset L.I.	44	818	13	85	31	733
18th. Gloucester Regt	40	705	17	63	23	642
34th. London Regt.	36	744	10	99	26	645
TOTAL.	120	2267	40	247	80	2020
11th. Hants Bn. (P)	41	705	4	42	37	663
GRAND TOTAL.	393	7922	107	991	286	6931
16TH. MACHINE GUN BN.	48	879	-	8	48	871
TOTALS ...						

R.N. Greenwood MAJOR,
D.A.A.G. 16th DIVISION.
Major General.
Commanding 16th. Division.

Headquarters.
16th. Division.
7th. September. 1918.

PRINTED IN FRANCE BY ARMY PRINTING AND STATIONERY SERVICES. PRESS A—4/18—6095D—3,000.

First Army Pro Forma No. 3—*continued.*

DETAILS OF OFFICERS "TAKEN ON" OR "STRUCK OFF" STRENGTH.

UNIT.	Rank.	Name.	Initials.	Remarks.
14th.Leic.Regt.	2/Lt.	CREW.	W.	Str.Off. Posted to 47th.L.T.M.B. A.G. G.H.Q. A.F./2158/5613(o) 28.8.18.
-do-	2/Lt.	WOOD.	G.	Posted to 11th.Hants.
9th.B.Watch.	2/Lt.	BELFORD.	C.R.	Killed in action.2.9.18
9th.B.Watch.	Lieut.	LAUDER.	J.N.	Joined 1.9.18.
22nd.N'land Fus.	2/Lt.	HODGE.	M.B.	Str.Off.Strength Med.Board ordered.
6th.Somerset L.I.	Capt.	KING.X.	E.	Transferred to England 23.8.18.
18th.Glos.Regt.	2/Lt.	ELLIS.	A.R.	Str.Off Strength. Probationer for Ind. Army.
34th.London Regt.	2/Lt.	EAST.	F.W.	To England.
	2/Lt.	BOND.	W.H.	Missing.
11th.Hants Bn.(P)	2/Lt.	WOOD.	G.	Joined from 14th. Leic.Regt.3.9.18

Appx IV

SECRET.

16TH DIVISION.

WEEKLY DISPOSITION REPORT No. 2.

Disposition of Units at 6 a.m. MONDAY, 9th SEPTEMBER 1918.

Reference Sheets 44A and 44B, 1/40,000, and LENS 11, 1/100,000.

Serial No.	Unit.	Location of H.Q.
1.	H.Q. 16th Divn.	K.25.c.4.2.
2.	16th Div. Arty.	K.25.c.4.2.
3.	177th Bde. R.F.A.	HOHENZOLLERN GROUP, CHATEAU DES PRES. F.27.d.20.65.
4.	180th Bde. R.F.A.	CAMBRIN GROUP. FOSSE No. 9, ANNEQUIN. F.29.c.3.3.
5.	16th D.A.C.	MAISNIL LES RUITZ. J.36.b.65.20.
6.	D.T.M.O.	CHATEAU DES PRES. F.27.d.20.65.
7.	X/16 T.M.B.	A.26.a.45.20.
8.	Y/16 T.M.B.	G.8.d.95.75.
9.	16th Div. Engrs.	K.25.c.4.2.
10.	155th Fd. Coy. R.E.	ANNEQUIN. F.23.d.9.2.
11.	156th do	SAILLY LABOURSE. L.3.a.2.8.
12.	157th do	ANNEQUIN. F.23.d. central.
13.	16th Div. Sig. Coy.	K.25.c.4.2.
14.	47th Inf. Bde.	Line - Right Section. CHATEAU DES PRES. F.27.d.20.65.
15.	14th Leic. Regt.	Line - Right Front. G.8.b.05.95.
16.	18th Welsh Regt.	Line - Left Front. A.25.d.75.25.
17.	9th Black Watch. (attd. 48th Inf. Bde.)	NOEUX-LES-MINES. K.24.b.9.9.
18.	47th T.M. Battery.	Line - G.3.b.0.2.
19.	48th Inf. Bde.	Reserve - SAILLY LABOURSE L.3.a.5.5.
20.	22nd North'd Fus. (att'd. 49th Inf. Bde)	Support (Left Section). A.21.c.1.7.
21.	18th Sco. Rif(" 47th Inf. Bde)	Support (Right Section) ANNEQUIN, FOSSE No.9. L.5.b.1.9.
22.	5th R. Ir. Fus.	NOEUX-LES-MINES. K.24.b.9.9.
23.	48th T.M. Battery.	NOEUX-LES-MINES. K.18.b.5.0.
24.	49th Inf. Bde.	Line - Left Section. ANNEQUIN, FOSSE No. 9. " " F.29.c.3.3.
25.	6th Som. L.I.	Line - Right Front. A.20.d.6.4.

P.T.O.

Serial No.	Unit.	Location of H.Q.
26.	16th Glouc. Regt.	Line - Left Front. A.21.b.05.30.
27.	34th London Regt. (K.R.R.C.) (attd. 48th Inf.Bde.)	CAMBRIN. A.19.d.5.2.
28.	49th T.M. Battery.	Line. A.26.b.5.6.
29.	11th Hants Regt. (P).	SAILLY LABOURSE. L.3.b.4.5.
30.	<u>16th Bn. M.G.C.</u>	BARLIN. K.33.b.05.25.
31.	"A" Coy.	" K.33.b.85.20.
32.	"B" "	" K.33.a.95.15.
33.	"C" "	Line - Left Front. ANNEQUIN, FOSSE No. 9. F.29.c.9.0.
34.	"D" "	Line - Right Front. SAILLY LABOURSE. F.27.d.1.0.
35.	<u>16th Div. Train.</u>	MAISNIL-LES-RUITZ. J.36.c.8.8.
36.	142nd Coy. A.S.C.	" " " J.36.a.9.4.
37.	143rd do	BARLIN. FOSSE No.7. J.31.c.
38.	144th do	MAISNIL-LES-RUITZ. J.36.b.2.5.
39.	145th do	" " " J.36.b.5.5.
40.	16th Div. M.T. Coy.	BARLIN, FOSSE No.9. Q.2.d.
41.	<u>A.D.M.S.</u>	K.25.c.4.2.
42.	111th Fd. Amb.	BARLIN, K.33.a.6.3.
43.	112th do	RUITZ, K.20.a.5.5.
44.	113th do	" "
45.	<u>D.A.D.V.S.</u>	K.25.c.4.2.
46.	47th Mob. Vet. Sec.	BARLIN, K.32.b.3.8.
47.	D.A.D.O.S.	BARLIN, K.33.a.5.8.
48.	D.A.P.M.	K.25.c.4.2.
49.	Camp Commandant,	do
50.	Div. Gas Officer,	do
51.	S.C.F., D.C.G's. Dept.	do
52.	S.C.F. P.C's. Dept.	BARLIN, K.27.d.0.1.
53.	16th Div. Salvage Coy.	SAILLY LABOURSE, L.3.b.3.8.
54.	217th Employment Coy.	BARLIN, K.27.c.2.1.
55.	Bath's Officer.	" "
56.	Burial Officer.	" "
57.	Canteen Officer.	" "
58.	Div. Reception Camp.	BOIS D'OLHAIN, Q.8. central.
59.	Transport Lines, 47th Inf. Bde.	K.31.d.8.2.
60.	" 48th Inf. Bde.	K.18.b.
61.	" 49th Inf. Bde.	K.18.b.9.8.
62.	" 11th Hants (P).	K.27.c.7.1.
63.	" 16th Bn. M.G.C.	K.33.b.3.4.

<u>Units affiliated to 16th Division.</u>

Serial No.	Unit.	Location of H.Q.
64.	18th Bde. R.G.A.	E.29.c.7.0.
65.	218th Siege Batty. (6 - 6" Hows.).	F.19.d.73.12.
66.	236th Siege Batty. (4 - 6" Hows.).	F.21.c.5.5.
67.	170th Tunnelling Coy. R.E.	MAISNIL-LES-RUITZ, J.36.b.8.8.

(Changes in position of Units in the line are notified as they occur on. 16th Div. Form G.1.)

[signature] Lt
for Lieut.Colonel,
General Staff 16th Division.

8th Sept., 1918.

APPENDIX V

	UNIT OR FORMATION	MOVE TO	DATE	DETAILS OF BILLETS.
(1).	Div.H.Q., Div.Sigs, Arty.H.Q. D.A.P.M. Postal Services, Div.Gas Offr.	DROUVIN CHATEAU.	23-9-18.	Div.Arty. take over exactly the same billets occupied by 55th Div.Arty. All billets detailed by Camp Commandant, 16th Divn.
(2).	A.D.M.S, C.R.E., D.A.D.V.S. Traffic Offr. Mob.Vet.Sect. French Mission, S.C.F.,D.C.G's Dept. D.A.P.M.Horse Lines & Billets	DROUVIN VILLAGE	23-9-18.	Billets same as those occupied by 55th Division.
(3)	D.A.D.O.S., O.C.Emp.Coy. Burials Offr. Baths Offr. S.C.F.,P.C's Dept. Div,Train, 4 Coys.of Train, Canteen Offr. & Theatre.	HOUCHIN.	Div.Train 22-9-18 Remainder 23-9-18.	O.C.Train has reconnoitred all billets to be occupied by him. O.C. Emplmt. Coy. has reconnoitred all remaining billets.
(4)	D.A.C.	HAILLICOURT.	22-9-18	Billets have been reconnoitred by D.A.C.
(5)	Artillery Horse Lines.	HOUCHIN & DROUVIN.	Under orders of C.R.A.	All horse lines in HOUCHIN except those occupied by Div.Train. To include Infy.Horse Lines previously occupied by 55th Divn. about K.16.a.3.9. Horse lines in DROUVIN previously occupied by 55th Div.Arty.
(6)	Reception Camp.	HOUCHIN	Date to be notified later.	
(7)	16th M.T.Coy.	Remains.		
(8)	Field Coy.Transport.	DROUVIN PARK.	Under orders of C.R.E.	All Standings previously occupied by Field Coys. 55th Divn. N. of Chateau Drive.
(9).	Salvage Officer	Remains.		

SECRET.

16th Div. No.A980/1.

With reference to 16th Div.Order No.250 dated 20-9-18, paragraph 3.

The attached table shows the necessary adjustments in the administrative area and the moves entailed.

R.N. Greenwood

H.Q.16th Divn.
HF.

Major,
A/A.A.& Q.M.G. 16th Division.

DISTRIBUTION :- G.O.C.
16th Div.Art.
16th Div.Engrs.
16th Div.Sig.Co.
47th Inf.Bde.
48th Inf.Bde.
49th Inf.Bde.
11th Hants.(P).
16th M.G.Bn.
A.D.M.S.
"G".
16th Div.Train.
16th M.T.Coy.
D.A.P.M.
D.A.D.V.S.
D.A.D.O.S.
D.G.O.
Camp Comdt.
O.C., 217th Emp.Coy.
Posts.
French Mission.
D.A.C. (S.A.A.Sect.)
Salvage Officer.
Canteen Officer,
Baths Officer.
Reception Camp.
S.C.F., D.C.G's Dept.
S.C.F., P.C's Dept.
Town Major, RUITZ,
" " BARLIN
" " NOEUX-LES-MINES,
" " VAUDRICOURT.
" " MAISNIL-LES-RUITZ.

Appendix VI

SECRET.

ADMINISTRATIVE INSTRUCTION NO. 8.

Administrative Instruction No. 2 dated 17.8.1918 is cancelled, and the following should be substituted:-

SUPPLIES.

Railhead - BARLIN.

Reloading is carried out by Train Wagons.

The usual system of refilling is for the Train Wagons to draw from the Broad Guage and deliver to the Transport Lines of Units: from then they are delivered by First Line Transport to the Light Railway fon the Units in the line. In the case of the Reserve Brigade supplies are delivered direct by motor lorries.

Refilling Points:-

Line Inf.Bde. Support " Divl.Troops.	HOUCHIN. K.15.b.5.5.
Res. Inf.Bde.	MARLES LES MINES.

Railhead for personnel is FOUQUIERES.
Fuel Dump - BARLIN.

RESERVE RATIONS AND WATER.

(a)	Inf. Bde. in the Line.	-	5100 rations.
(b)	Support Inf.Bde.	-	4450 "

WATER.

Each Infantry Bde. in the Line - 500 gallons.

The above is calculated on a basis of 1 day's supply per man.

LOCALITIES.

CAMBRIN - 250 galls. in petrol cans, plus 1000 galls in tanks.
ANNEQUIN.-200 galls. -do- 1000 galls -do-

S.A.A. & GRENADES.

Corps Dump is at HESDIGNEUL.

Divisional Dump is at WILLOW DUMP.

S.A.A., Grenades, etc., are sent up from Divisional Dump by Light Railway to

Brigade in the Line.
No. 1 HARLEY STREET. - A.20.d.35.15.
No. 2 Chemist's Shop, CAMBRIN. - A.19.d.8.2.

All requirements will be submitted to Divisional Headquarters, who will order the ammunition to be delivered to Brigade Dumps by the Advanced Echelon of D.A.C. which is being established at WILLOW DUMP.

The Light Railway will be used as far as possible.

SUPPLY OF R.E. STORES.

No.	Name.	Location.	Map Ref.	On authority of.
1	Corps Yard.	MINX.	K.5.b. central.	C.R.Es
2.	Main Divl. Dump.	SAILLY LABOURSE.	L.3.b.4.9.	-do-

P. T. O.

SALVAGE CORPS.

Area No.	Area.	Responsibility for clearing.
A. Brigade in the Line, Sector.	East of line running along HARLEY STREET A.20.d.2.5. to A.26.b.central, and then along road through A.26.b. & c. to G.2.d.5.2.	Bde in line.
B. Divl. Area.	West of the above line.	Divl.Sal.Coy.

LIGHT RAILWAYS.

Light Railways are used for transport of supplies and for reliefs. Trains for personnel are run as far as ANNEQUIN. Troops usually entrain and detrain at BARLIN and LABOURSE, but other stations can be utilized as required.

Application for trucks is made to C.L.R.O. Office at MINX, K.6.

TRENCH TRAMWAYS.

There is a system of Trench Tramways forward of CAMBRIN. R.T.O. at this point controls traffic and rolling stock on this system.

REINFORCEMENTS.

Reinforcements (except Artillery) are sent to FOUQUIERES.

They proceed by march route to the Divisional Reception Camp, HOUCHIN.

Transport for Officers' Kits and men's packs is provided daily.

Reinforcements are retained at the Divisional Reception Camp untill they have passed the necessary test in anti-gas precautions, when they are despatched to their units.

Artillery Reinforcements are sent from the First Army Artillery Reinforcement Camp according to the requirements of the Divisional Artillery under arrangements made by I Corps.

BATHS.

DROUVIN. K.4.b.3.4.
DROUVIN CHATEAU.
VERQUIN.K.4.b.9.9.
HOUCHIN. K.10.c.9.2.
VAUDRICOURT. K.4.b.2.5.
Bath at K.19.c.6.8. (just outside RUITZ).

Apply to Divisional Bath Officer for all Baths. Office at HOUCHIN.

LAUNDRIES.

Clothing is washed under Army arrangements.

SUPPLY OF CLEAN CLOTHING.

Corps Clean Clothing Depot. RUITZ.
Divl. -do- D.A.D.O.S. Stores, HOUCHIN.

O.C. Divisional Baths draws clean clothes from RUITZ and arranges for the delivery of the clothing to the Divisional Clean Clothing Store and Bath

H.Q. 16th Division.
26th September 1918.
FCR.

Major.
A/A.A. & Q.M.G. 16th Division.

D I S T R I B U T I O N.

I Corps.	Divl. Arty.	16th Div. Engrs.	16th Div.Sig.Co.R.E.
47th Inf.Bde.	48th Inf.Bde.	49th Inf.Bde.	11th Hants Regt.
16th M.G.B.	16th Div.Trn.	16th Div.M.T.Coy.	Div.Employ.Co.
Gen.Staff.	A.D.M.S.	D.A.D.O.S.	D.A.D.V.S.
D.A.P.M.	Camp Comdt.	Div.Sal.Officer.	

abt VII

16th **DIVISION.**

STRENGTH RETURN MADE UP TO 12 NOON SATURDAY, 28th September 1918 ... 21-9-..., 1919

UNIT.	(i.) Fighting strength for previous week, compiled in accordance with A.G.'s instructions.		(ii.) Increase during week, due to drafts, etc., taken on strength of unit.		(iii.) Totals from (i.) and (ii.).		(iv.) Decrease during week—Casualties, etc., deducted from strength of unit.		"A." Fighting strength compiled in accordance with A.G.'s instructions.		"B." Details. (Included in "A.").		REMARKS. [Brief notes regarding (ii.), (iv.), "B," etc.]	
	Officers.	O.R.	Officers.	O.R.	Officers.	O.R.	Officers.	O.R.	Officers	O.R.	Officers.	O.R.		
47th INFANTRY BRIGADE.													A minus B Offrs.	O.R.
14th Leicesters	40	863	-	3	40	866	-	10	40	856	6	53	34	803
18th Welsh.	34	795	3	10	37	805	-	33	37	772	7	53	30	719
9th Royal Highlanders.	33	539	1	15	34	554	1	31	33	523	9	40	24	483
TOTAL.	107	2197	4	28	111	2225	1	74	110	2151	22	146	88	2005
48th INFANTRY BRIGADE.														
22nd North'd Fus.	34	649	-	77	34	726	-	13	34	713	9	49	25	664
18th Scottish Rifles.	30	471	6	31	36	502	-	21	36	481	4	51	32	430
5th Royal Irish Rifles.	41	920	-	14	41	934	-	11	41	923	8	188	33	735
TOTAL.	105	2040	6	122	111	2162	-	45	111	2117	21	288	90	1829
47th INFANTRY BRIGADE.														
6th Somerset Light Inf.	42	760	-	7	42	767	-	19	42	748	10	75	32	673
18th Gloucesters	36	585	-	128	36	713	1	17	36	696	10	48	26	648
34th London Regt.	37	537	-	129	37	666	3	4	34	662	11	62	23	600
TOTAL.	115	1882	-	265	115	2146	4	40	111	2106	31	185	81	1921
11th Hampshire Regt.	41	697	5	5	46	702	-	11	46	691	8	42	38	649
GRAND TOTAL:-	368	6816	15	383	419	7235	5	170	378	7065	82	661	296	6404
TOTALS														
16th Machine Gun Bn.	48	874	-	13	48	697	1	18	47	876	2	18	45	837

ARMY PRINTING AND STATIONERY SERVICES. B. 528. 5000. 9/17.

CHANGES IN NOMINAL ROLLS OF OFFICERS.

Unit	Joined.	Struck Off	Cause.
9th Royal High'rs	Lieut J CALLA		Reinforcement.
		2/Lt G.L.S.Patullo	Wounded
18th Welsh	2/Lt H Stevens 2/Lt L.M.Watts 2/Lt C Wyatt.		Reinforcements
18th Scottish R.	2/Lt D.T. Forbes 2/Lt R.L. Paul 2/Lt J Ratcliffe 2/Lt J.F.C.Cassels 2/Lt H.L.M.Frew 2/Lt M Fulton		Reinforcements
18th Gloucesters		2/Lt G.E.Sankey	Evac. to Eng.
34th London Regt,		Capt. R.G. Race	Wounded
		2/Lt A Hood	Wd (gas) 16-0-18
		2/Lt Robertson	"B iii" Grade.
11th Hants Regt. (P)	Lieut.W.A. Weller 2/Lt B.S.Davies 2/Lt H.J.Pafford 2/Lt A.J.Mallard 2/Lt G.S. Roper		Reinforcements
16th M.G.Bn.		Major B.M. Puckle D.S.O.	Apptd to command 57th M.G. Bn.

Appx VIII

16th Div.No.Q.611/8.

SALVAGE ORGANISATION IN 16TH DIVISIONAL AREA.

PART I - GENERAL.

1. Salvage Administration will be in accordance with Salvage Pamphlet S.S.640 and amendments thereto.

2. Schemes for Salvage will be prepared by H.Q. of Brigades in the Line, and by the Divisional Salvage Officer.

3. AREAS.

Area No.	Area.	Responsibility for Clearing.
A. Brigade in the Line.	East of this Line. - HARLEY STREET, A.20.d.2.5., A.26.b.central, and along road thro' A.26.b. and d, G.2.b. and d.	Brigade in Line.
B. Div.Sector.	West of above Line.	Divl.Salvage Coy.

4. MAIN SALVAGE DUMPS.

Location.	Cleared by	Cleared to
CAMBRIN. A.20.c.4.3.	Divl.Salvage Coy.	Main Receiving Station. LABOURSE, L.2.c.cent. by Ration Trucks labelled "DADOS SPUR".
SAILLY LABOURSE. L.3.d.8.9.	Divl.Salvage Coy.	Main Receiving Station, LABOURSE.

5. All Units are responsible for the collection of Salvage in and around their Billets and Wagon Lines, and for sending it to the nearest Salvage Dump or Receiving Station.

6. Salvage returned by Light Railway will be clearly labelled to show destination (Salvage Receiving Station "DADOS SPUR") and name of Unit or Formation consigning it.

7. All salved articles and material will then be sent from LABOURSE to Corps Main Salvage Dump with the following exceptions:-

(1) R.E.material in Forward Areas handed over to nearest R.E.Dump.
(2) Ammunition empties (except S.A.A.) returned to Ammunition Railhead.
(3) Live S.A.A., cleaned , packed and returned to D.A.C.
(4) Gun ammunition to Divl.Ammunition Refilling Point, or D.A.C.
(5) Salved bombs and grenades to be dedetonated, cleaned, packed and handed over to D.A.C.
Doubtful grenades retained for inspection by Corps Ammunition Officer.

P. T. O.

8. RECOVERY OF LEAD FROM LEAD FOIL LININGS OF TEA BOXES.

The S.S.O. will arrange for all Lead Foil to be sent to Corps Main Salvage Dump, BARLIN, informing Divisional Salvage Officer.

9. EMPTY OIL DRUMS, PETROLEUM CASES, SACKS, etc. will be returned to Refilling Points.

10. DRIPPING.

Dealt with as per instructions in I Corps Area Memorandum, and particulars to be included in weekly return rendered by Salvage Officer.

11. WASTE PAPER.

Waste paper will be returned to Refilling Points, and despatched to Baling Press, as per instructions in I Corps Area Orders, Section 8, para.13.

12. HORSE HAIR.

Hair from the tails and manes of horses and mules is urgently required and will be handed in as Salvage.

13. EMPTY BOTTLES.

All Units, including Officers's Messes, will collect their empty bottles and deliver them to the nearest Salvage Dump or Receiving Station.

14. The whole system of salvage from the forward area hinges on the return of salvage by ration parties, empty transport, Light Railway Trucks, etc. All parties and individuals should be encouraged to carry back salvage when returning from forward areas.

15. Where ammunition and other articles have been specially dumped notices "NOT TO BE SALVED" are to be put up.

16. Weekly Return of Salvage, etc., which the Divisional Salvage Officer is called upon to render to Staff Captain, Salvage, I Corps, will be repeated to Divisional Headquarters.

28-9-18.

DIVISIONAL SALVAGE COMPANY ADMINISTRATION.

1. AREA OF BRIGADE IN THE LINE. The Brigade will be responsible for clearing its own area and for sending Salvage to Receiving Station, DADOS SPUR by Light Railway or by dumping it at CAMBRIN Salvage Dump. Divisional Salvage Officer will keep in touch with Brigades in this matter.

Salvage must not be allowed to accumulate at the Dump at CAMBRIN.

The Dump at SAILLY LABOURSE, will be used by each Brigade both for dumping salvage from that locality, and salvage carried back by individuals returning from the Forward Area. The Divisional Salvage Officer will be responsible for clearing this dump.

2. DIVISIONAL AREA. The Divisional Salvage Company will be responsible for clearing all the ground west of the Area mentioned in para 1.

A sketch map is attached explaining the method of working the Area.

3. METHOD OF OPERATING. Salvage Company personnel will be located at LABOURSE and NOEUX-LES-MINES, Salvage Receiving Stations, and CAMBRIN Salvage Dump.

Areas will be reconnoitred by O.C. Salvage Coy, and he will keep in touch with A.Cs., T.Ms., and Units regarding the location of any salvage. Work of collecting will be directed by O.C. Salvage Company.

One Salvage Company man will accompany all Transport used by the Salvage Company, for the purpose of loading and unloading, and picking up any Salvage that may lie along the roads.

The following will not be collected by the Salvage Company, but their position and quantity will be reported, to the formations concerned who will issue necessary orders:-

"Dud" Shell and Gas Cylinders.

A trained bomber will be permanently attached to the Salvage Company to deal with bombs etc.

4. RECOVERY OF SOLDER AND EMPTY BULLY BEEF TINS.

All salved empty Bully Beef Tins will be treated at the Salvage Receiving Stations, LABOURSE, where a kiln is in operation for this purpose.

Solder kilns are situated at the following places in the area:-

LABOURSE....................	)L.2.c.(central) Salvage Receiving Statio)F.27.c.5.2.
NOEUX-LES-MINES..............	K.18.b.8.5.
HOUCHIN......................	Town Majors Dump.
DROUVIN......................	-do-
VAUDRICOURT..................	-do-
VERQUIGNEUL..................	-do-

Units will deliver all empty Bully Beef Tins, Sliced Bacon Tins, Maconnackie Tins, Preserved Fish Tins to the nearest kiln as above indicated.

5. SCRAP METALS.

Scrap Metals of all sorts are now required at the Base, and will be collected and delivered to the nearest Salvage Receiving Station.

P. T. O.

6. SHIPMENT OF SALVAGE.

(a) All Salved Material from the Forward Area Dumps will be shipped by Light Railway every day by returning Ration and Supply Trucks, to the Main Divisional Receiving Station at LABOURSE, where the various materials will be checked, sorted and prepared, for shipment by Light Railway to Corps Main Salvage Dump, MARLES.

(b) All Town Majors Dumps, Canteens, Y.M.C.As in the Area will be visited once each week, and all Salvage collected, will be brought in by horse transport to either LABOURSE or ~~MARLES~~ NOEUX LES MINES, Divisional Receiving Stations according to locality. Transport will be arranged by O.C. Divl. Salvage Coy with H.Q. 16th Division.

7. The strength of the 16th Divisional Salvage Company is 1 Officer, and 50 other ranks.

8. The Officer Commanding 16th Divl. Salvage Company is Lieut. A.de R.S. REDMOND, Royal Dublin Fusiliers.

9. Headquarters, 16th Divl. Salvage Company is at SAILLY LABOURSE. Map Reference Sheet 44 B $\frac{1}{40,000}$ Sq. L.3.b.3.8.

28-9-18.

S K E T C H   M A P

illustrating

S A L V A G E   O R G A N I S A T I O N   I N   16TH   D I V L.   A R E A.

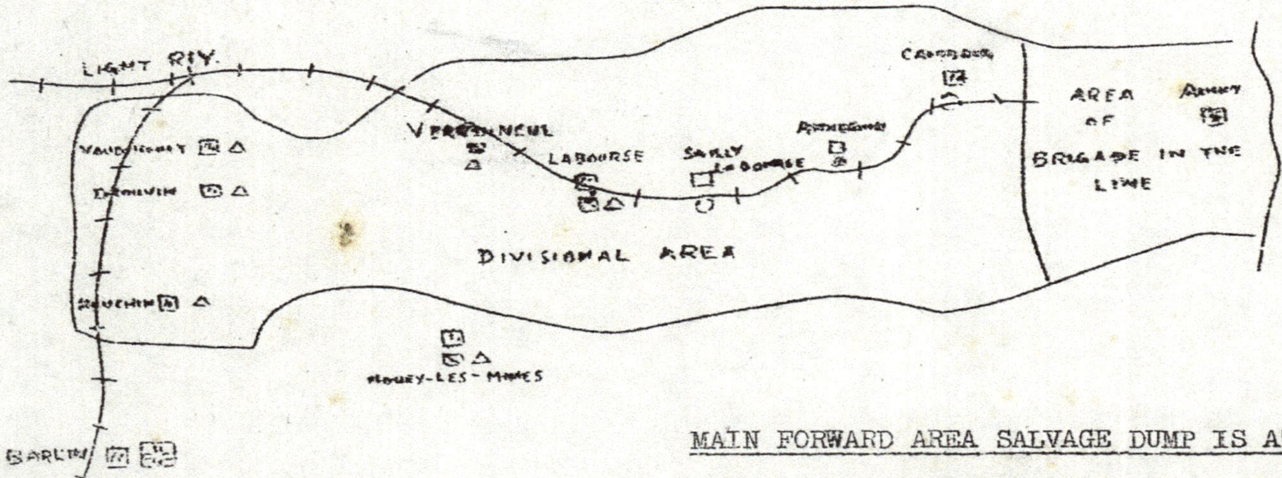

MAIN FORWARD AREA SALVAGE DUMP IS AT CAMBRIN.

MAIN DIVL. SALVAGE RECG. STATION IS AT LABCURSE.

I N D E X.

- ▣ CORPS MAIN SALVAGE DUMP.
- ☒ DIVL. SALVAGE RECG. STATIONS.
- ○ DIVL. SALVAGE DUMPS.
- △ TOWN MAJORS' SALVAGE DUMPS.

21

Instructions regarding War Diaries and Intelligence Summaries are contained in F. S. Regs., Part II. and the Staff Manual respectively. Title pages will be prepared in manuscript.

WAR DIARY
or
~~INTELLIGENCE SUMMARY.~~
(Erase heading not required.)

16 Division A & Q

Army Form C. 2118.

OCTOBER'

Vol 35

Place	Date	Hour	Summary of Events and Information	Remarks and references to Appendices
DROUVIN	1		Feeding Strength 14321. Casualties O R Killed 2 Wounded 11 Missing 1.	
	2.		Casualties O R Wounded 3 Enemy commenced retirement followed up by 48 Infy Bde. Administrative arrangements gone into & arrangements made for tracks tho' improved & pack animals fully used. Arrangements for collection of stores in case of an advance published.	Appendix I
	3		Casualties O R Killed 1 Wounded 8 Missing 1	
	4		Casualties Wounded Officers 3 O R 9. Ammunition dumps made forward in DOUVRIN. Administrative units all made arrangements for forward move.	

D. D. & L., London, E.C.
(A10266) Wt W5300/P713 750,000 2/18 Sch. 52 Forms/C2118/16.

Army Form C. 2118.

WAR DIARY
or
~~INTELLIGENCE SUMMARY.~~
(Erase heading not required.)

Instructions regarding War Diaries and Intelligence Summaries are contained in F. S. Regs., Part II. and the Staff Manual respectively. Title pages will be prepared in manuscript.

Place	Date	Hour	Summary of Events and Information	Remarks and references to Appendices
DROUVIN.	5		Casualties Wounded O.R. 9. Killed O.R. 4.	
	6		Casualties. Killed. Officers 1 O.R. 2 Wounded O.R. 8.	
CHATEAU DES PRES.	7		Casualties. Wounded O.R. 7. HQ. 16 Divn. moved to CHATEAU DES PRES. (SAILLY LABOURSE)	
	8		Fighting Strength 13400. Casualties. Wounded. Officers. 5. O.R. 4.	
	9		Casualties. Killed. Officers. 1. O.R. 1 Wounded. O.R. 8.	
	10		Casualties. Killed O.R. 2. Wounded. O.R. 6.	
	11		Casualties. Wounded. O.R. 1.	
	12.		Casualties. Wounded. O.R. 3. Fighting Strength. attached.	Appendix II

D. D. & L., London, E.C.
(A10266) Wt W5300/P713 750,000 2/18 Sch. 52 Forms/C2118/16.

Army Form C. 2118.

Instructions regarding War Diaries and Intelligence Summaries are contained in F. S. Regs., Part II. and the Staff Manual respectively. Title pages will be prepared in manuscript.

WAR DIARY

or

~~INTELLIGENCE SUMMARY.~~

(Erase heading not required.)

Place	Date	Hour	Summary of Events and Information	Remarks and references to Appendices
CHATEAU DES PRES	13		Casualties. Wounded O.R. 1.	
	14		Casualties. Killed. Officers 1. O.R 3. Wounded O.R. 13.	
	15		Casualties. Killed. Officers 1. Wounded O.R. 2. Feeding strength. 13191.	
	16		Casualties, ~~Nil~~. Wounded O.R. 3.	
BILLY	17.		Casualties. Wounded O.R. ~~7~~ 4. HQ 16 Divn moved to BILLY. Arrangements made for bridging HAUTE DEULE Canal.	
	18.		Casualties. Killed. O.R. 1. Wounded O.R. 11. HQ 16 Divn moved to PHALEMPIN on 19th	
PHALEMPIN	19.			
	20 21		Casualties. Killed. O.R. 3. Wounded. Officers 1. O.R. 20. HQ 16 Divn moved to TEMPLEUVE on 22nd	
TEMPLEUVE	22		Feeding Strength. 13284	

D. D. & L., London, E.C.
(A10266) Wt W5300/P713 750,000 2/18 Sch. 52 Forms/C2118/16.

Instructions regarding War Diaries and Intelligence Summaries are contained in F. S. Regs., Part II. and the Staff Manual respectively. Title pages will be prepared in manuscript.

WAR DIARY
or
~~INTELLIGENCE SUMMARY.~~
(Erase heading not required.)

Army Form C. 2118.

Place	Date	Hour	Summary of Events and Information	Remarks and references to Appendices
TEMPLEUVE	23		Casualties Wounded O.R. 5.	
	24		Casualties. Wounded Officers. 1. O.R. 8.	
	25		Casualties. Killed. O.R. 1 Wounded O.R. 10. Supply Railhead moved forward to DON.	
	26		Casualties. Killed. O.R. 2. Wounded O.R. 18. Fighting strength attached.	Appendix III
	27		Casualties. Wounded O.R. 5.	
	28		Casualties. Wounded O.R. 48. Supply Railhead moved forward to MARQUILLIES.	
	29		Casualties. Killed O.R. 1. Wounded Officers. 1. O.R. 5. Feeding strength. 12701.	
	30.		Casualties. Wounded O.R. 18. Missing O.R. 2. (believed prisoners) Arrangements made for supplies to be delivered from Railhead to TEMPLEUVE by Light Railway.	
	31.		Casualties Wounded O.R. 7.	

R.N. Greenwood Major for
Major General
Commdg. 16 Divn

D. D. & L., London, E.C.
(A10266) Wt W5300/P713 750,000 2/18 Sch. 52 Forms/C2118/16.

APPENDIX I

S E C R E T.   16TH DIVISION.   16th Div.Q.M.25.

ARRANGEMENTS FOR THE COLLECTION OF STORES IN EVENT OF AN ADVANCE.

1. The Divisional Salvage Officer will be in charge of the arrangements for the collection of Stores.
He will have the personnel set forth in Appendix A to carry out the work, in addition to the Divisional Salvage Company.
His Headquarters will be situated at SAILLY LABOURSE.

2. (a) On the necessary order being given all units will immediately collect at Unit Dumps (see Appendix B) all the stores which cannot be carried.
The exception to this will be that the trenches will not be dismantled of their tactical equipment without a definite order through the Corps that this may be done.
(b) On the Unit moving, the personnel shown in Appendix A will be detached and come under the orders of the Divisional Salvage Officer. One man per Battalion will be an expert in grenades etc.
(c) The Battalion personnel will at once prepare a list of stores in the Unit Dump or dumps.
(d) The Salvage Officer will arrange to clear the Unit Dumps into Main Dumps and as received the stores will be classified into:-
(i) Ordnance Stores.
(ii) Supplies.
(iii) R.E.Stores.
(iv) Medical.
(v) Veterinary.
(vi) Ammunition, Grenades, Rockets, etc.
(e) Trench Store Dumps will be formed on forward roads or Light Railways as needed.
(f) Personnel should be left by the Unit with three days rations. Thereafter Divisional Salvage Officer will ration. Train will leave with him 4 days preserved rations for all his personnel
(g) I Corps will subsequently arrange for all personnel to rejoin the Division.
(h) Personal kits, band instruments, surplus office kit, etc., may be stored in the Pioneer Workshop L.3.a.8.0 and will be guarded by Divisional Salvage Officer.
(i) French Mission will attach an Interpreter and Gendarme to the Divisional Salvage Officer.
(j) The Divisional Signal Company will leave behind a supernumerary or attached Officer if available to collect all Signal Stores as part of the general scheme.
(k) Area Officers will deal with the Baths and will send at once to the Salvage Officer any personnel of the Division whom he may have helping at the Baths, or in any other capacity under him.
(l) The Canteen Officer will remain behind and act as seems best according to the circumstances.

P.T.O.

(m) The C.R.E. will leave a R.S.M. and 2 Sappers at the Divisional R.E. Dump and one Sapper at each of the other R.E. Dumps. Lists of the contents of each subsidiary dump will be sent to the R.S.M. at the Divisional Dump.
All R.E. Stores in Unit Dumps will be collected as far as possible at the Divisional R.E. Dump.
The disposal of the R.E. Stores will be in accordance with the directions of C.E. I Corps.

(n) Heavy and Medium T.M.B's unless ordered to accompany the advance will concentrate at MAZENGARBE as will any L.T.M.B's ordered to remain behind. (See Administrative Notes in case of an advance).

(o) Anti-Gas Stores will be dealt with as directed by the D.G.O. to whom the Salvage Officer will attach 6 O.R. D.G.O. will normally form a dump on the best available line of communication ready to despatch all stores to the Advanced troops as soon as required.

(p) Divisional Salvage Officer will make as much use of the (p foreways system and Light Railways as circumstances permit.

3. DUTIES OF DIVISIONAL SALVAGE OFFICER.

(a) This Officer will be in general charge of the collection of stores and O.C. 217th Employment Company and Area Officers will co-operate in the work.

(b) He will keep in the closest touch with S/C. Salvage, I Corps.

(c) He will keep up to date the lists of Civilian Transport and Labour available in the Area. Requisition will be employed if necessary.

(d) Should other troops occupy the Area he will get into touch with them and arrange rationing, and accommodation for his men and give all necessary information as to the progress of his work etc,.

(e) He will co-operate with Area Officers in the protection of huts and tentage in the Area.

4. APPENDICES.

'A'. Personnel available under Divisional Salvage Officer.

(a) 217th Employment Company.
(b) Band Troups.
(c) Divisional Reception Camp.

'B'. DUMPS. (Giving Unit - Village and Map Spotting).

'C' CORPS DEPOTS.

(a)	All Stores except R.E.	NOEUX STATION.
(b)	" " " "	MAZINGARBE. L.24.a.37.
(c)	" R.E. Stores.	MINX YARD.

'D'. CIVILIAN TRANSPORT AVAILABLE BY VILLAGES.

'E'. CIVILIAN LABOUR AVAILABLE.

'F' HUTS AND TENTS IN AREA.

This is being obtained by all Area Commandants in accordance with I Corps No. Q.19/3 of 25.9.1918.

NOTE. Appendices not issued to Formations or Units etc.

W.B. Rennie

Lieut.Colonel.
A.A. & Q.M.G.16th Division.

H.Q. 16th Division.
2nd October 1918.

DISTRIBUTION.

16th Div.Artillery.
C.R.E.
16th Div.Sig.Coy.
47th Inf.Bde.
48th Inf.Bde.
49th Inf.Bde.
11th Hants.(P).
16th M.G.Bn.
16th Div.Train.
16th M.T.Coy.
"G".
A.D.M.S.
D.A.D.V.S.
D.A.D.O.S.
D.A.P.M.
Salvage Officer.
Camp Comdt.
O.C., 217th Emp.Coy.
French Mission.
Canteen Officer.
Baths Officer.
I Corps 'Q'.

Vaudricourt
Mazingarbe
Noyelles
Annequin.
Labourse.
Beuvry.
Gorre.

WAR DIARY. 16th DIVISION. No. A.22/1. appx II "B."

STRENGTH RETURN MADE UP TO 12 NOON SATURDAY 12th October, 1918. 12.10.18. 191

UNIT.	(i.) Fighting strength for previous week, compiled in accordance with A.Gs. instructions.		(ii.) Increase during week, due to drafts, etc., taken on strength of unit.		(iii.) Totals from (i.) and (ii.)		(iv.) Decrease during week—casualties, etc., deducted from strength of unit.		"A" Fighting strength compiled in accordance with A.Gs. instructions.		"B" Not present with unit. Details (Included in "A")		"A" Minus "B" Available Fighting Strength. Untrained in Corps Reinforcement Camp. (Included in "A")		REMARKS. (Brief notes regarding (ii.), (iv.) and "B," etc.)
	Officers	O.R.	Officers	O.R.	Officers	O.R.	Officers	O.R.	Officers	O.R.	Officers	O.R.	Officers	O.R.	
47th Infantry Brigade:-															
14th Leics. Regt.	40	850	2	-	42	850	1	2	41	848	12	94	29	754	
18th Welsh Regt.	38	767	1	22	39	789	-	6	39	783	19	100	20	683	
9th Royal Hdrs.	35	576	5	26	40	602	-	7	40	595	8	76	32	519	
TOTAL:-	113	2193	8	48	121	2241	1	15	120	2226	39	270	81	1956	
48th Infantry Brigade:-															
22nd North. Fus.	40	758	5	7	45	765	2	18	43	747	11	83	32	664	
18th Scott. Rif.	36	540	1	24	37	564	2	22	35	542	10	68	25	474	
5th R. Ir. Fus.	41	889	1	9	42	898	2	72	40	826	8	143	32	683	
TOTAL:-	117	2187	7	40	124	2227	6	112	118	2115	29	294	89	1821	
49th Infantry Brigade:-															
6th Som. L.Inf.	42	789	-	7	42	796	2	11	40	785	11	89	29	696	
18th Glos. Regt.	37	690	1	30	38	720	1	12	37	708	12	87	25	621	
34th Lond. Regt.	34	754	-	16	34	770	-	15	34	755	12	103	22	652	
TOTAL:-	113	2233	1	53	114	2286	3	38	111	2248	35	279	76	1969	(sd) R.N.GREENWOOD, Major,
11th Hants Rgt(P).	46	689	-	11	46	700	4	14	42	686	18	61	24	625	D. A. A. G., for Major-General,
GRAND TOTAL:-	389	7302	16	152	405	7454	14	179	391	7275	121	904	270	6371	Commanding 16th Division.
16th M.Gun Battn.	47	871	2	12	49	883	-	13	49	870	5	29	44	841	
TOTALS															

3rd Field Survey Co., R.E. 2336 20-11-17

appx III

WAR DIARY.

16th DIVISION.

STRENGTH RETURN MADE UP TO 12 NOON SATURDAY, 26th October, 1918. 26.10.18. , 191

UNIT.	(i.) Fighting strength for previous week, compiled in accordance with A.G.'s instructions.		(ii.) Increase during week, due to drafts, etc., taken on strength of unit.		(iii.) Totals from (i.) and (ii.).		(iv.). Decrease during week—Casualties, etc., deducted from strength of unit.		"A." Fighting strength compiled in accordance with A.G.'s instructions.		"B." Not present with unit. Details (Included in "A.").		"A" Minus "B" Available Fighting Strength.		REMARKS. (Brief notes regarding (ii.), (iv.), "B," etc.)
	Officers.	O.R.	Officers.	O.R.	Officers.	O.R.	Officers.	O.R.	Officers	O.R.	Officers.	O.R.	O.	OR.	
47th Infantry Brigade :-															
14th Leics. Regt.	40	848	-	-	40	848	-	36	40	812	17	90	23	722	
18th Welsh Regt.	36	763	-	7	36	770	1	22	35	748	18	127	17	621	
9th Royal Hdrs.	43	615	2	54	45	669	-	35	45	634	9	63	36	571	
TOTAL :-	119	2226	2	61	121	2287	1	93	120	2194	44	280	76	1914	
48th Infantry Brigade :-															
22nd North. Fus.	43	743	4	9	47	752	1	7	46	745	14	71	32	674	
18th Scott. Rif.	35	569	1	32	36	601	-	27	36	574	7	88	29	486	
5th R. Ir. Fus.	40	804	-	26	40	830	1	x16	39	814	13	125	26	689	
TOTAL :-	118	2116	5	67	123	2183	2	50	121	2133	34	284	87	1849	
49th Infantry Brigade :-															
6th Som. L. Inf.	41	807	1	15	42	822	1	14	41	808	10	84	31	724	
18th Glos. Regt.	38	777	1	-	39	777	-	7	39	770	13	110	26	660	
34th Lond. Regt.	34	769	1	4	35	773	-	9	35	764	8	91	27	683	
TOTAL :-	113	2353	3	19	116	2372	1	30	115	2342	31	275	84	2067	
11th Hants Rgt(P).	40	683	1	24	41	707	1	9	40	698	9	62	31	636	
GRAND TOTAL:-	390	7378	11	171	401	7549	5	162	396	7367	118	901	278	6466	
16th M. GUN Battn.	49	887	-	-	49	877	-	16	49	861	5	27	44	834	
TOTALS ...															

(sd) R.N. GREENWOOD, Major, D.A.A.G., for
Major-General, Commanding 16th Division.

ARMY PRINTING AND STATIONERY SERVICES. B. 528. 5000. 9/17.

Instructions regarding War Diaries and Intelligence Summaries are contained in F. S. Regs., Part II. and the Staff Manual respectively. Title pages will be prepared in manuscript.

WAR DIARY

or

~~INTELLIGENCE SUMMARY.~~

(Erase heading not required.)

16 Division A & Q

NOVEMBER

Army Form C. 2118.

36

Place	Date	Hour	Summary of Events and Information	Remarks and references to Appendices
TEMPLEUVE	1		Feeding strength. men 12900: horses HD 427. LD 3135. Casualties killed OR 1. wounded officers 1 OR 66.	
	2		Casualties killed OR 1. wounded officers 2 OR. 31.	
	3		Casualties wounded OR. 12.	
	4		Casualties killed OR 2 wounded OR 5.	
	5		Casualties wounded OR 2	
	6		Casualties killed OR 1 wounded officers 1 OR 14. missing officers 1 OR 1.	
	7		Casualties killed OR 1 wounded officers 2 OR 25.	

D. D. & L., London, E.C.
(A10266) Wt W5300/P713 750,000 2/18 Sch. 52 Forms/C2118/16.

Instructions regarding War Diaries and Intelligence Summaries are contained in F. S. Regs., Part II. and the Staff Manual respectively. Title pages will be prepared in manuscript.

WAR DIARY
or
~~INTELLIGENCE SUMMARY.~~
(Erase heading not required.)

Army Form C. 2118.

Place	Date	Hour	Summary of Events and Information	Remarks and references to Appendices
	8		Casualties Wounded OR 18 missing OR 4. Feeding strength men 12621: HD 376: LD 2214:	
	9		Casualties NIL. Fighting strength attached.	APPENDIX A.
TAINTIGNIES	10		Casualties NIL. DHQ "Q" moved to TAINTIGNIES.	
	11		Hostilities ceased 1100 hours. Casualties NIL.	
	12		Casualties NIL.	
	13		Casualties NIL.	
	14		Casualties NIL	
	15		Casualties NIL. Feeding Strength. men 12568: horses HD 440: LD 2228:	

Army Form C. 2118.

Instructions regarding War Diaries and Intelligence Summaries are contained in F. S. Regs., Part II. and the Staff Manual respectively. Title pages will be prepared in manuscript.

WAR DIARY
or
~~INTELLIGENCE SUMMARY.~~
(Erase heading not required.)

Place	Date	Hour	Summary of Events and Information	Remarks and references to Appendices
ATTICHES	16		Casualties NIL. DHQ moved to ATTICHES.	
	17		Casualties NIL.	
	18.		Casualties NIL.	
	19.		Casualties NIL.	
	20		Casualties NIL.	
	21		Casualties. NIL.	
	22		Casualties NIL. Feeding strength. Men 12351: horses HD 433: LD 3245	
	23.		Casualties NIL. Fighting strength attached.	APPENDIX B

D. D. & L., London, E.C.
(A10266) Wt W5300/P713 750,000 2/18 Sch. 52 Forms/C2118/16.

Army Form C. 2118.

WAR DIARY
or
~~INTELLIGENCE SUMMARY.~~
(Erase heading not required.)

Instructions regarding War Diaries and Intelligence Summaries are contained in F. S. Regs., Part II. and the Staff Manual respectively. Title pages will be prepared in manuscript.

Place	Date	Hour	Summary of Events and Information	Remarks and references to Appendices
ATTICHES	24		Casualties, NIL. AS.	
-	25		Casualties. NIL AS.	
	26		Casualties. NIL.	
	27		Casualties NIL.	
AVELIN.	28		Casualties. NIL. DHQ. to AVELIN to-day.	
	29		Casualties. NIL. Feeding strength. [illegible] horses HD 419: LD 3270:	
	30		Casualties. Killed O.R. 3. Wounded O.R. 3. by mine exploding at ALENNES. Final Casualty Report sent in. All units reported casualties checked to date.	

[illegible] Capt
for Brig-General,
Commdg. 16 Division

A7092 Wt. W128:9/M1293. 750,000. 1/17. D. D & L. Ltd. Forms/C2118/14.

www.ingramcontent.com/pod-product-compliance
Lightning Source LLC
Chambersburg PA
CBHW080908230426
43664CB00016B/2756